Turkey and the European Union

Also by Joseph S. Joseph

THE TREATY ESTABLISHING A CONSTITUTION FOR EUROPE: Introduction, Documents, Annotation (*editor*)

EURO–ATLANTIC RELATIONS AND THE EASTERN MEDITERRANEAN (*co-editor with Stephanos Constantinides*)

CYPRUS AND THE EUROPEAN UNION (*co-editor with Stephanos Constantinides*)

THE FIFTH EU ENLARGEMENT: Revisiting the Triangle of Cyprus, Greece and Turkey (*co-editor with Stephanos Constantinides*)

CYPRUS: Ethnic Conflict and International Politics, from Independence to the Threshold of the European Union

Turkey and the European Union

Internal Dynamics and External Challenges

Edited by

Joseph S. Joseph
Associate Professor of International Relations and European Affairs
Jean Monnet Chair in European Foreign and Security Policy
University of Cyprus

palgrave
macmillan

First published 2006 by
PALGRAVE MACMILLAN
Houndmills, Basingstoke, Hampshire RG21 6XS and
175 Fifth Avenue, New York, N.Y. 10010
Companies and representatives throughout the world.

PALGRAVE MACMILLAN is the global academic imprint of the Palgrave
Macmillan division of St. Martin's Press, LLC and of Palgrave Macmillan Ltd.
Macmillan® is a registered trademark in the United States, United Kingdom
and other countries. Palgrave is a registered trademark in the European
Union and other countries.

ISBN-13: 978-0-230-00549-5
ISBN-10: 0-230-00549-7

This book is printed on paper suitable for recycling and made from fully
managed and sustained forest sources.

A catalogue record for this book is available from the British Library.

Library of Congress Cataloging-in-Publication Data
    Turkey and the European Union : internal dynamics and external
challenges / edited by Joseph S. Joseph.
        p. cm.
    Includes bibliographical references and index.
    ISBN 0-230-00549-7 (cloth)
    1. European Union – Turkey. 2. Turkey – Foreign relations – European
Union countries. 3. European Union countries – Foreign relations –
Turkey. 4. Turkey – Foreign economic relations – European Union
countries. 5. European Union countries – Foreign economic relations –
Turkey. I. Joseph, Joseph S., 1952–
HC240.25.T8T8753 2006
341.242'209561—dc22   2006047485

10 9 8 7 6 5 4 3 2 1
15 14 13 12 11 10 09 08 07 06

Transferred to digital printing in 2007.

For Eleni and our daughters, Lina and Savina,
who are good at showing alternatives to
anger and confrontation.

In memory of my parents, who taught me that
listening can be better than talking

Contents

List of Tables

Preface

The object of this book is to make a scholarly contribution to the debate over Turkey's quest for EU membership and participation in the European integration process. It looks at various issues and aspects of EU–Turkish relations dealing with the past, present and future of Turkey's Western orientation and the EU's deepening and widening.

In selecting the topics addressed in the book, there was some emphasis on diversity and innovation. The theme of the book is quite broad and includes topics in history, politics, economy, society and culture. The various issues are presented and discussed in the context of the internal dynamics and challenges that both Turkey and the EU are facing in the light of Turkey's forthcoming membership in the Union. The regional context of Middle Eastern politics and the evolving transatlantic relations in a changing world of rising tensions between the West and Islam are also frameworks of reference for the presentation and analysis of some of the issues. The twelve chapters of the book provide a thorough picture of EU–Turkish relations and insightful analysis of the dynamics and complexities of these relations.

The first (introductory) chapter provides some background information on EU–Turkish relations and an overview of the main issues and challenges that Turkey presents to the EU and vice versa. In that sense, this chapter defines the theme of the book and provides a broader context for the more specialized chapters which follow.

In Chapter 2 Mehmet Ugur looks at the economic implications of Turkey's membership and tries to disentangle the costs and benefits for both Turkey and the EU. He concludes that accession is likely to benefit both sides, but further research on this critical aspect is needed.

In Chapter 3 Spyridon Kotsovilis explores the complex issue of democratic consolidation and the political role of Islam. The chapter has contemporary focus and concludes that Turkey can belong to both the East and the West, and be a truly democratic and Muslim country.

Chapter 4 is a study of the Turkish Grand National Assembly and some of the issues raised in Turkey's contentious march towards the EU. Neophytos Loizides and Elif Ersin conclude that there is increasing diversity in the views of parliamentarians, and that the stereotype of a monolithic political discourse lacking self-criticism and compromising voices is incorrect.

In Chapter 5 Wendy Weber looks at the relationship between civil society and the state in the context of Turkey's European aspirations and its forthcoming accession to the EU. She concludes that the pre-accession process has played a role in strengthening the civil society and the efforts of nongovernmental organizations in promoting human rights.

Chapter 6 provides an overview of the Kurdish problem and looks at its many aspects as a source of instability in the Middle East and beyond. Michael Gunter concludes that although currently the Kurdish situation remains highly uncertain, the importance of the Kurds in regional and international politics is increasing.

Chapter 7 deals with the Europeanization of Turkey's Kurdish question and looks at the EU's concerns about internal stability, democracy and respect for human rights. Nathalie Tocci provides an analysis of the political imperatives underpinning EU–Turkish relations and their impact on the handling of the Kurdish issue.

Chapter 8 looks at Greek–Turkish relations with particular emphasis on Greece's handling of Turkey's application for membership in the EU. Alexander Kazamias looks at the historical context and structural constraints which affect Greek policy towards Turkey's European course and other issues, including Cyprus and Aegean disputes.

Chapter 9 focuses on the Cyprus problem, which is high on the agenda of the Turkish government, in connection with Turkey's EU membership prospects. Tozun Bahcheli looks at the domestic constraints and external factors influencing Turkey's policy and handling of the Cyprus issue, with emphasis on the policy of the Erdogan government since 2003.

In Chapter 10 Mustafa Kibaroglu discusses some of the security implications that EU membership in the EU may have on Turkey. He does so in the context of a changing regional and global security environment, and by taking into account the American and European security sensitivities in the Middle East.

Chapter 11 looks at the triangle of Turkey–EU–US relations in the context of domestic Turkish politics and in the light of a changing global political environment. Omer Taspinar explores the dynamics of these relations and discusses the overall state of transatlantic relations and Turkey's growing frustration with both the US and the EU.

Chapter 12 is a case-study of the 2003 Iraq War and its implications for the troubled US–Turkish alliance and Turkey's European aspirations. Ozlem Kayhan and Dan Lindley suggest that Turkey's policy during the war was helpful in fulfilling its European objectives, but a balanced policy towards its Western partners is imperative.

My thanks and appreciation go to the many individuals who helped me in preparing this book. I am especially indebted to the contributing authors. Their contribution is greatly appreciated. I could rely on their background and expertise for preparing first-class chapters, but I also enjoyed interacting with them, exchanging views, and sharing constructive criticism. In a sense, this project has been an exercise in collective and constructive engagement. I may also add that the final product is the result of transnational cooperation among individuals with diverse backgrounds from several institutions in different countries.

I am also grateful to my colleagues in the Department of Social Political Sciences at the University of Cyprus. Our conversations often helped me give substance and shape to vague ideas. My students at the University of Cyprus have also provided inspiration and ideas. The long and occasionally intense debates we had in the classroom were stimulating and refreshing.

I am grateful to Alison Howson, publisher at Palgrave Macmillan, who provided valuable advice. Her professionalism was a source of support and enthusiasm for the project. I also express my thanks to the anonymous readers for their constructive criticism and feedback.

I am also thankful to the European Commission which provided support for this project through the funding of the Jean Monnet Chair in European Foreign and Security Policy at the University of Cyprus.

Last but not least, I am especially indebted and grateful to my wife Eleni and our daughters Lina and Savina. They were a constant source of support and inspiration. Without their patience and devotion to the project, its completion would have been long delayed.

While the contribution of many people was critical in completing this collective volume, I take full responsibility for its preparation and for any errors of omission or commission.

University of Cyprus   JOSEPH S. JOSEPH

Note on spelling and accents

In the English literature many Turkish words and names are used in their anglicized version (example: Ataturk instead of Atatürk). In this volume, some chapter contributors use the original Turkish spellings and accents while some others use the anglicized versions. The preference of each chapter author has been respected. As a result, there is some inconsistency among chapters in the use of spellings and accents of Turkish words and names.

Notes on the Contributors

Tozun Bahcheli is professor of political science at King's University College at the University of Western Ontario, London, Canada. He has written widely on Turkish foreign policy issues, Greek–Turkish relations and Cypriot politics. During 1995–96 he was senior fellow at the United States Institute of Peace in Washington, DC. He is the author of *Greek–Turkish Relations Since 1955* (1990) and co-editor of *De Facto States: The Quest for Sovereignty* (2004).

Elif Ersin studied political science and international relations at Bogazici University, Istanbul, Turkey, and worked for the Student Forum of the Center of European Studies on projects involving students from all regions of Turkey. She has a special interest in Turkish and European politics and is involved in research projects on EU–Turkish relations.

Michael M. Gunter is a professor of political science at Tennessee Technological University in Cookeville, Tennessee, USA. During the summer he teaches at the International University in Vienna, Austria. He is the author of several books on the Kurdish question, the most recent being *Kurdish Historical Dictionary* (2004); *The Kurdish Predicament in Iraq: A Political Analysis* (1999); and *The Kurds and the Future of Turkey* (1997). In addition, he is the co-editor (with Mohammed M. A. Ahmed) of *The Kurdish Question and the 2003 Iraqi War* (2005). He has also published numerous scholarly articles on the Kurds in leading periodicals including *Middle East Journal, Middle East Quarterly, Middle East Policy* and *Orient*. He was a senior Fulbright lecturer in international relations in Turkey and has been interviewed about the Kurdish question on many occasions by the international media.

Joseph S. Joseph is associate professor and holder of the Jean Monnet Chair in European foreign and security policy at the University of Cyprus. He received his BA from Panteion University (Greece); MA from the University of Stockholm (Sweden); and PhD from Miami University (USA). He was a post-doctoral fellow at Harvard and taught at the University of Alabama, Gustavus Adolphus College, and Miami University. His recent publications include *The Treaty Establishing a Constitution for Europe: Introduction, Documents, Annotation* (in Greek; 2006); *Cyprus: Ethnic Conflict and International Politics, from Independence* *to the Threshold of the European Union* (1997). He co-edited three special issues of the journal *Hellenic Studies/Études Helléniques* on *Transatlantic Relations and the Eastern Mediterranean* (2004), *Cyprus and the European Union* (2003) and *The Fifth EU Enlargement: Revisiting the Triangle of Cyprus, Greece and Turkey* (2003). He has published numerous chapters in books and articles in periodicals including the *Mediterranean Quarterly*, *Security Dialogue* and *Innovation*.

Ozlem Kayhan received her BSc degree in international relations from the Middle East Technical University, Ankara, Turkey, and her MA degree in political science from the University of Notre Dame, Indiana, USA. She is currently a PhD candidate at the University of Notre Dame. Her research interests revolve around the relationship between national security threats, civil–military relations, and state-building. She has given papers and talks on the foreign policy of Turkey, on democratic control of the Turkish Armed Forces, on the US war in Afghanistan and on Islam's compatibility with democracy. Prior to attending Notre Dame, she interned at the Ministry of Foreign Affairs of the Republic of Turkey.

Alexander Kazamias is senior lecturer in politics at Coventry University, United Kingdom. He specializes in Greek political and diplomatic history, Euro-Mediterranean relations and West European politics. He has written articles and book chapters in these areas including 'The Modernisation of Greek Foreign Policy and its Limitations' (*Mediterranean Politics*, 1997); 'L'Unione Monetaria Europea: Storia di una contro-egemonia?', in G. Campani and L. Sommo (eds), *L'Euro – Scenari Economici e Dimensione Simbolica* (2001); and 'The Rise and Fall of State-Partyism' (in Greek), in T. Pelagidis (ed.), *The Entanglement of Reforms in Greece* (2005). Since 1993 he has been a regular contributor to the Greek periodical *Anti*. He has taught as a visiting lecturer in Moscow State University, Warwick University and Cairo University. In 2005 he was a visiting research fellow at Princeton University.

Mustafa Kibaroglu is associate professor of international relations at Bilkent University, Isanbul. He has a BSc in industrial engineering and an MA in economics from Bogazici University in Istanbul. He received his PhD in international relations from Bilkent University in Ankara. He has held fellowships at the United Nations Institute for Disarmament Research, Switzerland; at the University of Southampton in the United Kingdom as a fellow of the International Atomic Energy Agency; at the Monterey Institute, California; and at Harvard University as a post-doctoral fellow. He has several chapters in books and articles in academic journals including *Security Dialogue, Nonproliferation Review, Bulletin of the Atomic Scientists, Middle East Quarterly, Middle East Journal, Brown Journal of World Affairs* and *European Security*.

Spyridon Kotsovilis is completing his PhD in political science at McGill University, Canada. A graduate of Athens College, Greece, he holds a BA from the University of Toronto in Peace and Conflict Studies and an MA from McGill in political science. His research interests include democratization, ethnic conflict and contentious politics in Southeastern Europe and the former USSR. He is a member of the executive council of the Canadian Association of Médecins Sans Frontières/Doctors Without Borders, and founder and former head of a group within MSF Canada that prepared and provided socio-political reports on the destinations of medical staff of the organization.

Dan Lindley is assistant professor of political science at the University of Notre Dame, Indiana, and a fellow at the Joan B. Kroc Institute for International Peace Studies. He received his BA degree in International Relations and French from Tufts University, Massachusetts. He received his PhD from MIT and his dissertation has become his book manuscript: *Promoting Peace with Information: Transparency as a Tool of Security Regimes.* He lectured at MIT and was a fellow in the International Security Program at the Belfer Center for Science and International Affairs at Harvard University. He has published on UN peacekeeping, ethnic conflict, the Cyprus problem and Greek–Turkish relations. His current research interests are in the areas of public diplomacy and the extent to which miscalculation and misperception can have an impact on the state's decisions for war.

Neophytos G. Loizides is currently a lecturer in the Department of Politics and the Hellenic Studies Program at Princeton University. He received his BA in international relations from the University of Pennsylvania and MA in economics from the Central European University in Budapest where he specialized in Southeast European studies. He received his PhD in political science from the University of Toronto. He was a fellow at the Belfer Center for Science and International Affairs, Kennedy School of Government, Harvard University. He has published on conflict and peace studies, Mediterranean politics and Greek–Turkish relations. His articles were published in international journals including *Security Dialogue, Southeast European Politics, Hellenic Studies* and *Weltpolitik*. He is currently working on a book manuscript on framing and communication strategies in the Greek and Turkish parliaments.

Omer Taspinar is the Director of the Turkey Program at the Brookings Institution's Center on the United States and Europe, and an adjunct professor at the School of Advanced International Studies, Johns Hopkins University. He received his BA in political science from Middle East Technical University, Ankara, and his MA and PhD in European Studies from Johns Hopkins University. His research focuses on Turkey–EU and Turkish–American relations; European politics; Transatlantic relations; Muslims in Europe; Islamic radicalism; and American foreign policy in the Middle East. His recent publications include *Fighting Radicalism with Human Development: Freedom, Education and Growth in the Islamic World* (Brookings Press, 2006); *Political Islam and Kurdish Nationalism in Turkey* (2005); *New Parameters in US–German–Turkish Relations* (AICGS Policy Report, 2005); 'The Anatomy of Anti-Americanism in Turkey' (*Insight Turkey*, 2005); *Turkey's European Quest* (Brookings Analysis Paper, 2004); 'Europe's Muslim Street' (*Foreign Policy*, 2003).

Nathalie Tocci is a Marie Curie Fellow at the Robert Schuman Centre for Advanced Studies, European University Institute, Florence. She received her PhD in international relations at the London School of Economics. She is currently researching a book on the role of the EU in conflict resolution in the Mediterranean region. She also collaborates with the Institute of International Affairs in Rome. She has been a research fellow at the Centre for European Policy Studies, Brussels. Her recent publications include 'Conflict Resolution in the Neighbourhood: Comparing the Role of the EU in the Turkish–Kurdish and Israeli–Palestinian Conflicts' (*Mediterranean Politics*, 2005), *EU Accession Dynamics and Conflict Resolution: Cayalysing Peace or Parition in Cyprus?* (2004); with A. Evin (eds), *Towards Accession Negotiations: Turkey's Domestic and Foreign Policy Challenges Ahead* (2004).

Mehmet Ugur is Jean Monnet reader in European Political Economy at the University of Greenwich Business School. He studied at the Middle East Technical University, Ankara, and the London School of Economics. His research focuses on institutional design for economic policy. In this context, he has researched and published in the areas of regional integration theory, integration–globalization linkages, EU–Turkey relations, corporate governance, and institutional determinants of economic performance. His recent publications include *Turkey and European Integration* (2004, edited with N. Canefe), *Open Economy Macroeconomics*

(2003) and *The European Union and Turkey: An Anchor/Credibility Dilemma* (1999). Currently he is working on the institutional determinants of economic performance in Turkey.

Wendy Weber is a visiting instructor at Macalester College, Minnesota, where she teaches courses in international relations. She is a PhD candidate at the University of Manitoba in Winnipeg and York University in Toronto. She is currently completing her dissertation on humanitarian intervention. Her research interests are in changing patterns of governance, especially in the areas of human rights and humanitarianism.

List of Abbreviations

AKP	Justice and Development Party
ANAP	Motherland Party
APD	Accession Partnership Document
CAP	Common Agricultural Policy
CEEC	Central and Eastern European Countries
CENTO	Central Treaty Organization
CFSP	Common Foreign and Security Policy
CGE	computable general equilibrium
CHP	Republican People's Party
CIA	Central Intelligence Agency
DEHAP	Democratic People's Party
DSP	Democratic Left Party
DTH	Democratic Society Movement
DYP	True Path Party (Correct Way Party)
EAGGF	European Agricultural Guidance and Guarantee Fund
EC	European Communities, European Community
ECHR	European Court of Human Rights
ECSC	European Coal and Steel Community
ECU	European currency unit
EEC	European Economic Community
EMU	Economic and Monetary Union
ESDI	European Security and Defence Identity
ESDP	European Security and Defence Policy
EU	European Union
EUISS	European Union Institute of Strategic Studies
EURATOM	European Atomic Energy Community
FBIS	Foreign Broadcast Information Service
FDI	foreign direct investment
FIR	Flight Information Region
FYROM	Former Yugoslav Republic of Macedonia
GDP	gross domestic product
GNP	gross national product
HADEP	People's Democracy Party
HCA	Helsinki Citizens' Assembly
IAEA	International Atomic Energy Agency
ICAO	International Civil Aviation Organization

ICJ	International Court of Justice
IDP	internally displaced person
IGO	intergovernmental organization
IMF	International Monetary Fund
ISAF	International Security Assistance Force (in Afghanistan)
KADEK	Kurdistan Freedom and Democracy Congress
LDP	Liberal Democratic Party
MHP	Nationalist Movement (Action) Party
NATO	North Atlantic Treaty Organization
NGO	nongovernmental organization
NPT	Non-Proliferation Treaty
NSC	National Security Council
NSP	National Order (Salvation) Party
OECD	Organisation for Economic Co-operation and Development
OHAL	State of Emergency Legislation
OLS	ordinary least square
OSCE	Organization for Security and Cooperation in Europe
OYAK	Armed Forces Pension Fund (Turkey)
PKK	Kurdistan Workers' Party
RP	(Welfare Party in Turkey)
RF	Welfare Party
SHP	Social Democratic People's Party
SP	Felicity (Contentment) Party (New Turkey Party)
SPO	State Planning Organization
TBMM	Turkish Grand National Assembly (also TGNA)
TGNA	Turkish Grand National Assembly (also TBMM)
TRNC	'Turkish Republic of Northern Cyprus'
TUSIAD	Turkish Industrialists' and Businessmen's Association
UK	United Kingdom
UN	United Nations
US	United States of America
USSR	Union of Soviet Socialist Republics
WB	World Bank
WEU	Western European Union
WTO	World Trade Organization

Chronology

1923	Establishment of the Republic of Turkey. Kemal Ataturk becomes president.
1925	Adoption of the Gregorian calendar. Prohibition of the fez.
1928	Turkey becomes a secular state.
1938	Kemal Ataturk dies. Ismet Inonu becomes president.
1945	Turkey joins the United Nations.
1952	Turkey joins NATO.
1959	Turkey applies to become an associate member of the EEC.
1960	May Army coup. The military takes power and rules until October 1961.
1961	New constitution establishes two-chamber parliament.
1963	Association agreement signed with EEC.
1965	Suleyman Demirel becomes prime minister, a position he is to hold seven times.
1971	Army forces Demirel to resign, following the escalation of political violence.
1974	Turkish troops invade Cyprus. US arms embargo imposed on Turkey.
1978	US arms embargo lifted.
1980 September	Army coup follows political violence. Military rules until November 1983.
1982	New constitution provides for seven-year presidency and single-house parliament.
1983	General election won by Turgut Ozal's Motherland Party.
1984	Kurdistan Workers Party (PKK) launches a separatist guerrilla war in southeast.
1987	Turkey applies for full EEC membership.
1989	European Commission issues *opinion* on Turkish application. It does not recommend opening of accession negotiations.
1990	Turkey allows the US-led coalition against Iraq to launch air strikes from Turkish bases.

1992	20,000 Turkish troops enter Kurdish safe havens in Iraq in anti-PKK operation.
1993	Tansu Ciller becomes Turkey's first woman prime minister.
1996	Customs union with the EU enters into force.
1996	Welfare Party leader Necmettin Erbakan heads the first pro-Islamic government since 1923.
1997 December	Luxembourg European Council declines to grant candidate status to Turkey.
1998	Welfare Party (the largest in parliament) banned.
1999	PKK leader Abdullah Ocalan captured in Kenya. Sentenced to death; sentence later commuted to life imprisonment.
1999 December	Helsinki European Council decides that Turkey is an EU candidate country.
1999 August	Devastating earthquake kills 17,000 people.
2000	Ahmet Necdet Sezer takes over from Suleyman Demirel as president.
2001 October	Parliament approves major amendments to the constitution to meet the Copenhagen political criteria.
2001 June	Constitutional Court bans the opposition pro-Islamic Virtue Party. New pro-Islamist party Saadet is set up by former Virtue Party members in July.
2002 January	Turkish men are no longer regarded in law as head of the family.
2002 July	Pressure for early elections as eight ministers including Foreign Minister Cem resign over the ailing PM Ecevit's refusal to step down amid growing economic and political turmoil.
2002 July	Cem launches new party committed to social democracy and EU membership.
2002 August	Parliament approves reforms aimed at securing EU membership. Death sentence abolished except in times of war. Ban on Kurdish education and broadcasting lifted.
2002 November	Islamist-based Justice and Development Party (AK) wins landslide election victory. The party promises to stick to the secular principles of constitution. Deputy leader Abdullah Gul becomes prime minister.
2002 December	Copenhagen European Council decides to review Turkey's European course in December 2004 with a

	view to opening accession negotiations without delay.
2002 December	Constitutional changes allow the head of the ruling AK, Recep Tayyip Erdogan, to run for parliament, and so become prime minister.
2003 March	AKP leader Recep Tayyip Erdogan wins a seat in parliament and becomes prime minister. Abdullah Gul resigns as prime minister and becomes foreign minister.
2003 March	Parliament decides not to allow the deployment of US forces ahead of the war in Iraq but allows US use of Turkish air space. It authorizes the dispatch of Turkish forces into Kurdish areas of northern Iraq.
2003 June/July	Parliament passes further laws easing restrictions on the freedom of speech, Kurdish language rights, and reducing the political role of military.
2004 January	Turkey signs the protocol banning the death penalty in all circumstances.
2004 May	PKK announces it plans to end its cease-fire because of what it calls annihilation operations against its forces.
2004 June	Turkish state television broadcasts first Kurdish language programme.
2004 June	Four Kurdish activists, including the former MP Leyla Zana, freed from jail.
2004 June	NATO heads of state gather for summit in Istanbul.
2004 September	Parliament approves penal reforms introducing tougher measures to prevent torture and violence against women. Controversial proposal on criminalizing adultery dropped.
2004 October	European Commission issues a report recommending that the European Council decides for the commencement of accession negotiations.
2004 December	European Council decides for the opening of accession negotiations in October 2005.
2005 January	New lira currency introduced.
2005 May	Parliament approves amendments to the new penal code after complaints that the previous version was too restrictive of media freedom.
2005 October	Accession negotiations with the EU launched.

1
Introduction: Turkey at the Threshold of the European Union

Joseph S. Joseph

From Westernization to Europeanization

The history of contemporary Turkey is characterized by change, the main causes of which have been external stimuli and incentives, particularly the drive for transformation from an oriental Islamic empire to a secular national state. This transformation – known as Westernization – has been slow and occasionally painful. It has been aptly called 'the Turkish revolution' and, as Bernard Lewis pointed out, it could be defined not only 'in terms of economy or society or government, but also of civilization'.[1] It gained momentum with the establishment of the Turkish Republic in 1923 and the ascent of Kemalism, when 'everything had to be rebuilt, above all a new identity'.[2] Its main goal was to move Turkey from being a medieval Islamic theocracy to becoming a modern capitalist Western democracy. At the centre of the Kemalist ideology and its state-building and nation-building efforts was the consolidation of the Turkish Republic which was based on a political system the core principles of which were 'heavily tainted by a historically developed authoritarian understanding of the unitary state and its functioning as well as an organic and homogenous understanding of the nation'.[3] Eventually the scope of Westernization was broadened to include economic, social and cultural changes which were intensified by industrialization efforts and rapidly increasing urbanization.

In the wake of the dismantling of the Ottoman Empire and in the process of reformation and socio-political reorientation

> the replacement of old, Islamic conceptions of identity, authority, and loyalty by new conceptions of European origin was of fundamental

1

importance. In the theocratically conceived polity of Islam, God was to be twice replaced: as the source of sovereignty, by the people; as the object of worship, by the nation.[4]

As a result of these changes, which have taken decades to consolidate, Turkey has become a secular democracy, although the politicization of Islam and the political role of the military are still features of the Turkish political landscape. The success or failure of these protracted reforms has been the topic of an ongoing debate with differing opinions. To this day, Turks are 'still struggling to digest the heavy burden of Ataturk's legacy'[5] while the prospect of accession to the EU is posing new challenges. Recently, French President Jacques Chirac commenting on Turkey's European aspirations suggested that it will have to undergo a 'major cultural revolution' to realize its dream of joining the EU.[6] It can be argued, however, that during the last few decades, in many areas of public life including government, economy, society and culture, changes and achievements have been remarkable and irreversible.

Today the challenge of Westernization is taking the form of Europeanization, that is, the reform of domestic structures, institutions and policies to meet the requirements of the systemic logic, political dynamics and administrative mechanisms of European integration. Turkey is, once again, facing a Western challenge as it is preparing to become a member of the EU and join the 'process of creating an ever closer union among the peoples of Europe'.[7] The role of Turkey in this process can be catalytic, as the EU will be welcoming its first Islamic member state. The deepening and widening of the integration process will acquire a new meaning as Europe will be redefining itself with reference to the future, not to the past. Indeed, the challenge and promise for both Islamic Turkey and Christian Europe is about seizing the moment and moving beyond the clash of civilizations as the *modus operandi* of history and the *modus vivendi* of governments and peoples.

A long road of ups and downs

Following a protracted period of ups and downs in EU–Turkish relations, accession negotiations started in October 2005. The decision for the commencement of accession negotiations was made by the Brussels European Council in December 2004 'on the basis of a report and recommendation from the Commission, that Turkey fulfils the Copenhagen political criteria'.[8]

Although accession negotiations and preparations will last for several years and accession is not expected to take place before 2014, in political terms Turkey is at the threshold of the EU.[9] Lest optimists point to the fact that although the objective of the negotiations is accession, there can be no guarantee in advance that they will be successfully completed. On both sides, however, there is positive predisposition and political will for successful conclusion of the negotiations and full membership of Turkey.

The commencement of accession negotiations was the culmination of a long relationship which goes back to the early years of the EU (Community). Turkey expressed an interest in institutionalizing its relations and becoming an associate member of the EU in the late 1950s. In 1959 it applied for associate membership and in 1963 it signed an association agreement which was intended to pave the way for full membership. The association agreement – known as the Ankara agreement – went into effect in 1964 and provided that when the relations of Turkey with the EU have 'advanced far enough to justify envisaging full acceptance by Turkey of the obligations of the [EC] Treaty, [the EC] shall examine the possibility of the accession of Turkey to the European Community'.[10] In 1971 an additional protocol was signed between Turkey and the EU aimed at further strengthening and broadening of their economic and political relations. The association agreement did not achieve its objective and failed to prepare Turkey for membership. It has been argued that the EU looked at it as a 'framework for its containment policy rather than a pre-accession strategy, because it had serious reservations about Turkey's prospects for EU membership on political and economic grounds'.[11] Despite its failure, the association agreement provided a useful link with the European integration process and bolstered Turkey's Westernization policy.

Following the two Mediterranean enlargements of the EU in 1980s – accession of Greece in 1981, and of Portugal and Spain in 1986 – Turkey applied for full membership in April 1987. The response of the EU was not positive and cited various reasons why 'it would be inappropriate for the Community ... to become involved in new accession negotiations [and] it would not be useful to open accession negotiations with Turkey'.[12] After the collapse of the Soviet Union and the end of the cold war, EU deepening and widening began accelerating. In 1995 the fourth EU enlargement took place with the accession of Austria, Finland and Sweden, while pre-accession preparations got under way with the countries of Central and Eastern Europe. In 1997, the European Council in Luxembourg decided for the commencement of accession negotiations with six countries – Cyprus, the Czech Republic, Estonia, Hungary, Poland and Slovenia – while excluding Turkey on economic and political grounds. A turning-point came two years later at the Helsinki European Council where it was decided that 'Turkey is a candidate State destined to join the Union on the basis of the same criteria as applied to the other candidate States'.[13] At the same time, the list of acceding countries was expanded to include Bulgaria, Latvia, Lithuania, Malta, Romania and Slovakia. At Helsinki, a decision was also made for the establishment of an Accession Partnership with Turkey which would serve as a road-map to accession. The Accession Partnership was adopted in 2001 and defined the principles, priorities, conditions and short- and medium-term objectives for Turkey's integration with the EU.

Another milestone in Turkey's European course was the publication in October 2004 of the positive 'Recommendation of the European Commission on Turkey's Progress Towards Accession'. The Recommendation concluded 'that Turkey sufficiently fulfils the political criteria and recommends that accession negotiations be opened'.[14] This was the first time an EU institution firmly and clearly recommended the opening of accession negotiations. As it was put by the *Washington Post*, 'Turkey seemed to shift geographically westward.'[15] The Commission, however, pointed out that accession negotiations would be an open-ended process the outcome of which could not be guaranteed in advance. It also warned that the negotiations could be suspended if there was a persistent violation of the principles of democracy, human rights and the rule of law.

Two months later, the Brussels European Council (16–17 December 2004) adopted the recommendation of the Commission and decided for the opening of accession negotiations on 3 October 2005. The message came clear and loud from Brussels that 'Turkey has taken its European destiny in its own hands.'[16] It is also interesting to note that the decision by the EU heads of state or government came at a time when the majority of the European public was not favouring accession of Turkey to the EU.[17] As was pointed out by the president of the European Commission, the challenge now for Turkey was 'to win the hearts and minds of those European citizens who are open to, but not convinced of Turkey's European destiny.'[18]

The accession negotiations were launched on 3 October 2005 and are expected to last for at least a decade. As the European Commissioner for enlargement put it, '[T]he journey is as important as the final destination.'[19] The negotiations and the pre-accession preparations are based on a strategy aimed at guaranteeing that harmonization with the *acquis communautaire* and the political reform process are consolidated, broadened and properly implemented.

Negotiating framework and principles governing the accession negotiations[20]

Accession negotiations opened on the basis that Turkey sufficiently meets the Copenhagen political criteria.[21] They are also based on Turkey's own merits and their pace depends on Turkey's progress in meeting the requirements for membership. The objective of the negotiations is accession, but they are an open-ended process, the outcome of which cannot be guaranteed beforehand.

While having full regard to all the Copenhagen criteria, including the absorption capacity of the Union, if Turkey is not in a position to assume in full all the obligations of membership, then it must be ensured that she is fully anchored in the European structures through the strongest possible bond.

Turkey is expected to sustain the process of reform and to work towards further improvement with regard to the principles of liberty, democracy, the rule of law and respect for human rights and fundamental freedoms, including relevant European case-law; to consolidate and broaden legislation and implementation measures specifically in relation to the zero tolerance policy in the fight against torture and ill-treatment and the implementation of provisions relating to freedom of expression, freedom of religion, women's rights, ILO standards including trade union rights, and minority rights.

In the case of a serious and persistent breach in Turkey of the principles of liberty, democracy, respect for human rights and fundamental freedoms and the rule of law on which the Union is founded, the European Commission will, on its own initiative or at the request of one-third of the member states, recommend the suspension of negotiations and propose the conditions for eventual resumption. The Council will decide by qualified majority on such a recommendation, after having heard Turkey, whether to suspend the negotiations and on the conditions for their resumption.

The advancement of the negotiations is guided by Turkey's progress in preparing for accession, within a framework of economic and social convergence. This progress is measured in particular against the following four sets of requirements:

1. The Copenhagen criteria, that is, (a) the stability of institutions guaranteeing democracy, the rule of law, human rights and respect for and protection of minorities; (b) the existence of a functioning market economy and the capacity to cope with competitive pressure and market forces within the Union; (c) the ability to take on the obligations

of membership, including adherence to the aims of political, economic and monetary union and the administrative capacity effectively to apply and implement the *acquis*.

2. Turkey's unequivocal commitment to good neighbourly relations and its undertaking to resolve any outstanding border disputes in conformity with the principle of peaceful settlement of disputes in accordance with the United Nations Charter, including if necessary jurisdiction of the International Court of Justice.

3. Turkey's continued support for efforts to achieve a comprehensive settlement of the Cyprus problem within the UN framework and in line with the principles on which the Union is founded, including steps to contribute to a favourable climate for a comprehensive settlement, and progress in the normalization of bilateral relations between Turkey and all EU member states, including the Republic of Cyprus.

4. The fulfilment of Turkey's obligations under the Association Agreement and its Additional Protocol (1964) extending the Association Agreement to all new EU member states, in particular those pertaining to the EU–Turkey customs union, as well as the implementation of the Accession Partnership, as regularly revised.

Parallel to accession negotiations, the Union engages with Turkey in an intensive political and civil society dialogue. The aim of the inclusive civil society dialogue is to enhance mutual understanding by bringing people together in particular with a view to ensuring the support of European citizens for the accession process.

Accession implies the acceptance of the rights and obligations deriving from the *acquis* and attached to the Union system and its institutional framework, such as (1) the content, principles and political objectives of the treaties on which the Union is founded; (2) legislation and decisions adopted pursuant to the treaties, and the case-law of the Court of Justice; (3) other acts, legally binding or not, adopted within the Union framework, such as interinstitutional agreements, resolutions, statements, recommendations and guidelines; (4) joint actions, common positions, declarations, conclusions and other acts within the framework of the common foreign and security policy; (5) joint actions, joint positions, conventions signed, resolutions, statements and other acts agreed within the framework of justice and home affairs; (6) international agreements concluded by the Communities, the Communities jointly with their member states, the Union, and those concluded by the member states among themselves with regard to Union activities.

Turkey's acceptance of the rights and obligations arising from the *acquis* may necessitate specific adaptations to the *acquis* and may, exceptionally, give rise to transitional measures which must be defined during the accession negotiations.

The financial aspects of the accession of Turkey must be allowed for in the applicable Financial Framework. Since Turkey's accession could have substantial financial consequences, the negotiations can be concluded only after the establishment of the Financial Framework for the period from 2014 together with possible consequential financial reforms.

In all areas of the *acquis*, Turkey must bring its institutions, management capacity and administrative and judicial systems up to Union standards, at both national and regional level, with a view to implementing the *acquis* effectively or, as the case may be, being able to implement it effectively in good time before accession. At the general level, this requires a well-functioning and stable public administration built on an efficient and impartial civil service, and an independent and efficient judicial system.

The EU will lay down benchmarks for the provisional closure and, where appropriate, for the opening of each chapter.[22] Turkey will be requested to indicate its position in relation to the *acquis* and to report on its progress in meeting the benchmarks. Turkey's correct transposition and implementation of the *acquis*, including effective and efficient application through appropriate administrative and judicial structures, will determine the pace of negotiations.

Issues, prospects and challenges

The accession negotiations and the forthcoming Turkish accession present challenges to both Turkey and the EU. It is widely accepted that 'Turkey's accession would be different from previous enlargements because of the combined impact of Turkey's population, size, geographical location, economic, security and military potential.'[23] The negotiations are taking place in the framework of an intergovernmental conference and decisions are made by unanimity which requires the participation and approval of all member states. Keeping in mind that by the time of Turkish accession the EU will include at least 27 members – Bulgaria and Romania are expected to become full members in January 2007 – the issue of unanimity becomes a critical and complicated one. The case of Turkey will be different and more challenging from previous accessions for a number of reasons, some of which are presented below.[24]

Turkey is a country with a large population and geographic area. With a population of 71 million today, it is projected that it could be the largest member state at the time of accession. It is worth mentioning that the last enlargement included ten countries with a total population of 75 million. As a Moslem secular country, Turkey will also add a new demographic and religious dimension to the EU. Also, the presence of a large number of Turkish immigrants in European countries raises the issue of possible additional migration, as a natural consequence of accession, which may affect the labour market and demography of small member states. The social repercussions of such a development raise sensitivities and pose challenges with political ramifications.

The EU, in an effort to address cultural and religious differences at the grass roots level, is promoting political and cultural dialogue between the people of Turkey and EU member states. This dialogue will address concerns and perceptions on issues such as 'difference of cultures, religion, issues relating to migration, concerns on minority rights and terrorism'.[25] The view from Brussels is that although 'the negotiation process will be essential in guiding further reforms in Turkey ... the civil society should play the most important role in this dialogue'.[26] This is an interesting and innovative strategy, which upgrades the role of the civil society which is moving to the centre of the political stage in the EU and can also make a difference in Turkey's Europeanization process. In this regard, the strengthening of civil society in Turkey is a major objective of the EU pre-accession strategy.

The Kurdish question is a multifaceted challenge that is becoming more and more an accepted reality and an item on the agenda of EU–Turkish relations. As a 'major fault line within Turkish democracy' and a problem without 'a solution on the horizon', it is a source of concern at home and in the EU.[27] The EU assessment is that 'progress has been slow and uneven. In some cases, it has even deteriorated.'[28] The Kurdish issue has also ramifications in some EU member states where Kurdish immigrants live and have established active political and cultural organizations. Another transnational aspect of the Kurdish issue is the fact that developments in the neighbouring countries of Iraq, Iran and Syria – where also Kurds live – can easily have an impact on Turkey. As Andrew Mango, put it, 'Kurdish nationalism is a many-headed [*sic*] hydra, and it will survive somewhere, if not everywhere'.[29]

The strategic location of Turkey presents a unique challenge to the EU's external role and policies as 'it lies at the epicenter of a series of conflicts, real and potential'[30] in the region. Turkish accession will bring closer to the EU the instability and tensions of a strategically vital region with strong, conflicting energy-related interests. The unstable neighbour-hoods of the Middle East, Caucasus and Central Asia will become the immediate neighbourhood of the EU and its member states. As a major power in the region 'Turkey could be drawn into conflicts that work against European, Central Asian, and Middle Eastern integration and peace.'[31] In conjunction with this point, the addition of new long exter-nal borders will present a major challenge to the EU as it will involve critical policies and issues such as migration, asylum and drug-smuggling.

Turkey's participation in the European common foreign and security policy can also be controversial. Its role in NATO is a central one and so far it 'has not witnessed a strong "Europeanization" of its foreign policy'.[32] Its large military force will make it a major military power in the EU with the largest number of military personnel. Turkey – like other member states – has already shown that on issues of vital national interest it is not willing to compromise and align its foreign and security policy with the positions of other states. The willingness and ability of Turkey to meet European expectations on issues of security and defence are also largely determined by domestic factors such as civil–military relations and secular–religious dichotomies.

The discussion over external policy and orientation points to the fact 'that modern Turkey has functioned as part of several systems – European, Middle Eastern, Eurasian – while remaining on the cultural and political periphery of each'.[33] It cannot go unnoticed that Turkey has uneasy bilateral relations with some of its neighbours and has been characterized a 'reluctant neighbour'.[34] For example, relations with Syria have been bad in recent decades for various reasons, including water resources and Kurdish connections. Iran's Islamic political orientation and nuclear ambitions are sources of concern for Turkey. Turkey's policy of expanding its influence in the Turkic states of the Caucasus and Central Asia have alarmed Russia, while Armenia has no diplomatic rela-tions with Turkey and the border between the two countries has been closed.

Turkey has unresolved issues and unstable relations or no relations at all with some EU member states. Greece and Cyprus are cases in point. In recent years, Greek–Turkish relations have improved considerably and Greece's policy towards Turkish accession is a positive one, but this depends on the political barometer over the Aegean and Cyprus. The fact that Turkey does not recognize the Republic of Cyprus – a full member of the EU since May 2004 – has been a source of legal controversies and political complications. In that regard, there is still an open question: how can a candidate country conduct accession negotiations and sign an international treaty (like the accession treaty) with a country it does not recognize?

The Cyprus problem has been a source of difficulties for EU–Turkish relations and Greek–Turkish relations. The Mediterranean island has been a flash point in the region since 1963 when intercommunal fighting broke out. In 1974 a Greek *coup d' état* and a Turkish invasion took place which led to ethnic segregation and the *de facto* division of the island. Besides the division of the island, the presence of a sizeable Turkish army in the northern part of the island and a shared feeling of insecurity among the two local communities are also striking features of the problem. Several efforts for a solution made so far by the UN, or in the name of the UN, have failed. The most recent one culminated in the submission of a comprehensive plan for a settlement in 2004 – known as the Annan Plan – which provided for the establishment of a new state of affairs on the island based on a bizonal bicommunal federation.[35] The two Cypriot communities held separate, simultaneous referenda on the Annan Plan, but it was rejected by the Greek Cypriots.[36] Apparently the majority of the Greek Cypriots believed that the plan was not fair. Especially the provisions on security, the Turkish settlers, the gradual withdrawal of the Turkish army, the exchange of properties, and the return of refugees made the Greek Cypriot voters unhappy. There were also serious questions about the implementation and viability of the plan which created feelings of uncertainty among the Greek Cypriots.[37] The failure of the Annan Plan, the accession of Cyprus to the EU and the commencement of accession negotiations with Turkey have created a new reality, additional urgency and a promising prospect. Sooner or later a momentum will emerge for the reunification of the island which is too small to remain divided, but big enough to accommodate its people as a reunited EU member state. In this regard, besides the UN, the EU can also play a key role in the search of a settlement which will address the concerns of all parties involved. Turkey, in particular, can expect major political benefits from a solution on Cyprus as it will improve its European stature and be in a better position to pursue its goal of accession to the EU.

Turkey has a level of economic development well below that of the EU average and its accession will have a considerable budgetary impact on the EU. Among the economic consequences Turkish accession will have for the EU is the creation of a regional economic disparity and financial burden for other member states. On the basis of current regulations and practices, Turkey will be receiving considerable support from the cohesion and structural funds at the expense of other member states which may no longer be eligible for these funds. The prospect of such a development presents another challenge with political and economic ramifications. Along these lines, Turkey's huge agricultural sector also receives special attention.

The participation of Turkey in the EU institutions will affect dramatically the allocation of power and influence on decision-making, policy formulation and the dynamics of the broader European political arena. As a large member state, Turkey will have a powerful voice in the European Parliament and the Council of Ministers where decisions are mostly made by qualified majority. This shift of power from the Western Christian capitals to the eastern Islamic frontier is already causing scepticism and reactions in some countries.

Besides the above issues, which are discussed in detail in the following chapters, there are topics and aspects inherent in the EU itself and its ability to absorb a new member state like Turkey. Already in 1993, the Copenhagen European Council, besides defining the political and economic criteria, also raised the issue of the EU's capacity to enlarge without undermining the integration process; as stated by the heads of state or government, 'the Union's capacity to absorb new members, while maintaining the momentum of European integration, is also an important consideration in the general interest of both the Union and the candidate countries'.[38] Structural, political and economic developments in the EU during the next decade may affect the deepening and widening of the EU in a way that can have an impact on further enlargement, including the accession of Turkey.

Conclusion: Oriental past vs. Western future

While accession talks and preparations are under way, the debate over Turkey's European prospects is heating up and a variety of perspectives, positions, opinions and arguments are put forward. The president of the European Commission, Romano Prodi, asked Turkey to show 'determination in pursuing further reforms and wisely conducting an accession process which, like all the others, will display both periods of progress and moments of tension and unavoidable difficulties'.[39] He also appealed to the member states and the European public to demonstrate equal perseverance, as 'Europe has nothing to fear from Turkey's accession'.[40]

Europe's confusion and ambivalence about Turkey is not a new phenomenon, although recently it has been becoming more visible. A few years ago, the fear of many Europeans about Turkish accession were expressed and stirred up by the former French president and head of the European constitutional convention Valéry Giscard d'Estaing, who in a blunt and provocative manner declared that Turkey was 'not a European country' and that its inclusion in the EU 'would be the end of Europe'.[41] In a similar vein echoing Turco-scepticism, a European commissioner brought back memories of the Ottoman siege of Vienna by stating that 'the liberation of 1683 would have been in vain'[42] if Turkey joins the EU.

On the other hand, there are strong voices arguing that Turkey can play the role of 'a cultural and physical bridge between the East and West. ... [and] become one of Europe's most prized additions'.[43] Across the Atlantic, the United States has a clear pro-Turkish position that cannot be ignored. In June 2004, during the NATO Summit in Istanbul, the American President George W. Bush underlined that position and called on Europe to prove that it 'is not the exclusive club of a single religion' and that 'as a European power, Turkey belongs in the EU'.[44]

The increasingly polarized discussion over Turkey's position and role in Europe will continue for years to come at various levels. The debate may even outlast the protracted period of accession negotiations during which not only negotiations on the *acquis* chapters will be conducted, but also a lot of diplomatic manoeuvring and political twisting will take place. Throughout this period, the Christian and Islamic worlds will have to show that they can accommodate each other and prove false Samuel Huntington's argument about 'the clash of civilizations' and the reconfiguration of the political world 'along cultural lines'.[45] Both Europe and Turkey will find out what they expect from each other and whether they can share a common future that will reconcile their different their pasts. The real question will be whether the internal socio-political dynamics and external orientations of Turkey can be compatible with the changing dynamics of European integration, which aims at deepening the solidarity among peoples 'while respecting their history, their culture and their traditions', and creating 'firm bases for the construction of the future Europe'.[46]

In the long run and in a broader sense, the challenge for the EU will be to develop a forward-looking world-view based on a multicultural civilization that has ample room for different religions including Islam. In a shrinking world of increasing interdependence this may no longer be a political option, but an urgent imperative for European integration which is a process of building unity through diversity.

Notes

1. Bernard Lewis, *The Emergence of Modern Turkey*, 2nd edn (London: Oxford University Press, 1968), p. 486.

2. Nicole Pope and Hugh Pope, *Turkey Unveiled: A History of Modern Turkey*, 2nd edn (Woodstock, NY: Overlook Press, 2004) p. 59.
3. Heinz Kramer, *A Changing Turkey: The Challenge to Europe and the United States* (Washington, DC: Brookings Institution Press, 2000), p. 9.
4. Lewis, *The Emergence of Modern Turkey*, p. 486.
5. Pope and Pope, *Turkey Unveiled: A History of Modern Turkey*, p. 67.
6. Jacques Chirac talking at a press conference on October 4 (the day after accession talks with the EU were launched); see *Guardian Unlimited* (The Guardian digital edition), 5 October 2005.
7. Treaty on European Union (consolidated version), art. 1.
8. Brussels European Council, 16–17 December 2004, Presidency Conclusions, paragraph 17.
9. The European Commission recommended that: 'The EU will need to define its financial perspectives for the period from 2014 before negotiations [with Turkey] can be concluded.' See European Commission, Communication from the Commission to the Council and the Parliament, 'Recommendation of the European Commission on Turkey's Progress towards Accession' (6 October 2004), p. 5. The Recommendation was issued together with the 2004 'Regular Report on Turkey's Progress Towards Accession.'
10. Agreement Establishing an Association Agreement between the European Economic Community and Turkey, art. 28. The Association Agreement (known as the Ankara Agreement) was signed on 12 September 1963 and went into effect on 1 December 1964.
11. Harun Arikan, *Turkey and the EU: An Awkward Candidate for EU Membership?* (Aldershot: Ashgate, 2003), p. 74.
12. Commission of the European Communities, 'Commission Opinion on Turkey's Request for Accession to the Community', issued 18 December 1989, paragraphs 10 and 11.
13. Helsinki European Council, 10–11 December 1999, Presidency Conclusions, paragraph 12.
14. European Commission, Communication from the Commission to the Council and the Parliament, 'Recommendation of the European Commission on Turkey's Progress Towards Accession,' p. 8.
15. *Washington Times*, 'Turkey's Continental Drift,' 10 October 2004.
16. José Manuel Barroso, President of the European Commission, statement at a press conference, 17 December 2004.
17. The results of a poll carried out in October–November 2005 showed that 55 per cent of the Europeans are against Turkish accession, 31 per cent in favour, and the rest 14 per cent do knot know. Source: Standard Eurobarometer 64, published by the European Commission in December 2005. These results are consistent with similar findings of polls carried out in recent years.
18. José Manuel Barroso, president of the European Commission, statement at a press conference, 16 December 2004.
19. Olli Rehn, 'Accession Negotiations with Turkey: The Journey Is as Important as the Final Destination', speech at the European Parliament, 28 September 2005.
20. This section of the chapter is a compilation of the main points included in the EU paper 'Negotiating Framework for Turkey: Principles Governing the Negotiations' (2005). It also draws on the 'EU Opening Statement for the Accession Conference with Turkey' (2005).

21. The 'Copenhagen criteria' were decided by the Copenhagen European Council, 21–22 June 1993, and spelled out in the Presidency Conclusions as follows:

    Membership requires that the candidate country has achieved stability of institutions guaranteeing democracy, the rule of law, human rights and respect for the protection of minorities, the existence of a functioning market economy as well as the capacity to cope with competitive pressure and market forces within the Union. Membership presupposes the candidate's ability to take on the obligations of membership including adherence to the aims of the political, economic and monetary union.

22. For the purposes of the accession negotiations, the *acquis* has been divided into the following chapters: 1. Free movement of goods; 2. Freedom of movement for workers; 3. Right of establishment and freedom to provide services; 4. Free movement of capital; 5. Public procurement; 6. Company law; 7. Intellectual property law; 8. Competition policy; 9. Financial services; 10. Information society and media; 11. Agriculture and rural development; 12. Food safety, veterinary and phytosanitary policy; 13. Fisheries; 14. Transport policy; 15. Energy; 16. Taxation; 17. Economic and monetary policy; 18. Statistics; 19. Social policy and employment (including anti-discrimination and equal opportunities for women and men); 20. Enterprise and industrial policy; 21. Trans-European networks; 22. Regional policy and coordination of structural instruments; 23. Judiciary and fundamental rights; 24. Justice, freedom and security; 25. Science and research; 26. Education and culture; 27. Environment; 28. Consumer and health protection; 29. Customs union; 30. External relations; 31. Foreign, security and defence policy; 32. Financial control; 33. Financial and budgetary provisions; 34. Institutions; 35. Other issues.

23. European Commission, 'Recommendation of the European Commission on Turkey's Progress Towards Accession' (6 October 2004), p. 3.

24. An elaborate presentation of the issues and challenges arising from the prospect of Turkish accession is included in the Commission staff working document: 'Issues Arising from Turkey's Membership Perspective', SEC (2004) 1202.

25. European Commission, 'Recommendation of the European Commission on Turkey's Progress Towards Accession' (6 October 2004), p. 7.

26. Ibid., p. 9.

27. Kramer, *A Changing Turkey: The Challenge to Europe and the United States*, p. 52.

28. European Commission, 'Turkey: 2005 Progress Report' (9 November 2005), p. 38.

29. Andrew Mango, *The Turks Today* (London: John Murray, 2004), p. 211.

30. John W. Mountcastle, 'Foreword', in Stephen J. Black, Stephen C. Pelletiere and William T. Johnsen, *Turkeys's Strategic Position at the Crossroads of World Affairs* (Honolulu, HI: University Press of the Pacific, 2002), p. v.

31. Black *et al.*, *Turkey's Strategic Position at the Crossroads of World Affairs*, p. 2.

32. F. Stephen Larrabee and Ian O. Lesser, *Turkish Foreign Policy in an Age of Uncertainty* (Santa Monica, CA: Rand Corporation, 2003), p. 65.

33. Ibid., p. 189.

34. From the title of a book by Henri J. Barkey, ed., *Reluctant Neighbor: Turkey's Role in the Middle East* (Washington, DC: US Institute of Peace Press, 1996).

35. For an extensive account on the developments which led to the shaping of the Annan Plan and its failure, see the 'Report of the Secretary General on His Mission of Good Offices in Cyprus', UN doc. S/2004/437 of 28 May 2004.

36. At the referenda, which were held on 24 April 2004, the majority of the Greek Cypriots (75.83 per cent) voted *no* and the majority of the Turkish Cypriots (64.91 per cent) voted *yes*.

37. An elaborate account of the Greek Cypriot positions on the weaknesses and rejection of the Annan Plan was presented in a long letter by the president of the Republic of Cyprus to the UN secretary-general dated 7 June 2004.

38. Copenhagen European Council, 21–22 June 1993, Presidency Conclusions, paragraph 7(A)iii.

39. Romano Prodi, president of the European Commission 'The Commission's Report and Recommendation on Turkey's Application', presentation to the European Parliament, 6 October 2004.

40. Ibid.

41. Valéry Giscard d'Estaing, 'Pour ou contre l'adhésion de la Turquie à l'Union Européenne', interview with *Le Monde*, 9 November 2002.

42. Frits Bolkenstein, European Commissioner for Internal Market, speech at the University of Leiden, 6 September 2004. In his speech, Bolkenstein cited the pre-eminent historian and Islamic expert Bernard Lewis.

43. *Washington Times*, 'Turkey's Continental Drift'.

44. Remarks by President George W. Bush, 29 June 2004.

45. Samuel Huntingon, *The Clash of Civilizations and the Remaking of World Order* (New York: Simon & Schuster, 1996), p. 20.

46. Treaty on European Union (consolidated version), Preamble.

2

The Economic Dimension of Turkey's EU Membership: A Stock-Taking Exercise at the Start of Accession Negotiations

Mehmet Ugur

Introduction

The public debate on European Union (EU)–Turkey relations tends to focus on the political dimension of Turkey's EU membership and on the quality with which recent political reforms are likely to be implemented. To some extent, this focus on political issues has been at the expense of detailed work on economic issues in EU–Turkey relations. Part of the reason for this asymmetry has been the assumption that Turkey is well placed to carry out economic reforms given the post-1980 liberalization efforts and the customs union with the EU. Another reason has been the fact that IMF and/or World Bank conditionality since the mid 1990s has already led to a significant degree of economic policy convergence towards EU norms. However, the IMF conditionality is likely to be phased out from the end of 2007 onwards. In addition, the EU has begun accession negotiations, which will require the adoption of not only trade-related EU legislation but also the *acquis communautaire* in its entirety. Given these developments, the economic costs and benefits of accession will acquire added significance for both Turkey and the EU.

The economic effects of accession on the EU can be expected to be small for two reasons. First, EU imports from Turkey account only for about 3 per cent of total EU imports. In addition, about 70 per cent of Turkish agricultural exports already enter the EU without tariffs or quantitative restrictions. Therefore, the impact of further trade liberalization in sectors not covered by the customs union (mainly agriculture and services) will be small. Second, free movement of people will be introduced gradually and the transition may take longer than the seven-year period imposed after previous enlargements. Nevertheless, the main impact of Turkish accession on the EU will be budgetary. Turkey will be a net beneficiary and the extent of transfers from the EU budget will depend on the reform of the Common Agricultural Policy (CAP) and the speed with which agricultural and structural support to Turkey is aligned with the regime that applies to other member states.

Nonetheless, Turkey's accession is a source of major concern for the EU for well-known reasons. First, Turkey is by far the largest and least-developed candidate compared with new member states. Therefore, the budgetary implications for the EU are expected to be significant. Second, Turkey has a large agricultural sector that employs about 33 per cent of her labour force and accounts for 12 per cent of her GDP. In addition, Turkey's official unemployment rates are high (over 10 per cent) and the transformation of agriculture is expected to add further to the numbers of unemployed. The combination of a large agricultural sector and already high levels of unemployment is expected to create a high level of migratory pressure.

As far as Turkey is concerned, the impact of accession will also be felt through a number of channels. First, the transformation of economic policy framework will imply significant adjustment costs in all sectors of the Turkish economy. These adjustment costs will result from increased competition and from compliance with higher regulatory standards within a single market. These costs can be expected to be higher in sectors that have been less exposed to EU rules and competition within the customs union – mainly agriculture, energy, and services. Second, accession will alter the rules of the game that determine the expectations of the economic actors in Turkey. The speed at which expectations are revised will affect not only the profitability of the micro level economic units, but also the country's macroeconomic performance. Finally, budgetary transfers from the EU will affect agriculture and the regions where reliance on agriculture is significant.

This chapter aims to disentangle the potential economic costs and benefits of Turkey's accession and provide a basis for further research. To achieve this aim, we draw on existing findings and provide additional evidence on factors that may affect the costs and benefits of Turkish accession. The chapter is organized in four sections. In the next one, we examine the likely impact of accession on economic growth and adjustment costs in Turkey. Here, we will see that EU membership will constitute a structural break for the Turkish economy, leading to significant adjustment costs and potentially higher growth rates. Given that adjustment costs are temporary, it will be argued that accession is highly likely to improve the welfare of Turkish citizens and may well lead to a less inequitable distribution of income in Turkey. In the third section, we examine the impact of Turkish accession on the EU. We will see that the cost of Turkish accession for the EU will be mainly of a budgetary nature. The cost due to migration is likely to be very small, but it will be borne by low wage-earners. However, the overall impact of Turkish accession on the EU is highly likely to be positive given the scope for increased trade and investment flows. Finally, in the fourth section we will note the main findings and indicate the areas where further research is necessary.

Impacts of EU accession on Turkey

The traditional literature on regional integration focused on the effects of trade creation and trade diversion, using comparative static methods of calculation. The pioneering study by Viner concluded that regional integration would lead to an increase in welfare if the trade-creating effect dominates the trade-diversion effect.[1] Empirical studies on the EU found that the welfare effect of the EU-wide customs union would be small, usually less than 1 per cent of the benchmark GDP.[2] Studies of the EU–Turkey customs union obtained similar results: the welfare gain for Turkey would be between 0.5 to 1.5 per cent of the benchmark GDP, depending on the accompanying tax reforms and other structural reforms.[3]

These findings suggest that the gains from regional integration are likely to be small and conditional on a number of reforms. Therefore, they raise the question as to why countries choose to join regional blocs and why regional blocs proliferated in the 1990s. To explain this conundrum, a new generation of research on regional integration suggests that there may be additional effects of regional integration that are not captured in the traditional approach. One of these effects – the dynamic effect of integration over time – has been noted by earlier studies, but it was considered as too uncertain to be quantified. Baldwin, in a widely discussed paper, attempted to capture this effect by examining the effect of static gains on investment and future growth.[4] He demonstrates that the static gains from integration will act like a positive shock to the capital stock, leading to higher growth rates in the future. Although this was an innovative method of trying to capture the dynamic effect, it overlooks the institutional effects of deepening integration on existing members as well as the institutional effects of accession on new members.

Fernandez made the first attempt to tackle the institutional effects of regional integration on economic performance, which he describes as non-traditional gains from regional integration.[5] Among those, two are particularly relevant to new EU members in general and Turkey in particular: signalling and policy credibility. In this context, the signalling effect results from the fact that EU membership enables the government of the day to signal to domestic and foreign investors that: (1) the economy is resolute enough to cope with competitive pressure in a single market; (2) the government is willing and able to cope with the adjustment costs of membership; and (3) the government's future economic policies will be compatible with the EU-wide policy choices. The policy credibility effect, on the other hand, results from the government's willingness to rely on the EU as a commitment mechanism that would reduce the risk of policy reversals in the future. Fernandez suggests that both signalling and policy credibility may have positive effects on the rates of investment and growth in the future.

Against these potential gains, producers in the acceding country will incur adjustment costs. These costs can be classified into two groups. First, there are adjustment costs caused by increased exposure to competition from EU producers. As competition from EU producers increases, uncompetitive producers will lose market share in both the EU and the domestic market. The fall in market shares will initially lead to an increase in average costs as less output is now produced with the given amounts of capital and labour. As increasing average costs bite into profit margins, firms will start to lay off employees or the latter will have to accept lower wages. Hence, eventually the cost of increased exposure to competition will be observed as a combination of falling profit rates for companies and higher risks of unemployment and/or falling wages.

The other type of cost is related to the adoption of new regulatory and environmental standards. The acceding country will have to adopt all the EU rules and regulations concerning health and safety at work, employment protection, environmental protection, product health and safety standards, and so on. These regulatory standards will increase the firms' cost of production in the acceding country. The increase in the cost of production is a once-and-for-all increase (a static cost) if the regulatory burden does not lead to lower overall growth rates in the future. The regulatory cost however may acquire a dynamic feature if the overall growth rates fall owing to the increase in regulatory burden.

In what follows, we will try to provide evidence on the relative significance of the expected benefits and costs of Turkey's EU membership. We first begin with the trade-related benefits and costs. Then, we examine the impact of accession on economic growth through the 'signalling' and 'credibility' effects of integration. After this macro level assessment, we focus on agriculture as a specific area where the adjustment cost of accession is relatively high.

Trade-related effects of Turkey's EU membership

The first impact we examine here is that of EU accession on sectoral profits. Bekmez conducted a computable general equilibrium (CGE) analysis to trace the implications of different scenarios for sectoral profits, average variable costs and profit/capital ratio.[6] He assumes that capital is fixed and the change in average variable costs is due to changes in the demand for labour. We draw on his findings for the scenario involving EU membership. As can be seen from Table 2.1 below, the impact of EU accession on sectoral profits is small but positive. Overall profits are estimated to increase by Turkish lira (TL) 1505 billion relative to the base-year profits in 1990. This is equivalent to an increase of about 0.8 per cent. What is important here is not the magnitude of the positive impact *per se*, but the distribution of costs and benefits that underpins this overall result. As predicted by the theory, EU accession will have different effects on different sectors, depending on the initial conditions that exist before membership. The figures in Table 2.1 suggest that the sectors most likely to lose are those that had been protected in 1990, that is, before trade liberalization. These are the tobacco industry, transport equipment, petroleum products, and general services. Because of significant profit declines in these sectors, the positive impact of EU accession on sectoral profits remains small.

Yet this finding can be qualified in a number of ways. First of all, the decline in some sectoral profits is not necessarily an undesirable outcome. This would be especially the case had the sectors that experience profit declines been protected before trade liberalization. To the extent that this is the case, these sectors must have been extracting monopoly profits and the decline in those profits does not necessarily imply a loss of welfare. In fact, social welfare may increase if the profit decline has been due to lower prices, which increases consumers' welfare by more than the decline in producers' welfare.

Second, the estimates above are based on two restrictive assumptions: (1) EU membership will affect sectoral profits only through the change in trade patterns; and (2) the supply of capital is fixed. In other words, sectors faced with increased competition are assumed to be able to change only their demand for labour. However, EU accession can be expected to have a positive effect on capital flows through foreign direct investment

Table 2.1 Impact of EU membership on sectoral profits

Sector	Base-year profit (1990, bn TL)	Per cent change due to EU membership	Change (bn TL)
Basic agriculture	28,889.46	2.05	592.23
Agribusiness	4,274.20	5.09	217.56
Mining	3,148.34	11.11	349.78
Beverage industry	1,353.20	−0.42	−5.68
Tobacco industry	1,425.67	−17.47	−249.06
Textiles	5,717.65	12.83	733.57
Wearing apparel	1,755.56	14.63	256.84
Leather & fur products	817.40	11.81	96.53
Wood & furniture	2182.72	1.26	27.50
Paper & publishing	1,429.70	−3.59	−51.33
Chemical products	4,575.21	0.38	17.39
Petroleum products	4,605.71	−4.73	−217.85
Glass and glass products	776.36	0.71	5.51
Non-metallic products	4,728.28	0.11	5.20
Metal industry	4,354.45	5.94	258.65
Non-electrical machinery	2,579.88	3.62	93.39
Electrical machinery	1,956.39	−3.24	−63.39
Transport equipment	1,723.23	−10.97	−189.04
Electricity–gas–water	5,148.68	−0.87	−44.79
Construction	7,562.06	1.55	117.21
Transportation–communication	42,688.84	3.97	1,694.75
Other services	54,850.24	−3.90	−2,139.16
Total	186,543.23		1,505.81

and joint ventures. To the extent that this is the case, the supply of capital can no longer be taken as constant. Therefore, EU accession may affect not only the demand for labour but also the demand for capital. As a result, the sectors that appear to suffer from declining profits in Table 2.1 may be able to reverse this trend by restructuring.

Finally, the fall in the profits of initially protected sectors may coexist with increased profits as well as wages in other sectors. In other words, EU membership may be affecting not only the distribution of profits between sectors, but also the distribution of the value added between labour and capital in individual sectors. In fact, Bekmez provides results which suggest that this may be the case.[7] Most of the sectors with increased profits in Table 2.1 are the very sectors where the average variable costs – that is, labour earnings – are also expected to increase. Because profits are net of costs, the effect of EU membership on total value added (profits + wages + rents) is bound to be larger than the 0.8 per cent mentioned above.

A study by Togan enables us to go beyond the impact of EU membership on sectoral profits reported in Table 2.1.[8] He uses ordinary least squares (OLS) estimates of a gravity model of trade between the EU-15 to forecast bilateral trade between Turkey and the EU-15 after accession. The forecast indicates that Turkish trade (average of exports and imports) with the EU-15 would have been $26.1 billion in 2000. Given that the actual trade was $18.5 billion on average over 1999–2001, Togan concludes that EU accession can be expected to lead to an increase of 41 per cent in Turkish trade with the EU-15. This estimated increase will be partly due to trade liberalization in agriculture and services (sectors not covered by the customs union) and partly because of the trade-creating effects of the single market beyond the customs union.

This estimate, however, is subject to uncertainty – as reflected by the long range between the lower limit ($9.7 billion) and upper limit ($70.3 billion) of a 95 per cent confidence interval. Therefore, Togan provides an alternative estimate based on convergence of Turkey–EU trade towards the share of intra-EU trade in total trade of large EU members. Currently, large EU members conduct about 58 per cent of their trade (the average of exports and imports) with other EU members. Turkish trade with the EU, however, is about 50 per cent of total trade. Therefore, there is a potential for increased trade openness between Turkey and the EU, which is equivalent to about 5 per cent of the benchmark GDP. In addition, the existing work on trade openness and economic growth suggests that there is a positive association between the two. For example, Frankel and Rose estimate that a single percentage point increase in trade openness (the average trade/GDP ratio) is associated with a 0.3 percentage point increase in GDP growth rate.[9] Then, we can expect Turkish GDP to increase 1.5 per cent faster as a result of increased trade openness.

The estimates above are in addition to what Harrison *et al.* have estimated for the customs union.[10] These authors have estimated that the customs union would increase Turkish GDP by 0.5 to 1.5 per cent of the benchmark level in early 1990s. Further integration in the single market can also be expected to generate trade-related benefits. These benefits can be estimated to be around 1.0 to 1.5 per cent of Turkish GDP at the end of the 1990s. However, existing theories also suggest that EU membership can affect Turkish GDP growth through other channels too. Two such channels are especially significant: (1) the policy credibility channel, and (2) the signalling channel. What underpins the accession's impact through these channels is the structural break with the old policy framework. The expected impact on GDP growth is positive and will be due to improved institutional quality. This likely effect is examined below.

The institutional effects of Turkey's EU membership

Throughout the 1980s and 1990s, the Turkish economic policy framework was based on a symbiotic relationship between discretionary policies and rent-seeking behaviour. This symbiotic relationship was underpinned by institutions (that is, rules, regulations, norms and conventions, and so on) that provided perverse incentives, increased the risk of economic instability and worked against economic growth. As a result, Turkey's macroeconomic performance has deteriorated over time and the prospect of EU membership has become increasingly problematic.[11] The deterioration in Turkey's economic performance can be seen in Table 2.2 below. Average growth rates in Turkey declined from 4.76 per cent in the 1970s to 3.93 per cent in the 1990s, whereas the coefficient of variation increased from 51 per cent to 137 per cent over the same period.

There is extensive work indicating that macroeconomic instability in the 1990s went hand in hand with low institutional quality in Turkey. Low institutional quality was evident in the degree of discretion (that is, absence of transparent and enforceable rules),[12] the opacity of fiscal rules and procedures,[13] the absence of a credible monetary policy framework,[14] high levels of corruption, and high levels of rent-seeking activities organized around distributive policies of the central and local government.[15] As a result of low institutional quality, attempts at stabilization have lacked credibility and the risks associated with long-term investment have increased. Stated differently, low institutional quality has generated incentives against long-term investment and growth, and encouraged pro-cyclical policies and rent-seeking.

Table 2.2 Declining growth rates and increasing volatility in Turkey: decade averages

Decade	(1) Average growth (%)	(2) Standard deviation	(3) Coefficient of variation (%) (2) / (1) × 100
1970–79	4.76	2.43	51
1980–89	4.04	2.70	67
1990–99	3.93	5.37	137

Source: Calculated from GDP data at 1987 prices.

As is well known, EU membership essentially implies imports of institutions through the adoption of the EU's *acquis communautaire*. The economic *acquis* will imply a significant improvement in institutional quality as discretion is replaced by rules and the scope for populist policies is reduced. These improvements will increase the credibility of economic policies and induce economic actors to revise their expectations accordingly. As a result, we can expect a reduction in economic volatility and an improvement in economic performance.

Cross-country studies reported by the IMF demonstrate that macro economic instability (measured as the standard deviation of GDP growth rates) is inversely related to institutional quality. According to the IMF, the volatility of GDP growth would fall by approximately 25 per cent should a country's institutional quality improve by one standard deviation.[16] This finding is relevant for Turkey's experience in 1990s, when low institutional quality was associated with three successive crises and increased volatility. In addition, recent work also suggests that reduced economic volatility is conducive to better economic performance.[17] Given these findings, we can see that an increase in institutional quality due to EU membership is likely to dampen economic volatility and improve economic performance in terms of GDP growth. This is what we described earlier as the 'policy credibility effect' of EU accession.

If we assume that Turkey had been able to join the EU in 1990 and had membership led to a 16 per cent (one standard deviation) convergence of Turkey's institutional quality towards the EU average, then the volatility of Turkish GDP growth in the 1990s would have been reduced by $(5.37) \times (25$ per cent$) = 1.35$ units. Hnatkovska and Loayza report that a one-unit fall in the standard deviation (that is, volatility) of GDP growth is conducive to a 2.2 per cent increase in the per capita GDP growth rate. Given that improved institutional quality could have reduced GDP growth volatility by 5.37×25 per cent $= 1.35$ units then per capita GDP growth rate would have increased by $2.2 \times 1.35 = 2.97$ percentage points over and above the actual growth rates recorded in the 1990s.

Turkish GDP increased by 3.93 per cent in the 1990s (Table 2.2), whereas population growth was 1.83 per cent.[18] Therefore, the average per capita GDP growth in Turkey in the 1990s was $3.93 - 1.83 = 2.1$ per cent. Given that improved institutional quality could have increased per capita GDP growth by $2.2 \times 1.35 = 2.97$ percentage points over and above the actual growth rates recorded in the 1990s, the annual increase in per capita GDP would have been $2.97 + 2.21 = 5.18$ per cent per year. If we normalize the level of per capita income at the beginning of the decade to 1, then the difference between low-volatility and high-volatility incomes would be $(1 + 0.0518)^{10} - (1 + 0.021)^{10} = 0.426$. This means that per capita GDP under EU membership would have been $[0.426/(1 + 0.021)^{10}] \times 100 = 34.6$ per cent higher than the actual per capita GDP recorded at the end of the 1990s. Put differently, at the end of the 1990s, Turkish citizens would have been more than one-third better off had Turkey joined the EU in 1990 and had EU membership led to improvement in institutional quality.

This estimate must be qualified because it is based on findings of cross-country regression results. As is well known, cross-country regression analysis is similar to a snapshot taken at a certain point in time and is not necessarily valid for making reliable predictions for a particular country over time. Despite this qualification, however, there are three reasons why the positive impact of EU membership on per capita GDP cannot be overlooked.

First, the estimate above relates only to the indirect impact of institutions on per capita GDP – that is, to the impact that comes about as a result of reduced volatility. However, improved institutional quality can also have a direct effect on GDP growth. For example, Nsouli et al. report that a one-point increase in the ICRG's 'investment profile rating' (a rating based on perceived institutional quality) is associated with a 1 per cent increase in the growth rate.[19] This is net of any positive effect that may result from the implementation of the IMF-sponsored stabilization programmes that aim to reduce volatility. In addition, Rodrik et al. report that a one-unit improvement in the institutional quality is conducive to a 2.0 to 2.15 per cent improvement in per capita GDP.[20] Second, there is also an extensive range of empirical findings indicating that an improvement in institutional quality is associated with increased investment and technological deepening. For example, Clarke[21] and Hall and Jones[22] report that technological deepening, capital accumulation and productivity are all positively associated with institutional quality.

Finally, the estimated static effect of institutional improvement for Turkey is positive. Using a computable general equilibrium model, Lejour et al. report that Turkish GDP could increase by 5.6 per cent between 2015 and 2025 if Turkey's ranking on the 'corruption perception index' of Transparency International improves from 64 to 25.[23] This static effect excludes any dynamic effect that may result from economies of scale or from technological spillovers usually associated with integration. Therefore, the institutional impact of EU membership we estimated above (an additional GDP increase of 2.97 per cent per year) may not be exact but there is extensive evidence to suggest that improved institutional quality due to adoption of EU rules and regulations would have a positive effect on GDP growth as well as GDP per capita growth. This impact is likely to be between 1.0 and 2.0 per cent per year, in addition to any trade-related effect.

Another institutional effect of EU membership on Turkish GDP growth is related to what we described as signalling. By joining the EU, Turkey would signal to domestic and foreign investors that the Turkish economy is resolute enough to cope with competitive pressure and that the government is willing to carry out the necessary structural reforms. It would also signal that sectors less likely to cope with competitive pressure cannot expect special treatment in terms of protectionist trade policies or sector-specific subsidies. That is because the economic *acquis* either prohibits such protection or makes it time-limited and conditional on structural change. Then, these signals will have two effects on investor strategies. On the one hand, they will induce domestic and foreign investors to increase their investment in relatively competitive sectors. On the other hand, they will induce the incumbents of the relatively less-competitive sectors to engage in productivity-enhancing investment aimed at preventing bankruptcy.

We do not have direct estimates for the growth of net capital for Turkey before and after accession. However, a recent report by ABN-AMRO, a Dutch investment bank, provides figures for net capital stock and foreign direct investment (FDI) flows into the peripheral members of the EU: Greece, Ireland, Portugal and Spain. ABN-AMRO (2004) reports that the net capital stock in these countries increased by 1–1.9 per cent per year faster than the EU average after accession.[24] One reason for the relatively higher growth rates is the fact that these countries were relatively capital-scarce before accession. Given relative capital scarcity, the returns on capital were higher than the EU average and this led to relatively higher levels of investment in the new members. The other reason, however, was that EU membership constituted a change in the business environment and signalled to investors that the risk of policy reversals is low as a result of adopting the EU *acquis*. ABN-AMRO report similar trends in FDI flows too. Whereas net FDI flows to Portugal and Spain were 1.5 per cent of GDP during the decade before accession, FDI flows during the decade after accession increased to about 2.5 per cent of GDP. In other words, accession was associated with an additional net FDI flow of 1 percentage point of GDP per year. These figures suggest that EU membership does indeed have a signalling effect, which encourages both domestic and foreign investment after accession.

The analysis above demonstrates that EU membership is likely to have a positive impact on Turkish economic growth beyond the impact that may be associated with further trade openness. A rough estimate would suggest that this positive impact will be about 1.0–2.0 per cent per year in addition to the growth rates that would be attainable in a Turkey that remains outside the EU. However, the caveat here is that this positive impact will take place only if EU membership leads to a significant improvement in the quality of institutions in Turkey. Although the reforms undertaken to meet the Copenhagen criteria and the adoption of the economic *acquis* are likely to act as positive shocks to institutional quality in Turkey, they do not necessarily prevent political instability nor do they necessarily eradicate the anti-institutional bias of populism. Therefore, we must treat these estimates as potential gains that depend on the extent to which the positive institutional shock of EU membership is not unravelled by political instability and populism in Turkey after accession.

A further question that arises in the debate on Turkey's EU membership is whether or not accession will be followed by a worsening of income inequalities. This question is pertinent because EU membership essentially boils down to increased exposure to competition in a single market where freedom of movement for goods and capital is the norm. In this environment, firms and employees less endowed with physical and human capital are likely to lose out whereas well-endowed firms and employees are likely to gain. This environment will be conducive to worsening income distribution if two conditions are satisfied: (1) EU membership is followed by relatively lower economic growth compared with the historical trend of the country, and (2) the government's taxation transfer policies become regressive.

The existing evidence suggests that the probability for the first condition to obtain is very low. As indicated above, the existing evidence suggests that new member countries are highly likely to benefit from trade-related and/or institutional effects of regional integration. In addition, the experience of earlier enlargements that involved Greece, Ireland, Portugal and Spain (countries with initial conditions similar to those of Turkey) suggests that less-developed new members tended to grow faster than their historical trends (and the EU average) after they acceded to the EU.[25] We do not have evidence on the change in taxation transfer policies of the member states comparable to Turkey, but we do have evidence on indicators of income inequality after accession, which is presented in Table 2.3.

Table 2.3 Indicators of income inequality: Gini index[a]

	Early 1980s	Mid 1980s	Early 1990s	Mid 1990s	Year 2000
Greece	36.6	36.1	32.6	34.5	32.3
Ireland	36.6	38.8	36.8	30.9	32.1
	(1973 = 38.2)				
Portugal	35.7[b]	34.8[b, c]	34.7[d]	36.8[d]	34.7[d]
Spain	35.6	25.9	34.5	35.2	32.9
Turkey	48.5	44.0	n.a.	45.7	39.8

Source: UNU/WIDER Database (United Nations University, World Institute for Development Economics Research).

Notes:
[a] Figures for years nearest to the beginning, middle and end of decade, except 2000. Simple averages, when two or more Gini indices are given for a year.
[b] Continental Portugal only.
[c] Source: TUSIAD (Turkish Industrialists' and Businessmen's Association)[26]
[d] Continental Portugal and overseas territories.

As can be seen from Table 2.3, there is no uniform trend in income inequality immediately after EU membership. In two countries, income inequality has remained constant after accession. This is the case for Greece (accession in 1981) and Portugal (accession in 1985). In one country (Ireland), income inequality seems to have fallen from the date of accession (1973) to the early 1980s, but to have increased in the mid 1980s. Finally, in one country (Spain) income inequality seems to have increased from mid 1980s (accession in 1985) to the early 1990s. These trends do not allow us to claim that EU accession has been accompanied by a decrease or increase in income inequality. However, when we move into the long run after accession, there is an evident trend towards falling income inequality in all EU countries included in the table. Therefore, we can conclude that EU membership may be conducive to reduced income inequality in the long run. This conclusion is in line with the existing evidence as well as theory, which suggests that sustained economic growth (which is assisted by EU membership) is conducive to less income inequality.

Another conclusion we may derive from Table 2.3 is that income inequality in Turkey has been higher historically than in the comparison group. In addition, income inequality in Turkey remained high throughout the 1980s and 1990s. This is not surprising given the relatively slower growth rates and the increased growth volatility reflected in Table 2.2 above. The combination of low growth rates and high economic instability is usually associated with increased income inequality.[27] Given this aspect of income inequality and its relevance for Turkey, we expect EU membership to have a neutral effect on income inequality in Turkey in the short run and to reduce income inequality in the long run. This positive impact in the long run can be expected to come about as a result of reduced economic instability and relatively better economic performance after accession.

Structural adjustment costs: the special case of agriculture

The sector expected to experience a major accession shock is agriculture, for a number of reasons. First, agriculture is not included in the EU–Turkey customs union. Nevertheless, currently about 70 per cent of Turkish agricultural exports to the EU already enjoy free entry whereas agricultural exports from the EU are subject to high tariffs in Turkey. Therefore, the agricultural sector in Turkey will experience the highest level of exposure to competition after accession.

Second, agriculture is still a major contributor to Turkish GDP and employment. As of 2004, agriculture accounts for 12 per cent of Turkish GDP and 33 per cent of total employment. In the EU-25, the corresponding figures are 2.1 and 5 per cent. This contrast implies that the ongoing decline in relative shares of Turkish agriculture in GDP and employment can be expected to continue after EU membership. The decline is highly likely to increase the level of unemployment, which is currently about 10 per cent in official statistics but could be much higher if underemployment is taken into account.

The third reason for high adjustment costs in Turkish agriculture is related to low productivity. In Turkey, as of 2003, 33 per cent of the total work force employed in the agriculture produces 12 per cent of the total output. Therefore, the ratio is 12/33 = 0.36. In the EU-25, 5 per cent of the total work force employed in agriculture produces 2.1 per cent of total output. This gives a ratio of 2.1/5 = 0.42, which is comparable to the ratio in Turkey. These ratios indicate that a one-unit increase in agricultural employment would produce less than one-unit of increase in total output in both Turkey and the EU. However, this comparison is misleading because the number of people employed in agriculture is 7 million in Turkey and 10 million in the EU-25. Agricultural output, on the other hand, is €25 billion in Turkey and €204 billion in the EU.[28] Therefore, the agricultural output per worker in Turkey would be 25 billion/7 million = €3,600 whereas the agricultural output per worker in the EU would be €204 billion/10 million = €20,400. In other words, the average agricultural worker in the EU-25 produces about six times what the average agricultural worker in Turkey does.

The final reason for high adjustment costs in Turkish agriculture is the small enterprise size. As can be seen from Table 2.4, 65 per cent of agricultural enterprises in Turkey consist of farms that are less than 5 ha in total. In addition, the 2001 agricultural survey indicates that each agricultural enterprise consists of 4 to 5 plots on average. Therefore, the average size of plots is much lower than the average enterprise size. This high level of fragmentation is a significant obstacle to improving productivity through higher levels of mechanization and capital invest-ment. In addition, the high level of farm fragmentation in Turkey stands in contrast to much larger farm size on average in EU countries. At the end of the 1990s, the average farm size in the EU was 17 ha whereas the average farm size in Turkey was 5 ha.[29]

Given the evidence examined above, we can expect continuity in the declining shares of agriculture in total output and employment. In other words, the exit from agriculture will continue and the level of surplus labour (unemployed and underemployed labour) will remain high. According to the official figures, the rate of surplus labour was 14.4 per cent in 2001, increased to 16 per cent in 2003 and remained at 15.5 per cent in 2004 despite a 9.5 per cent increase in GDP.[30] It is a widely held view that actual figures are higher than the reported official figures. Given these trends, the adjustment cost in agriculture can be expected

Table 2.4   Agricultural enterprise size in Turkey

	Enterprise size (ha)	*% of farms*	*% of area*
1.	No land	2.50	0.00
2.	<0.5	6.19	0.29
3.	0.5–0.9	9.37	1.08
4.	1–1.99	18.49	4.32
5.	2–4.99	31.33	15.77
Less than 5 ha (2 to 5)	65.38	21.46	
6.	5–9.99	17.53	20.11
7.	10–19.99	9.42	21.17
5 – < 20 ha (6+7)	26.95	41.28	
8.	20–49.99	4.27	19.99
9.	50–99.99	0.59	6.44
10.	100–249.99	0.25	5.96
11.	250–499.99	0.05	2.81
12.	500+	0.01	2.06
20 ha or more (8 to 12)		5.17	37.26

Source: State Institute for Statistics, Turkey, 2001.

to take two forms: (1) a fall in small-farm incomes and (2) a continuous addition to surplus labour in the short and medium terms.

EU accession can enable Turkey to ameliorate these costs through three channels. First, Turkey will be eligible for common agricultural policy (CAP) support from the Guarantee and Guidance sections of the European Agricultural Guidance and Guarantee Fund (EAGGF). For 2020, this support is estimated to be around €7.4 billion, of which €6.4 billion is from the Guarantee section and €1 billion from the guidance section.[31] This estimate is highly optimistic because it is based on the assumption that the CAP regime will remain as it is. This is not likely to be the case as the EU is already discussing the reform of the common agricultural policy. Second, Turkey will be eligible for structural fund support, which is estimated to be around €7.9 billion in 2020.[32] A significant proportion of the structural fund support will be channelled to less developed regions where agriculture accounts for 50 per cent or more of the employment in 2004. Finally, current transfers to agriculture in Turkey are about 8.3 per cent of GDP. This is much higher than the EU-15 average of 1.5 per cent. However, the share of Turkish agriculture in Turkish GDP is 12 per cent whereas that of EU agriculture is 1.5 per cent. In other words, the intensity of the transfers in Turkey (8.3 % / 12 % = 0.7) is actually lower than in the EU (1.5 % / 1.5 % = 1). Therefore, Turkey will not be under pressure from the World Trade Organization (WTO) to reduce agricultural support in magnitude terms. As Turkish GDP increases, the proportion of agricultural transfers to GDP will decline even if current levels of support are maintained. Given that the share of agriculture in GDP is declining, the current levels of transfers will amount to higher levels of transfers per unit of agricultural income.

The transfers from the EU and Turkish budgets are not likely to reverse the exit from agriculture or the additions to surplus labour that this exit will entail. The economic cost of the exit from agriculture will be reversed only if EU accession delivers the expected benefits of higher output growth, which will absorb the surplus labour in the long run. Nevertheless, budgetary transfers from the EU and Turkish budgets can counterbalance the fall in small-scale farmers' incomes. The tendency towards decoupling agricultural support from production in the EU and the WTO's insistence on direct income support are likely to enable Turkey to target farming families faced with falling incomes. However, the extent to which this will be the case remains uncertain as Turkey's newly introduced agricultural income support policy is still in its infancy and the future direction of the CAP is still unknown.

The impact of Turkish accession
on the EU: budgetary transfers and migration

As indicated above, the impact of Turkish accession on the EU economy is likely to be small for three reasons. First, EU imports from Turkey account only for about 3 per cent of total EU imports. Second, about 70 per cent of Turkish agricultural exports already enter the EU without tariffs or quantitative restrictions. Finally, Turkish accession will have no impact on institutional quality in the EU. Nevertheless, Turkish accession will have some distributional effects on the EU through two channels: the EU budget and migration from Turkey. In this section, we will elaborate on these distributional effects and the factors that may reduce their significance.

It is quite difficult to estimate the net budgetary implications of Turkish accession to the EU for a number of reasons. First, the amount of net budgetary transfers will depend on the future shape of the CAP, the rules governing the distribution of structural support, and the rules governing the member states' contributions to the EU budget. This information will be available only after 2013, when the EU will have to decide on the new medium-term financial perspective. Second, the amount of agricultural and structural support to be received by Turkey will depend on the change in the structure of the Turkish economy. This amount will decline as regional disparity and the share of the Turkish agriculture in total output decline, but will increase as Turkey's GDP increases. The positive association between budgetary transfers and regional disparity as well as share of agriculture in GDP is self-explanatory, but the positive association between budgetary transfers and the level of Turkish GDP may require some explanation. In the last enlargement, the EU has established a link between the two by imposing an upper limit to the level of structural fund support at 0.69 per cent of a member country's GDP. This upper limit is taken as the measure of a member country's capacity to absorb the structural support effectively. As a result of this linkage, it is possible for Turkey to obtain higher levels of structural support as its GDP increases. Finally, the amount of Turkey's contributions to the EU budget will not be known until the post-2014 financial perspective is in place.

Therefore, net transfers from the EU budget can be estimated only on the basis of assumptions about the future rules of the game, the growth of Turkish GDP, the status of the Turkish agricultural sector and the level of regional disparity in Turkey. Given this complexity, it may be better to begin with the simplest scenario in which we assume Turkey joins the EU in 2015 and the rules of the game remain the same. Under this scenario, Turkey would contribute to the EU a budget an amount equal to 1.2 per cent of its GDP, which is assumed to be 4 per cent of EU GDP in 2015. Under this assumption, Turkey's budgetary contribution would be equal to $0.012 \times 0.04 = 0.048$ per cent of EU GDP in 20015. Dervis *et al.* estimate that Turkey's receipts from the EU budget in this scenario would amount to 0.25 per cent of EU GDP in the same year.[33] Therefore, net budgetary transfers to Turkey would be about 0.20 per cent of EU GDP. Given that EU GDP in 2003 was €9716 billion and assuming that EU GDP would increase by 2 per cent per year until 2015, then the net budgetary transfers can be calculated as follows: $0.002 \times 9716(1+0.02)^{12} = €24.6$ billion.

It must be indicated that this is an upper-bound limit because it is based on the assumption that the rules governing CAP and structural fund support would remain the same. However, there are indications that structural fund support will be capped at less than 1 per cent of the recipient country's GDP. There are no clear-cut rules for capping the structural fund support, but the cap is supposed to reflect the recipient country's absorption capacity. For 2005, the new member states' absorption capacity is estimated to be 0.69 per cent of their GDP. Taking this as a benchmark, the State Planning Organization of Turkey estimates that Turkey's net budgetary receipts would be about one-fourth of the upper bound at €5.9 billion. If the cap is set at one per cent of Turkey's GDP, the corresponding amount is estimated to be €7.8 billion. If the time horizon is extended to 2020, net transfers would increase to €6.5 billion if the absorption capacity is 0.69 per cent of Turkish GDP and to €10 billion if the absorption capacity is assumed to be 1 per cent of Turkish GDP.[34]

Another way of estimating the budgetary implications of Turkish accession is to use the financial packages the EU has agreed in the last enlargement for Bulgaria and Romania. Following such an approach, Hughes estimates that the gross budgetary transfers to Turkey in 2015 can be expected to be €10.5 billion.[35] According to the SPO, Turkey's budgetary contributions in the same year would be €4.9 billion.[36] Therefore, net budgetary transfers to Turkey would be €5.6 billion – close to the SPO estimate of €5.9 billion.

The estimates presented above suggest that net budgetary transfers to Turkey could range between €6 and 25 billion per year. However, we must place the net budgetary transfers to Turkey into context. The sum of €6 to 25 billion is a significant amount, but relative to EU GDP it represents a very small percentage, which is between 0.05 and 0.2 per cent. In addition, the net budget transfers to Turkey are more or less similar to budgetary transfers to the 10 new members. Therefore, there is no a priori economic reason to suggest that the budgetary cost of Turkish accession is not manageable. There is, however, a political issue here as the budgetary cost of integrating 1 country (Turkey) is equal to the budgetary cost of integrating 10 countries from Central and Eastern Europe.

It is difficult to ascertain whether or not the EU will be able to recover the net budgetary transfers to Turkey. As indicated at the beginning, the impact of Turkish accession on the EU GDP is likely to be insignificant. Lejour *et al.* confirm this in their estimation of a small welfare gain of $3.8 billion by 2025.[37] However, there are two channels through which the EU stands to benefit from Turkish accession. One channel is the relatively higher returns on capital invested in Turkey. As we indicated in the previous section, FDI flow to Turkey is estimated to increase by 1 per cent of Turkish GDP after accession. Given that more than half of FDI flow to Turkey originates in the EU, EU investors are likely to benefit from higher returns on investment in a relatively capital-scarce Turkey.

The second channel is the positive effect of Turkish migration on EU GDP and fiscal balances in member states. In a comprehensive survey, Krieger (2004) establishes that potential migrants from Turkey are better educated than those from Central and Eastern European members and tend to be drawn from the 15–39 year age bracket.[38] Brücker reports that net tax payments (that is the balance between tax payments and social security transfers plus government expenditures) by migrants are positive over the life cycle if the age of immigrants is between 11 and 48.[39] The net contribution of a representative immigrant over the life cycle is around €50,000. These findings are parallel to those of Storesletten, who finds that the net present value of the positive contribution of a young working immigrant to Swedish public finances is $23,500.[40]

This brings us to another issue with evident political connotations in EU–Turkey relations: the impact of Turkey's accession on migratory flows into the EU. The issue occupies the public debate in two ways: (1) the number of Turkish migrants expected to move to core EU countries after the introduction of free movement, and (2) the impact of Turkish migrants on wages and employment chances of the incumbent labour force. In what follows, we will try to address these issues in turn.

One estimate of migration from Turkey to the EU-15 is provided by Lejour *et al.*, who predict that the migration potential (which does not take account of return migration) by 2025 is 2.7 million.[41] This is similar to the number of migrants estimated to move from Central and Eastern European members to the EU-15, which is estimated to be 2.9 million. This is equivalent to 0.7 per cent of the EU-15 population in the reference year. The estimate for Turkey is based on overall historical migration data for the EU-15, which includes Turkish and non-Turkish migration. Therefore, it may not be reliable even though it takes account of demographic developments in Turkey and the income gap between the latter and the EU-15. Another study by Erzan *et al.* is based on different scenarios concerning the EU's migration regime and migration data used.[42] In the scenario where Turkish migration data is used and free movement of labour is granted in 2015, Erzan *et al.* estimate net migration to the EU-15 to be 1.07 million by 2030. Interestingly, the free movement estimate is lower than the guest-worker regime estimate, which is 1.83 million by the same year. When migration data for Turkey and cohesion countries (Spain, Portugal and Greece) are used, the net Turkish migration is estimated to be 0.96 million in the case of a free movement scenario and 1.92 million in the case of a guest-worker regime similar to that implemented by Germany in the 1960s. The highest estimate provided by Erzan *et al.* is a net migration of 2.13 million by 2030, on the basis of an ordinary least square (OLS) estimation for Turkey only.

Krieger follows a radically different method for estimating the number of migrants from Turkey and Central and Eastern European countries to the EU-15.[43] His estimate is based on face-to-face interviews with 15,000 people across the focus countries. Questions were asked to establish the general intention for migration (the 'soft' indicator of migration to the EU-15) and the strong intention for migration (the 'hard' indicator of migration to the EU-15). The interview results suggest that the number of people willing to migrate from Turkey to the EU-15 ranges between 0.4 million (strong intention) and 3.03 million (general intention). This estimate suggests that the number of people who contemplate to migrate under a free movement scenario may be high, but the number of actual migrants is likely to remain much smaller.

We think that this finding is more reliable than the estimates derived from econometric models because it reflects the rationality implicit in migration decisions. Potential migrants will commit to migrate not only on the basis of push and pull factors such as unemployment in the country of origin and wages as well as chance of employment in the destination country. They will also take into account other risks associated with migration, which can include stigmatization, marginalization and cultural rupture. In fact, the experience of earlier enlargements lends support to this reasoning. The number of migrants from Mediterranean members remained lower than what was expected at the time.[44] Given past experience and the range of estimates reported above, we would argue that the level of net migration from Turkey to EU-15 can be expected to vary between 1 and 1.5 million by 2030. This is hardly an unmanageable flood as it would constitute about one-third of one per cent of the EU-15 population and about half of one per cent of the EU-15 labour force.

The other issue that occupies the public policy debate in the EU has been the impact of migration in general and Turkish migration in particular on the EU labour market. Specifically, to what extent could migration from new member states lead to lower wages and higher risks of unemployment in the old member states? There is an extensive range of studies suggesting that the impact of migration on the labour market is usually less significant than what is implied by the policy debate. In fact, some of the existing findings suggest that any adverse effect from migration is very likely to be small whereas some others suggest that migration could have a positive effect on the labour market. For example, Smolny reports that migration into West Germany had positive employment and output effects, and alleviated labour demand pressure on wage and price inflation.[45] Similarly, Straubhaar and Weber found that this is the case for Switzerland.[46] Finally, 10 empirical studies cited by Brücker reflect similar results.[47] 9 out of the 10 studies show that 'a 1 per cent increase in the labour force through migration yields a change in native wages in a range ... between −0.3 per cent and +0.3 per cent'.[48] These empirical studies also report that individual unemployment risks increase in a range between zero and 0.2 per cent.

Findings establishing an adverse effect tend to report that the effect is fairly small. For example, in a study on the impact of migration in the US, Borjas *et al.* report that a 10 percentage point increase in the relative number of immigrants reduces the employment-to-population ratio of the natives only by 0.45 percentage point.[49] They also report on the combined effect that trade and immigration might have had on wage differentials between high- and low-skill US workers. *The combined effect accounts for less than 10 per cent of the increased wage differential.* Other factors, such as 'acceleration of skill-biased technological change, a slow down in the growth of the relative supply of college graduates, and institutional changes in the labour market' and so on are likely to be more important in explaining the widening wage differential in the US since the late 1970s.[50]

A report by the European Integration Consortium provides similar insights into the likely consequences of free movement within an enlarged European Union.[51] Focusing on Austria and Germany, the two countries expected to attract a disproportional share of the migrants from new member states, the Consortium's final report states the following:

> Against the background of empirical knowledge on the labour impact of migration, the projected flows and stocks of migrants will affect neither wages nor employment in the host countries strongly ... One should recall that an increase of the foreigner share in one branch by one percentage point reduced wages by 0.25 per cent in Austria and 0.65 per cent in Germany. The risk of unemployment is increased by 0.8 per cent in Austria and 0.2 per cent in Germany.[52]

The empirical findings cited above enable us to conclude that the negative effect, if any, of Turkish immigration on wages and employment is highly likely to be very small – much less than 1per cent. Let us bear in mind that the highest estimate of Turkish migration suggests that it will constitute only 0.7 per cent of the EU-15 population, which is equivalent to 1.1 per cent of the labour force. If we take a less pessimistic view and estimate the number of Turkish migrants at 1.5 million, this will be equivalent to 0.35 per cent of the EU-15 population and 0.6 of the EU-15 labour force. Taking the worst estimates provided by the European Integration Consortium, the impact of Turkish migration would be 0.3 per cent fall in wages and 0.4 per cent increase in the unemployment risk.[53] These are very small impacts that can hardly be distinguished from zero. Nevertheless, we must bear in mind also that these risks can be higher for individual host-country workers with very low human capital endowment. We should also bear in mind the fact that the earning capacity of this minority is already low. Therefore, the challenge for EU policy-makers is to find ways for compensating the small number of low-skill workers who are likely to be affected by Turkish migration without falling hostage to demands for suspending the free movement of labour indefinitely.

Conclusions

One conclusion that can be derived from the analysis above is that the benefits and adjustment costs (risks) of Turkey's EU membership are correlated. The party that is expected to derive high levels of benefit is also the party that is expected to bear high adjustments costs (or vice versa). The evidence examined above suggests that Turkey is likely to derive significant benefits, but it is also likely to bear high adjustment costs resulting from structural change in the economy and from the adoption of new institutions. The EU, on the other hand, is likely to derive smaller economic benefits in return for lower risks. The main benefits for the EU will arise from higher returns on capital invested in Turkey and the positive effect of young and educated migrants on EU GDP and national budgets. The risks faced by the EU are limited to budgetary transfers and very small adverse effects on the wages and employment chances of workers with low human capital endowment. A simple cost–benefit analysis based on these dynamics suggests that Turkey's EU membership is likely to be a positive-sum game for both parties.

The other conclusion that can be derived from the evidence examined above is that Turkey will be able to secure the expected benefits of EU membership if the signalling and policy credibility effects of integration are not undermined by political instability and if there is no return to populist economic policies after accession. Unless these conditions are satisfied, Turkey may be faced with high levels of unemployment resulting from the exit from agriculture and from low levels of per capita GDP growth. In this worst-case scenario the income gap between the EU and Turkey will persist, migratory pressure will increase and there will be less scope for FDI flows from the EU to Turkey. Put bluntly, Turkey's failure to capitalize on the signalling and credibility effects of integration carries the risk of rendering its EU membership a negative-sum game for both parties.

The final conclusion to be derived from the analysis above is a call for caution and further research. Although the estimates reported above are based on state-of-the-art estimation techniques, they should in no way be taken as certain results. The estimates are based on a large number of assumptions which we endeavoured to state explicitly. However, there are still other assumptions that are not stated explicitly due to space constraints and concerns about legibility of the text. In addition, some of the estimates are extrapolations, which should be considered as less certain than the model predictions on which they are based. Although these shortcomings do not necessarily invalidate the direction of the estimated effects, they may well reduce the reliability of the reported magnitudes. Therefore, we conclude this chapter by indicating that there is an evident need for further research on the sectoral, the fiscal and also the macro level impacts of Turkey's EU membership.

Notes

1. Jacob Viner, *The Customs Union Issue* (New York: Carnegie Endowment for International Peace, 1950).
2. See Bela Balassa, 'Trade Creation and Diversion in the European Common Market: An Appraisal of the Evidence', in Bela Balassa, ed., *European Economic Integration* (Amsterdam: North-Holland, 1975), pp. 79–118.

3. See Glenn W. Harrison, Thomas W. Rutherford and David G. Tarr, *Economic Implications for Turkey of a Customs Union with the European Union* (Washington, DC: World Bank, 1996).
4. Richard E. Baldwin, 'Measurable Dynamic Gains from Trade', *Journal of Political Economy* 100 (1992), 1: 162–74.
5. Raquel Fernandez, 'Returns to Regionalism: An Evaluation of Non-Traditional Gains from Regional Trade Arrangements', Centre for European Policy Studies, Working Paper No. 1634 (1997).
6. Selahattin Bekmez, 'Is Integration with Europe Good Enough for Turkish Producers?', paper presented at the International Conference of Policy Modelling, Brussels, 4–6 July 2002.
7. Ibid., p. 24.
8. Subidey Togan, 'Turkey: Towards EU Accession', *World Economy* 27 (2004), 7: 1013–46.
9. Jeffrey Frankel and Andrew Rose, 'An Estimate of the Effect of Common Currencies on Trade and Income', *Quarterly Journal of Economics* 117 (2002), 2: 437–66.
10. Harrison *et al.*, *Economic Implications for Turkey of a Customs Union with the European Union* (1996).
11. Mehmet Ugur, 'Economic Mismanagement and Turkey's Troubled Relations with the EU: Is There a Link?', in Mehmet Ugur and Nergis Canefe, eds, *Turkey and European Integration: Accession Prospects and Issues* (London: Routledge, 2004), pp. 75–99.
12. Ibid.
13. World Bank, 'Turkey: Public Expenditures and Institutional Review – Reforming Budgetary Institutions for Effective Government', Report No. 22530 (2001); and Sayistay (Court of Accounts, responsible for auditing), '2000 Yılı Mali Raporu' (Fiscal Report for Year 2000).
14. Selahattin Dibooglu and Aykut Kibritcioglu, 'Inflation, Output, and Stabilization in a High Inflation Economy: Turkey, 1980–2000', Office of Research, University of Illinois at Urbana-Champaign, Working Paper No. 01–0112 (2001); and Oreste Napolitano and Alberto Montagnoli, 'Inflation Persistence and Credibility in Turkey During the Nineties' (manuscript), Brunel University, UK (2001).
15. İzak Atiyas and Şerif Sayın, 'Siyasi Sorumluluk, Yönetsel Sorumluluk ve Bütçe Sistemi: Bir Yeniden Yapılanma Önerisine Doğru' (Political Accountability, Administrative Accountability and the Budgetary System: Towards a Restructuring Proposal) (Istanbul: TESEV [Turkish Economic and Social Studies Foundation], 1997).
16. IMF, *World Economic Outlook* (2003), 104–8.
17. See Viktoria Hnatkovska and Norman Loayza, 'Volatility and Growth', in Joshua Aizenman and Brian Pinto, eds, *Managing Economic Crises: A Practitioner's Guide* (Cambridge University Press, 2005), pp. 65–100.
18. DIE (State Institute of Statistics), *Turkey: General Census, 2002*, http://www.die.gov.tr (accessed November 2005).
19. Saleh M. Nsouli, Rouben Atoian and Alex Mourmouras, 'Institutions, Programme Implementation and Macroeconomic Performance', IMF Working Paper No. WP/04/184 (2004).
20. Dani Rodrik, Arvind Subramanian and Francesco Trebbi, 'Institutions Rule: the Primacy of Institutions over Geography and Integration in

Economic Development', *Journal of Economic Growth*, 9 (2004), 2:131–65, p. 140.

21. George R.G. Clarke, 'How the Quality of Institutions Affects Technological Deepening in Developing Countries', Policy Research Working Paper No. 2603 (Washington, DC: World Bank, 2001).

22. Robert E. Hall and Charles I. Jones, 'Why Do Some Countries Produce so Much More Output per Worker than Others?', *Quarterly Journal of Economics*, 114 (1999), 1:83–116.

23. Arjan M. Lejour, Ruud A. de Mooij and Clem H. Capel, 'Assessing the Economic Implications of Turkish Accession to the EU', CPB Netherlands Bureau for Economic Policy Analysis, Working Paper No. 56 (2004).

24. ABN-AMRO, 'Opportunities Beyond the Bosphorous: Exploring Growth, FDI and Trade Flows in View of Turkey's EU Accession' (Amsterdam, 2004), http://www.abnamro.com/pressroom/releases/media/pdf/abnamro turkeyreport 27may2004.pdf (accessed June 2005).

25. Ibid.

26. TUSIAD (Turkish Industrialists' and Businessmen's Association), 'Turkiye'de Bireysel Gelir Dagilimi ve Yoksulluk; Avrupa Birligi ile Karsilastirma' (Income Distribution and Poverty in Turkey: A Comparison with the European Union), Publication No. T/2000–12/295 (2000), p.119.

27. IMF, *World Economic Outlook* (2003).

28. European Commission, 'Issues Arising from Turkey's Membership Perspective', Staff Working Paper, COM (2004), 656, http://www.deltur.cec.eu.int (accessed October 2005).

29. SPO (State Planning Organization), 'Tarimsal Politikalar ve Yapisal Duzenlemeler Ozel Ihtisas Komisyonu Raporu' (Report of the Commission for Agricultural Policies and Structural Measures), Publication No. DPT: 256 – OIK: 534 (2000).

30. SPO, '2004 Yili Programi' (The Programme for 2004), http://ekutup.dpt.gov.tr/program/2004.pdf (accessed October 2005); and SPO, '2005 Yili Programi' (The Programme for 2005), http://ekutup.dpt.gov.tr/program/2005.pdf (accessed October 2005).

31. SPO, 'Turkiye'nin Uyeliginin AB'ye Muhtemel Etkileri' (Possible Impacts of Turkish Membership on the EU) (2004) http://ekutup.dpt.gov.tr/ab/uyelik/etki/olasi.pdf (accessed October 2005).

32. SPO, 'Turkiye'nin Uyeliginin AB'ye Muhtemel Etkileri' (Possible Impacts of Turkish Membership on the EU) (2004).

33. Kemal Dervis, Daniel Gros, Faik Oztrak and Yusuf Isik,'Turkey and the EU Budget: Prospects and Issues', Centre for European Policy Studies, EU–Turkey Working Paper No. 6 (2004).

34. SPO, 'Turkiye'nin Uyeliginin AB'ye Muhtemel Etkileri' (Possible Impacts of Turkish Membership on the EU) (2004), pp. 33–4.

35. Kirsty Hughes, 'Turkey and the European Union: Just Another Enlargement?' A Friend of Europe Working Paper (2004), http://www.friendsofeurope.org/pdfs/TurkeyandtheEuropeanUnion-WorkingPaperFoE.pdf (accessed October 2005).

36. SPO, 'Turkiye'nin Uyeliginin AB'ye Muhtemel Etkileri' (Possible Impacts of Turkish Membership on the EU) (2004).

37. Lejour *et al.*, 'Assessing the Economic Implications of Turkish Accession to the EU'.

38. Hubert Krieger, 'Migration Trends in an Enlarging European Union', paper presented at the Conference on Immigration Issues in EU–Turkey Relations, Bogazici University, Istanbul, 8–9 October 2004.
39. Herbert Brücker, 'The Impact of International Migration on Welfare and the Welfare State in an Enlarged Europe', paper presented at the Oesterriche Nationalbank East–West Conference, 3–5 November 2002.
40. Kjetil Storesletten, 'Fiscal Implications of Immigration: a Net Present Value Calculation', *Scandinavian Journal of Economics*, 105 (2003), 3:487–506.
41. Lejour *et al.*, 'Assessing the Economic Implications of Turkish Accession to the EU', pp. 35–6.
42. Refik Erzan, Umut Kuzubas and Nilufer Yildiz, 'Growth and Migration Scenarios: Turkey–EU', paper presented at the Conference on Immigration Issues in EU–Turkey Relations, Bogazici University, Istanbul, 8–9 October 2004.
43. Krieger, 'Migration Trends in an Enlarging European Union' (2004).
44. See International Labour Organization, 'Informal Consultation on Migrants from Non-EEC Countries in the Single European Market After 1992', Informal Summary Record, Geneva, 27–28 April 1989.
45. Werner Smolny, 'Macroeconomic Consequences of International Labour Migration: Simulation Experience from an Econometric Disequilibrium Model', in Hans-Jürgen Vosgerau, ed., *European Integration in the World Economy* (Berlin: Springer, 1991), pp. 376–412.
46. Thomas Straubhaar and Rene Webber, 'On the Economics of Immigration: Some Empirical Evidence from Switzerland', *International Review of Applied Economics*, 8 (1994), 2: 107–29.
47. Brücker, 'The Impact of International Migration on Welfare and the Welfare State in an Enlarged Europe'.
48. Ibid., p. 20.
49. George Borjas, Richard B. Freeman and Lawrence Katz, 'How Much Do Immigration and Trade Affect Labour Market Outcomes?', Brookings Paper on Economic Activity No. 1 (1997), http://web22.epnet.com/citation.asp (accessed May 2004).
50. Ibid., p. 18.
51. European Integration Consortium, 'The Impact of Eastern Enlargement on Employment and Wages in the EU Member States – Analysis', Milano and Berlin, 2000.
52. Ibid., p. 130.
53. Ibid.

3

Between Fedora and Fez: Modern Turkey's Troubled Road to Democratic Consolidation and the Pluralizing Role of Erdoğan's Pro-Islam Government

Spyridon Kotsovilis

> After a century of Westernization, Turkey has undergone immense changes – greater than any outside observer had thought possible. But the deepest Islamic roots of Turkish life and culture are still alive, and the ultimate identity of Turk and Muslim in Turkey is still unchallenged.
>
> Bernard Lewis, *The Emergence of Modern Turkey*

Introduction[1]

In October 2003, the Turkish Republic celebrated its eightieth anniversary, and for many believers in the Kemalist principles under which it was founded, the election a year earlier of Tayyip Erdoğan's pro-Islam Justice and Development Party (AKP) did not contribute to the festive mood at all. Still, after more than three years into its mandate, Erdoğan's government has arguably proven to be far from as negative a development as had been widely feared. On the contrary, AKP's tenure has presented a significant opportunity towards the reconciliation – that is, coexistence – between Islamic and Kemalist republican elements regarding the character of the Turkish state, and therefore towards the pluralizing of a hitherto monolithic, laicist, top-down prescribed identity to reflect the modern socio-political, cultural and demographic realities of modern Turkey. While its outcome is by no means certain or complete, this latest endeavour to expand the Turkish socio-political and civic space may strengthen substantially the pace for democratic consolidation in modern Turkey.

This chapter deals with democratic consolidation and pluralism in modern Turkey. It is divided into three parts. The first part provides a broad account of contemporary Turkish political history, combined with an analysis of the socio-political conditions that, during the period between the founding of the republic in 1923 and the 2002 election that brought AKP to power, witnessed the bifurcation of nationalist and religious traits of the Turkish identity. The second part, after providing a brief theoretical framework for conceptualizing democracy, offers an assessment of modern Turkey's road to democratization and discusses the impact of AKP's ascent to power on the process of democratic consolidation. The third part presents a discussion on the prospects for Erdoğan's government to further foster and enhance a more liberal democracy in Turkey as well as on the challenges ahead. This is possible, the chapter concludes, through the reconceptualization and gradual pluralization of Turkish national identity as a more inclusive one that incorporates and accounts for the social, cultural and ethnic diversity in the modern Turkish state.

Bearers of Kemalism and Islam: strangers in the same land

The social and political history of modern Turkey has witnessed an uneasy, ambiguous, and problematic relationship between religious and secularist forces. Throughout the history of the Turkish Republic, the pendulum marking attitudes towards Islam has swung more than a few times, from rigorous containment, to openness, to suppression, to cooptation, to cooperation and to conflict.

The new republic and de-Islamization

1923, the year of the founding of the republic, was to be the year zero for the new Turkish nation, and Mustafa Kemal's intentions became clear from its very beginning: to build a new national identity for Turkey, one which came into direct conflict with the Ottoman one and its emphasized Islamic traits.[2] Modern Turkey would be the mirror-image of the collapsed empire. Whereas the old political entity was a transethnic, transpolitical social amalgam held together by the faith of universal Islam, the sword of its tired armies and the disconnected high culture and archaic bureaucracy of its often ethnic elites, the new one would be a solidly Turkish, uniform republican state brought together by unconditional faith in the nation, its (new) nationalist culture and a historical mission of Westernization and modernization.[3]

Radical reforms contain Islam

With this vision in mind, in 1924, soon after the establishment of the new Turkish Republic, the nationalist leader Mustafa Kemal commenced a series of radical reforms aimed directly at the heart of Ottoman identity, especially its prominent Islamic element. Initially, the new republican government moved to make symbolic reforms, to abolish the caliphate (1924), to adopt Western clothing, to change the calendar and the day of rest of the week (1925), and introduce the adoption of surnames (1934). It also proceeded with a series of reforms – institutional (for example the reorganization of the ministry of religious affairs, and the dissolution of religious associations in 1925),[4] functional (for example the placement of schools under secular direction) and legal (for example the abolition of Sharia courts and the adoption of the Swiss civil code in 1926) – all of them aimed at curbing the influence of Islam in society.[5] De-Islamization continued and was pursued vigorously in the 1930s, to the point of severely punishing dissenters. The intention seems to have been 'the double replacement of God, as source of sovereignty, by the people, and as an object of worship, by the nation'.[6]

Nation-building from the top, religion surviving underneath

All in all, these efforts were a monumental task aimed at constructing a new Turkish nation-state and a new national identity, amid the ruins of a collapsed empire, vesting the people with new history, language and symbols. With the nation becoming the new object of worship, under the auspices of Kemal's second-in-command Ismet Pasha (later, Inönü), etatism (*Devletçilik*) became the new official ideology and *modus operandi* of the new Turkish state.[7]

Etatism

As imposed and centrally enforced as it may have been, the new national culture – complete with its invented national mythology – never seriously attempted to monopolize culture as it did violence.[8] Because this was a top-down, elitist process, it was not embraced or actively promoted by the whole of the population; while official Islam was checked (with the abolition of the official clerical bureaucracy of the *ulema*), folk Islam persevered, almost as an underground movement. The primarily cultural, symbolic changes that were introduced aimed to upset traditional lifestyles and support systems, without replacing or coopting them. Hence, culturally it did not touch the whole of society, especially rural areas, where a competing folk-Islamic element remained in operation.

Culture before economy

Central in Kemal's belief was the notion that cultural modernization must precede sweeping structural socio-economic changes involving any bottom-up mobilization of the population.[9] In turn, this meant that, in a centrally–planned modernizing economy with limited infrastructure, while urban centres readily espoused the triptych of nationalism, industrialization and modernization, the remote periphery remained largely untouched by that ideology. Instead, it continued to mobilize and function through the familiar Ottoman-era tools of clientelism and patronage. Thus, in essence, the periphery remained localized and rural, lagging behind in economic development. Its continuing economic backwardness ensured that the old-fashioned safety and social networks provided by religion, and religious associations and orders (*tarikats*), prevailed despite their official abolition in 1925.[10] Forcefully asked to adopt a mostly novel national identity, while ignoring and instantaneously doing away with strong identity traits of the old (religion), many simply did not make that choice. While the centre continued to prescribe and pontificate the new ways and means of Turkish identity from above, the periphery changed only on the surface, and an urban/secular–rural/religious chasm developed.

The post-Kemal era: Islam's early rehabilitation steps

The one-party-state nature of the regime under Kemal and its official vehicle, the Republican (People's) Party, also meant that dissent was not permissible, and religion went underground, where it hibernated but did not wither away. The charismatic personality of Mustafa Kemal 'Atatürk' – the father of the Turks – conferred legitimacy (of the charismatic type[11]) to his political projects while he was alive. But subsequent developments after his death in 1938 began eroding the monopoly and credibility of the laicist ideology of the State. Starting with his successor, Inönü, especially after World War II, the unconditional belief in the staunchly secularist project slowly began to give some way to the reality that the popular religious aspects of Turkish identity could be neither completely eradicated nor completely ignored; some efforts to integrate them to the national project of state-building would follow.[12]

Islamic identity resurges

In 1946, the first debate over reintroducing religious education took place in the Turkish Grand National Assembly and in 1948 it became a reality. With the introduction of a multi-party system in 1950, the first genuinely contested elections (the first ones in 1946 were not) and the surprise electoral victory of the Democratic Party opposition resulted in a greater degree of liberalization of society and led to a renaissance of religion. This was reflected by government actions such as lifting the ban on *tarikats*, allowing the return of prayer in Arabic, and sanctioning the mushrooming Islamic publications, especially as Prime Minister Menderes tried to exploit Islam as a vote-getting tool.[13]

Two solitudes

From the 1950s onwards, with Turkey's population having tripled in three decades, the demographic and socio-political effects of the postwar period helped this flourishing of Islam to continue, especially in the periphery. Also, as the country began experiencing sustained periods of economic growth, this trend contributed to a large segment of the population following a divergent path from the secularization process. One could begin to talk about not one unitary Turkish identity but two fragmented ones, developing into solitudes occupying the same land: the urban, secularist, 'White', and the 'other' 'peasant', 'Black', traditional 'Anatolian' one.[14] While the next decades would bring the two closer in contact, they would continue to develop and grow apart, like strangers in the same land.

The troubled postwar decades: the parallel universes merge

In the 1960s, rapid industrialization (via import substitution industrialization) and urbanization arrived in Turkey with the classic symptoms of dislocation, mobility and acute inequality.[15] It took place at the expense of rural development (for example land reforms were systematically ignored) and the rural population.[16]

Perils of uneven development

The uneven developmentalism fostered by the etatist model of state capitalism increased the booming urban–poor-rural chasm and contributed to the gradual alienation of an increasing number of the population from the nationalist secularist project. Specifically, rapid urbanization resulted in mushrooming urban centres without the capacity adequately to absorb the influx of internal migrants, who, in turn, settled in the periphery of cities – in urban shantytowns (the so-called night settlings, or *gecekondu*), where religious associations provided a parallel social safety network.[17] The Kemalist success of higher education reforms also exacerbated the situation, since the inability of urban centres to absorb qualified urban migrants turned them to Islamic schooling. The uneven redistribution of profits from industrialization contributed to greater societal inequality and poverty and an increased sense of alienation and marginalization.[18] The Turkish state was modernizing, but at the expense of a large part of its population. Overall, the model was developmentally anti-rural and politically elitist, and sociologically it aimed at the creation of a state-sponsored middle class that depended upon state subsidy and protection.

Fiscal etatism: end with a bang

While such a type and source of modernization was instrumental for the successful launching of the nationalist project in the first decades of the republic at a difficult era, by the 1960s and 1970s it clearly became an outdated model of lopsided growth and development that seriously failed to promote and deliver social justice alongside modernity. More specifically, 'Turkish developmental strategy [also] lacked accountability to masses, and, consequently, institutionalized a new socio-economic order of structured inequality ... with income concentration on the top and mass poverty at the bottom'.[19] By the end of the 1970s, at a time of severe economic crisis and *de facto* bankruptcy of the Turkish economy,[20] the economic component of etatism had fully outlived its usefulness, eroding, in the process, the legitimacy of the orthodox political-secular ideology of the state, and rendering its mainstream parties vulnerable to the lure of competing ideologies both from the left (communists) and the right (political Islam).

The custodians of Kemalism and the rise of political Islam

Traditionally a political player in the waning decades of the Ottoman empire (for example in promulgating or restoring the constitution in1876 and 1908 respectively[21]), the army remained active in the modern political scene of Turkey.

More Kemalist than Kemal

In spite of Kemal's explicit proclamation of the incompatibility between military and political identities,[22] over the course of the republic's history, gradually the military *de facto* and eventually *de jure* assumed the role of custodian of the state, and of Kemalism itself. Within a period of four decades, directly or indirectly, the military interfered four times (1960, 1971, 1980 and 1997) with the democratic process. Despite its professed intentions to correct the democratic path of the country and provide the stability necessary for democracy to flourish, the political, structural and social results of such interventions hindered the overall process of democratic transition and consolidation in Turkey. 1960 witnessed the first of such interventions, targeting governmental corruption along with re-Islamizing trends. Following the trial and execution of Menderes, the army was instrumental in crafting a new, fairly liberal constitution (1961) which sought to render the regime more democratic (for example by the introduction of bicameralism and the Constitutional Court) and the society more pluralist (for example by the recognition of the right of association).[23]

A 'state' within the state

However, this came at the cost of establishing the National Security Council – composed of the armed forces chiefs, the Joint Chief of Staff, and top government officials – which grew to become the *de facto* executive body of the Turkish state. At the same time, the rent-seeking behaviour of the military elites manifested itself that same year in the establishment of OYAK (the Armed Forces Pension Fund – a holding company managing the largest private retirement fund; also one of the largest institutional investors in Turkey to which all military personal must contribute a small percentage of their salaries – which over the decades has sought and received lucrative public contracts).[24] This entrenchment constituted a double blow to political and economic liberalization. It marked a period of prolonged praetorianism in Turkish politics, amid an era of political instability that reflected the explosive mix of relaxed political pluralism and uneven economic growth. The army's active involvement was highlighted by the 1971 'coup by memorandum',[25] followed by an all-out coup in 1980 that installed the National Security Council regime in power and proceeded radically to restructure Turkish politics.

The 1980s: back to the future

Among the goals of the military's 'repossession of the public domain' was the checking not only of political violence and the radicalization of leftist politics in Turkey but also of political Islam.[26] Indeed, the political liberalizing trends in the 1970s had given rise to the first expressions of political Islam, in the form of the NSP (National Order Party) (established in 1969 and dissolved in 1971) and its successor the National Salvation Party (1973–81).[27] Despite its relatively small numbers (11.8 per cent in 1973 and 8.6 per cent in 1977),[28] the latter had managed to hold the balance of power in coalition governments, and it had been tolerated by the NSC as a way of reintegrating Turkish society via a Turkish–Islamic synthesis to confront leftist and Kurdish threats to the state.[29] Still, while a junior partner in government, the NSP under Erbakan's leadership had extracted some reforms, and itself started challenging the staunchly secularist ideology of the state with its rhetoric 'on moral values of family and religion'.[30] As a result, it too was swept away by the 1980 military government.

The NSC regime

The National Security Council regime (1980–3) led by General Evren succeeded in ending ideological violence, and depoliticizing the political scene, by virtually forbidding all interest groups from pursuing political aims, and banning established political parties from running in the elections set for 1983.[31] In promulgating a new illiberal constitution (1982) (which always referred to the state with a capital 's'), the army further entrenched itself in the political arena, strengthened the role of the NSC and the office of the president (reserved for General Evren until 1987) and reaffirmed the sacred character of the Turkish state (*Kutsal Türk Devleti*).[32] Still, despite the new emphasis on the secularist elements of Kemalism brought forth by this latest military intrusion in Turkish politics, public and increasingly political expressions of Islam prevailed and flourished.

On the surface, the surprise victory in the 1983 election of the new party of Turgut Özal – once an NSP candidate in the 1970s, and with family ties to the religious orders – produced the first president (after his election to the office in 1987) to restart an extensive mosque construction project, and to attend Friday prayers in a mosque.[33] Symbolic politics, however, were not enough of a remedy for the continued socio-economic inequalities, triggered by Özal's neo-liberal fiscal policies – ones that had steered the Turkish economy into an export-driven, market-oriented direction.[34] The liberalization of the economy – that witnessed the withdrawal of the traditional etatist protective umbrella of the state in a number of sectors of the economy – in combination with a bloated bureaucracy, endemic business corruption and an even less accountable executive meant the continuous weakening of the welfare state from within, the widening of the gap between the affluent and poor, and the fleeing of those fiscally and socially disfranchised to the arms of Islamic parallel social providence. Adding to the picture, the mixed economic results of the economic liberalization of the decade produced a tumultuous socio-economic picture with high inflation, unemployment, widespread governmental corruption and social inequalities that continued well into the 1990s, triggering a reaction wave that swelled the *tarikats*. Alienation from the state rendered attractive not only the social mission but also the political message of Islam, and this practical estrangement is directly responsible for Islam's political, often radical manifestation.

The 1990s: the challenge by Islam as a political force

More challenges to the national identity

At the same time, one cannot ignore a variety of other challenges to the concept of the Turkish nation-state, both internally and externally. Internally, with cultural aspects of their ethnic identity suppressed and largely unrecognized for the past half-century by the nationalist project, in 1984 Kurdish rebels in the southeast of the country launched a guerrilla war; during the next ten years they forced the Turkish military to conduct huge military operations (notably in 1992, and 1995) to meet their challenge at a substantial cost in lives and material resources for both sides, before the termination of hostilities in 1999.[35] Externally, the advent of globalization, especially after the end of the cold war, initiated a post-modern era, during which the salience of multiple interests and particular identities (both supranational and subnational, but different from the state's) increased.[36] Globalization's dual cultural effects – a localizing one, of cultural retreat to traditional identities to counter the phenomenon, and a universalizing one, of embracing its transnational pop culture – combined with global economic trends, further eroded the credibility, relevance and most importantly the control of the nation-state over its citizens. Spearheading the challenge was the rise of political Islam.

The many political lives of Neçmetin Erbakan: the
Welfare government and its demise

From 7.2 per cent in the 1987 elections, the political Islamic movement, revived under Erbakan's new Welfare Party, skyrocketed to 17 per cent in 1991[37] to 28 out of 72 centres of municipal government in 1994 (including Istanbul and Ankara) and to first place in 1995 with 21.4 per cent.[38] By the mid-1990s, religious organizations assumed 'many of the social functions of the rapidly delegitimizing secular welfare state, whose provisions had been sacrificed in the liberalization programme of the

1980s'.[39] Along with such functions, Islamic politics took over the welfare state's rhetorical mantle; it is not coincidental that the latest political reincarnation of Erbakan and political Islam was called the 'Welfare Party'.

If the etatist element of Kemalism had crumbled after 1979, the ascent of an explicitly Islamic party in power – as happened with Erbakan's Welfare Party in 1996 after the collapse of a right-wing coalition minority government – shattered and shocked the sacred secularist aspect of modern Turkish national identity.[40] The shock became greater once the threefold political platform of the new Welfare-led government was unveiled, and actively pursued. Its targets for (1) advancing grass-root populist democracy, ending the centralist Kemalist model of ruling, (2) restoring authority and power to the National Assembly away from the NSC, and (3) integrating *political* principles of Islam with the state and reorienting Turkish politics away from liberal Europe towards authoritarian regions of the Muslim world, were all seen as challenges to the state and its secularist foundations.[41] Particularly, Erbakan's opposition to association with the European Union,[42] his declaration of intention to rid Turkey of all Western influences, his proposal for loosening ties with NATO, his calls for international Islamic cooperation, and a number of highly publicized trips to states like Libya and Iran appeared particularly inflammatory. Despite pledges to democracy and the secularist principles of the republic, many worried about the viability of his 'political Islamic third way to modernization', a rumoured secret radical Islamization agenda, and the influence of hardliners within the Welfare Party.[43] Thus, a year into his tenure, Erbakan was 'persuaded' by the military, a number of political leaders and professional associations and unions to step down, in what has been characterized as the first post-modern coup.[44] The Welfare Party was banned, but the influence and transformation of Islamic identity in the public sphere would soon resurface under new political vehicles.

'Pure' victory

With the Turkish democracy tainted by another military intervention, and the national economy plagued by a continuing acute crisis of huge price increases and the plummeting of real wages, the post-Erbakan political landscape did not improve.[45] Successive coalition governments were consumed by the continuing fiscal crisis, endemic corruption and internal bickering between veteran, 'mainstream' politicians. They failed, as the electoral results of 2002 were to attest, to convince the Turkish populace that their political remedies were worthy of renewed popular trust. Amid growing turmoil, the collapse by mid 2002 of the latest coalition headed by ailing Prime Minister Ecevit witnessed the emergence of new parties, which contributed to further fragmentation of the Turkish political scene and paved the way to power for another party with a strong association with Islam.

The new Party of Justice and Development (Adalet ve Kalkinma, or AK Party – the acronym of which alluded symbolically to 'white', 'clean' or 'pure') was seen as a milder version of, spin-off from and, for some, heir to successive political reincarnations of the Welfare Party (like the also banned Virtue Party). Despite being threatened with a ban by the Constitutional Court, and with its leader Recep Tayyip Erdoğan barred from running, the AKP still achieved an astonishing 34.2 per cent of the popular vote in the late 2002 elections, which in turn gave it an overwhelming majority of 364 out of 550 seats in the Turkish Grand National Assembly.[46] While AKP was feared and reviled by many, ironically, the future of Kemal's dreams for modernization and Westernization, together with democratic consolidation, may rest with this very party's fate and performance in government.

The troubled road of modern Turkish democracy

Some theoretical background on democracy

Amid a plethora of designations, types and subtypes of the phenomenon, and investigations through the ages by scholars like Aristotle, Machiavelli, Rousseau, Kant and others, the modern approaches of democracy fall into two categories and generally involve a representational regime, or system of governance, the presence of elected rulers, the open public realm, the active and free participation of citizens in the affairs of the polity and the institutionalization of competition and cooperation.

Definitions 'thick' and 'thin'

The contemporary-political-science, classic, 'thin' definition of democracy has been put forward by Schumpeter, as an 'institutional arrangement for arriving at political decisions in which individuals acquire the power to decide by means of a competitive struggle for the people's vote'.[47] It is a definition that lists the minimum requirement for democracy – a procedural one, regarding participation and contestation between party elites – and it has been adopted by a variety of scholars.[48] This minimalist approach, equating it with regular elections, fairly conducted and honestly counted, is the most popular definition that commonly identifies democracy with majority rule; it is also the most contentious,[49] in that, if considered alone as a necessary and sufficient condition, it comes perilously close to 'electoralism' – 'the faith that merely holding elections will channel political action into peaceful contests among elites and accord public legitimacy to the winners'.[50]

On the opposite definitional pole there exists another classic: Dahl's 'thicker' definition of 'polyarchy'. For him, the free-contestation criterion is but one of the numerous procedural conditions, or 'institutional guarantees', that, together with a free, civic atmosphere of pluralism, political competition and active public participation and check, must be present for modern democracy to exist. These consist of (1) control over government decisions about policy that is constitutionally vested in elected officials; (2) frequent and fairly conducted elections – in which coercion is comparatively uncommon – for choosing any elected official; (3) the right of universal suffrage for each citizen of the polity; (4) the universal right for any citizen to run for elective office in the government; (5) the universal right of the citizen to freedom of expression, without the danger of punishment on political matters broadly defined; (6) the citizen's right to seek out alternative sources of information (those that not only have a right to exist, but which are also protected by law); (7) the right of civil society, that is, the citizens' right to form relatively independent associations or organizations, including independent political parties and interest groups.[51] To these criteria scholars have also added; (8) the imperative for any popularly elected official to be able to exercise their constitutional powers uninhibited by overriding (formal, or not) opposition from non-elected officials; (9) the self-governing – able to act independently of constraints imposed by some other overarching political system – nature of the polity;[52] and (10) an uncontested national territory that clearly defines the voting population.[53] In contrast to the 'thin' one, this 'thicker' version is of a *liberal* democracy.[54]

Both sets of approaches demonstrate that democracy's definitions vary by degree, and this places them on a conceptual continuum, stretching from the end of authoritarian rule[55] through democratic transition and electoral democracy to the other end of a liberal (both procedurally and substantively consolidated, or 'persistent') democracy.

In a way, the difference between a 'thick' and a 'thin' definition of democracy – the gap that *electoral* democracies have to fill before they become *liberal* – amounts to the process and period of consolidation.[56]

The trials and tribulations of Turkish democratization

According to a 'thin', procedural definition, since 1950 Turkey has experienced almost continuous periods of democracy, interspersed with military intrusions into the political arena (most notably, 1961 and 1980). However, assessed by 'thicker' criteria, the Turkish democratic experience in the twentieth century virtually fails almost all of the standards listed above, at best approximating, instead, to a sterile electoralism that is quite remote from a consolidated liberal democracy.[57] A great share of responsibility for this poor standing rests with the self-appointed, overzealous guardians (military, politicians and bureaucracy) of the nationalist project. Their persistently staunch secularism and the exaltation of a rigid, monolithic and unassailable conception of the Kemalist identity and the state, aimed in large part to safeguard modernization against a 'backward-looking', traditional, religious way of life, have instead insulated an elitist state and excluded a large part of the society from its political, social and economic discourse. Stated in theoretical terms, since its conception in the early 1920s, the religion-suppressing aspect of the nation-building project conflicted with what could be termed 'the right to equal recognition of identity in the public sphere'.[58] By attempting to monopolize the character of the new Turkish identity, this move undermined a priori one of the foundations for a genuinely democratic, 'Western-type' society, namely the liberal ideas of citizenship, and set the tone for the incontestably illiberal and anomalous Turkish path to democratization after the introduction of democracy in 1950.

Indeed, it seems ironic that the guardians of the spirit of 'Westernization' themselves bear responsibility for Turkey's lagging behind in the democratic aspect of that very goal. In entrenching themselves within the mechanisms of a centrist state, they embarked on and persisted in a course of political action that failed to account for the complex socio-economic and cultural realities of postwar Turkey, further isolating, alienating and even radicalizing competing identities (among them, political Islam). To prevent deviation from the sacred course, the political and military custodians of the state developed a logic and modus operandi that amounted to a regime which, upon evaluation using the 'thick' constitutional requirements listed earlier, consistently failed to meet most of them. This failure was manifested most often at the expense of free expression of other cultural (for example Islam) or ethnic (for example Kurds) identities, with occasionally serious infringements of human and civil rights. At the same time, their asphyxiating grip on the modern Turkish state apparatus prevented a healthier development of the political, constitutional, civil, bureaucratic and economic societies – themselves behavioural and attitudinal measures of democratic consolidation. A case in point of containing political and civil society was the frequent prohibition of political parties and politicians (as recent as the 2002 elections, with the banning of Erdoğan from running and the threat to outlaw AKP because of their affinities with Islam). Another example from the constitutional realm is the recurrent interventions of the military in the political scene, the suspension of constitutional order and its replacement by constitutional arrangements institutionalizing (1961) and strengthening (1980) the involvement of unelected and unaccountable officials (the army) in the running of the state (via the National Security Council).[59] Prime examples of the deleterious effects of the state custodians on the economic and bureaucratic spheres include, first, the *Devletçilik* policies and their state and military–company monopolies that atrophied private competition, and, later, the unregulated liberalization that encouraged widespread corruption.

Overall, then, this legacy yielded strongly qualified versions of democracy (for example praetorianism, illiberal and delegative democracy).[60] It seriously tainted the republic's democratic record and reputation abroad – for example in hindering its past efforts to gain membership in the European Union – and set grave obstacles in the road for genuine and complete democratization of the society. According to Freedom House, an organization dedicated to monitoring and evaluating democracy around the globe for the last three decades, Turkey has consistently scored low, earning only six classifications of its regime as 'free' (1973–9) in more than thirty years.[61]

To be fair, there have been some encouraging, if mostly recent, steps forward in Turkey's first five decades of agonizing with democratization, especially when compared with the dismal political record of neighbouring Middle Eastern states. For example, in 2000, despite the sitting president's efforts to remain in power by tampering with the constitution, a normal succession did take place, and for the first time in the history of the republic the elected head of the Turkish state was neither a military man nor a professional politician. Also, during sweeping overnight-legislated reforms in 2002, women finally achieved full legal equality with men, a series of restrictions were lifted on the right to associate and form civil associations, and deliberations began on lifting the ban on Kurdish education and broadcasting.[62] Still, the fate for most of these reforms rested in their diligent implementation rather than simply their expeditious legislation, especially as actual progress on the ground towards democratic consolidation was concerned. The government of Tayyip Erdoğan has had an unusually crucial role to play towards this goal, not despite its Islamic affiliation, but precisely because of it.

Turkish politics in the new millennium:
Islam as a moral motive force

The Erdoğan phenomenon

Formally at the helm of the new government since a by-election in early March of 2003, the formerly banned popular leader of AKP could well personify the social profiles of a vast number of his supporters, as well as embodying their aspirations for inclusion in society – through justice, fairness and representation. Relatively young at 49 when elected prime minister, Erdoğan is a dynamic if not cosmopolitan Turk who grew up in Istanbul's Kasimpaşa's *gecekondu* under the influence of religion. His tenure as mayor of Istanbul in the mid 1990s had been marked by more radical Islamic rhetoric, but also by his efficient administration that saw the improvement of municipal services in the city.[63] He had former associations with the Welfare Party but practical reality subsequently moderated his views.[64] With a new, temperate view on the type of the role of Islam in the public sphere – decidedly less political and polemical in style and substance than Erbakan's – a decidedly pro-European-Union stance and a disciplined electoral campaign that focused on reinstating trust in the Turkish political system, fighting corruption and ameliorating the economic situation, he was seen by many in the electorate more as a competent, populist, pragmatist socially conservative politician, rather than an Islamist one. The same could be said about many in his party and most of its executive body (for example Abdullah Gül, the AKP government's foreign minister), which, unlike the Islamic 'Welfare' one has been widely described only as 'pro-Islam'. Once in AKP was power, the vast majority of its policies would indicate that, despite the fears of the bureaucracy and the warnings of the army,[65] it was not about to confront the secular character of the state but eventually to compromise with it. Religion might still figure prominently in its character, but this time it is emphasized predominantly as a system of personal values or, at most, a common cultural–moral background: again, to help situate individual moral choices – a private Islam – rather than one of political governance. In the words of a Turkish professor of politics, the estimation is that

> he [Erdoğan] will continue to represent the views of Islam, but more as a moral force than an outright political one ... He thinks that for the individual you need ethics derived from Islam. He also thinks that at the community level, Islam should to some extent regulate interpersonal relations. This is the extent to which he wants to use Islam.[66]

Re-acquainting political Atatürk with moral Islam

It may come as a surprise to some, but the role of Islam as a personal moral compass envisioned by the AKP government is not incompatible with Atatürk's own prescription for the Turkish national identity. For Kemal, the basis for the Turkish national identity was to be 'historical and natural facts, including political unity, linguistic unity, territorial unity, unity of lineage and roots, and shared history and shared morality'.[67] Both the notion of 'unity of lineage and roots' and – especially – that of a 'shared morality' point unmistakably, at least partially, to Islam. Therefore, as Erdoğan's government has continued to impress Islam's influence on a moral rather than political plane of the Turkish public space – that is, as a culture and a system of moral values for the individual, rather than a political ideology for the community – hitherto incompatible secular and religious elements of modern Turkish identity have found mutual accommodation for the first time since the national project severed them in the 1920s. Such an accomplishment – the reconceptualization of modern Turkish national identity to legitimize the affiliation with Islam as a way of belonging to and participating in the affairs of the Turkish state – would, in itself, be as momentous for the Turkish Republic as was its foundation eighty years ago. All the more remarkable, such a synthesis could help to pluralize Turkish society and substantially augment the consolidation of the Turkish democracy.

On the path towards further democratization

Assessing the AKP government's first years in power

In the words of the European Union official in charge of EU expansion commenting on Erdoğan's electoral platform and his party's success in the 2002 elections, 'If he is sincere, Mr Erdoğan may usher in 'one of the most interesting experiences in the future, whether we can have a modern democratic party in an Islamic country, a party based on religious values.'[68]

More than halfway into his government's mandate, it has been proved to be exactly such an interesting experience for Turkey, as Erdoğan and his Justice and Development Party have demonstrated they remain committed to their declared path of separating the socio-cultural from the ideological Islam, adopting the former over the latter in their style and substance of government. Despite a few instances where legislation with explicit religious overtones has been promulgated,[69] analysts and scholars concede that in the first two years of his tenure Erdoğan has 'passed more democratic reforms than previous Turkish governments had in the past two decades'.[70] It is a positive change, also reflected in improved scores by Freedom House,[71] that can be mapped in three phases and themes spanning from the immediate to the distant future.

1. Symbolic and economic inclusion of the proximate 'other' in Turkish society: the 'Black' Turks

The immediate positive effect for democratization in Turkey from the electoral victory of AKP has been on a symbolic level. The ascent to political power of a pro-Islamic populist party and its *gecekondu*-bred leader with his strong religious sympathies heralded a new era of inclusion, acceptance and legitimacy for the large part of the population that shared a similar background and popular beliefs. Erdoğan has been quoted as saying: 'In this country, there is a segregation of Black Turks and White Turks. Your brother Tayyip belongs to the Black Turks.'[72] With his victory, 'Black' Turks could symbolically lay claim to the co-ownership of state power. Indeed, following his electoral victory, the leader of Justice and Development emphasized the fact that a large part of the population could now have its champion representative in government: 'AK is the party of the people. It is reliable, honest, respects and protects basic rights and freedoms. It is the voice of the silent masses, protector of the defenseless.'[73]

The fact that this was a pro-Islamic government meant it formally embraced aspects of an Islamic social identity, one whose tenets can be interpreted to accommodate, and even encourage pluralism.[74] Consequently, it would serve as the voice of a hitherto socially disfranchised, large part of the population with similar affinities – by no means a negligible segment of the Turkish population, ranging from 'Anatolian peasants' to 'second-class urban citizens'.[75] By virtue of the moral aspects of their religious identity, they could finally claim to be incorporated symbolically by both *participating in* and *identifying with* the Turkish state and its politics now that, for the first time in the history of the republic since Atatürk, a non-establishment politician was at the helm.

In addition, economic aspects of this identity have become more prominent since AKP's ascent to power, as the changing economic realities in modern Turkey are spearheaded by the same socially conservative AKP supporters and encouraged by the government.[76] Turkey's new economy is most energetically and successfully propelled by private entrepreneurs and their non-state-backed industries and companies, most of them outsiders to the economically outdated, underperforming statist model. A sizeable number of these entrepreneurs are wealthy conservative Anatolians and share Erdoğan's values, both economic (anti-corruption, self-efficiency)[77] and social (for example many have assumed local development roles by performing the Muslim *zakat*, that is charitable work prescribed by Islam towards improving the local community).[78] This element of AKP support helps further situate the role of religion in Erdoğan's political outlook. His motivation and agenda appear more similar to the religion-inspired social conservativism of the contemporary American and Canadian right, or of early European Christian Democrats, than to any radical Islamic government of the Middle East.[79] In many ways, then, his party's ascent to power and rising popularity also represent the social and economic shift and rise of these hitherto under-represented rural and suburban conservative groups.

2. A bold legislation record: AKP's judicial and political reforms

The volume of the government's liberalizing legislation and actual policies – ranging from empowering the legislative body to reforming a lethargic, hypertrophic state bureaucracy – has also incrementally contributed to the strengthening of democratic practices in Turkey. In accordance with the Copenhagen criteria for membership in the European Union, Erdoğan's government has continued on and vastly expanded the path of reforms of its predecessor. AKP reforms have significantly limited the role of the armed forces in the politics of the nation, abolished the death penalty, revised the criminal code (mostly unchanged since 1926) and improved the freedom of expression and individual rights. Characteristically, National Security Council reforms have restricted the role of the military in the Council (modification of art. 118, ratified by the TGNA in June–July 2003), and since August 2004 the post of NSC secretary-general has been held by a civilian. The most recent budget placed fiscal allocations to the armed forces under civilian control, and for the first time in the republic's history education received a bigger share of the national budget than the military.[80] The penal code has also been revised to abolish the death penalty scrap state security courts and end random searches without court orders. Some steps have also been taken to decriminalize freedom of expression regarding some hitherto punishable offences (revision of law 4809 on 'press' crimes) and to expand civil rights (for example increasing penalties for torture and violence against women).[81]

3. The prospect of inclusion for distant 'others': the Kurds and other ethno-religious minorities

Finally, in the long run, the combination of the previous contributions can produce an even more substantial one: the actual inclusion of previously disfranchised and alienated groups in the social, economic and political discourses of the Turkish state. Spanning the spectrum of 'Turkishness' beyond the 'Black Turk', one finds what some have even called 'Mountain' Turks – the Kurds; and further away, non-Muslim ethnic minorities. Franchising these groups presents the ultimate challenge for the AKP government's ambitious programme of completely opening up the political space in Turkey, especially as non-Muslim minorities in Turkey still face civil rights restrictions, for example in property acquisition and legal standing for schools.[82]

A case in point is the question of the fate and place of the sizeable Kurdish population in the Turkish Republic. After a succession of dark chapters in the history between the modern Turkish state and its Kurdish population[83] there is renewed hope for turning the page. Under the recent package of reforms, a glimmer of progress has been registered towards language rights, even with a meagre half-hour per week of television broadcasting in Kurdish, and with the permission for the language to be taught in private schools. Also, a symbolically important, if so far practically unsuccessful, process has been set up for compensatory claims for damages during the period of the conflict.[84] Erdoğan himself has expressed the desire to move further towards accommodation. In what represents a startling departure in policy from his predecessors, he has admitted to a hitherto taboo 'Kurdish problem' and diagnosed it as a result of a democratic deficit.[85] During a landmark 2005 visit to Diyarbakir, he stated:

> A great and powerful nation must have the confidence to face itself, recognize the mistakes and sins of the past, and march confidently into the future ... We accept it [the Kurdish issue] as real, and are ready to face it ... we are ready to listen to anyone who has something to say, and ready to consult anyone who has a sense of justice ... Turkey will not retreat from the point we have reached. We will not step back from our process of democratization.[86]

What is more, Erdoğan spoke of the need for a supranational identity, that of *citizen* of a Turkish Republic, that could accommodate the diversity of the country's populace and accompany or complement rather than antagonize other, particular identities. As he put it: 'The government expresses the view of equality of citizens with different religious beliefs, since the problems of the various national groups are common problems of the citizens of the Turkish Republic.'[87]

The dual pursuit of a liberalizing agenda to render the society more pluralistic, with the maintenance of the availability of more than one symbolic representation in defining what it means to be a Turkish national, could provide one with the option of participating in the state, either in an associative (*Gesellschaft*) or in a communal (*Gemeinschaft*) form, thereby allowing for optimizing and enriching the socio-political functions of its citizens.[88] This is what the political philosopher Charles Taylor has termed 'deep diversity' – the acknowledgement and acceptance of a plurality of ways of belonging to a country.[89]

This argument is usually discussed with respect to multiculturalism, but it could also apply to the Turkish example, by virtue of the distinctly cultural component of the Kemalist revolution and the deep division between secular and religious – let alone ethnic – 'cultures' in Turkey. Opening up the identification with the state to more than one affiliation, in tandem with a liberalizing political platform, could thus give real voice (as an alternative to potential exit),[90] and actual participation to social, cultural and ethnic groups that may well have been excluded and ignored by a monolithic, elitist, insular nation-state official ideology. In fact, expanding the ways to belong to the Turkish state might be the best way to accommodate otherwise potentially disruptive or centrifugal forces.

Future promise and challenges

The deepening of democracy benefits from external encouragement and support, like the political and financial backing by the European Union, or the economic assistance from multilateral organizations. Undoubtedly, the prospect of membership in the European Union and the conditionality attached to this process – for example the Copenhagen criteria – has been instrumental in having provided the impetus for drastic changes and reforms in Turkey. Despite the promise of being a complicated, arduous and long process, the opening of accession talks in October 2005 has provided additional incentives for the government and guarantees for civic and ethnic groups to mutually foster and enlarge Turkey's overlapping constitutional, political, civil, bureaucratic and economic society. It is no accident that the composition of the pro-EU membership domestic forces includes Islam-friendly AKP supporters, business interests and local NGOs.[91] Many Kurds have found the prospects for improved human rights and freedoms within a more democratic Turkey acceptable under the aegis of the European Union accession process and related criteria. In the words of one Kurd from Diyarbakir, describing the positive influence of the EU membership process, 'We're becoming part of Europe ... If we're European, we can say whatever we want.'[92]

However, the success or failure of democracy, both as a system of political contestation and as a civic value, is primarily a domestic affair – one that depends upon political and social forces arriving at a fair and respectful balance in the vibrant, civil discourse between competing but also coexisting interests, preferences, rights and identities within the polity. Such an affair requires political capital and the will to spend it. Questioned on the link between the fate of democratic reforms and the state of the Turkish application in the EU, Erdoğan replied: 'I would be pushing these reforms anyway.'[93] This statement both summarizes the complementarity between national and international objectives and conditions, and hints at the paramount importance of domestic input. As he pursues the European Union dream, Erdoğan has taken a series of foreign policy initiatives in dissonance with the old political and military guard – from pressuring the former Turkish Cypriot leader Rauf Denktash to end his obstructionist stance on Cyprus negotiations, through encouraging a settlement on the island, to further cultivating relations with Greece.[94] But the most striking and potentially provocative developments coming from his government have been domestic, a series of broken taboos about the ethnically and linguistically homogeneous Kemalist vision of the Turkish Republic: the open acknowledgement of the 'Kurdish problem' and of the inefficacy of a military solution to it; the effective dropping of criminal charges against a celebrated Turkish author for 'un-Turkish' remarks;[95] the restoration with public funds of an old Armenian church; and, despite initial public commotion and repeated cancellations, the acquiescence to a hitherto unimaginable event – an academic conference in Istanbul on the role of the Ottoman Empire in the fate of the Armenian population during World War I.

This delicate balancing act of combining a socially conservative and economic and civic-minded liberal agenda entails the double danger of alienating radical members within Erdoğan's party (with demands for a more prominent, public role for Islam), and the coalescence or mobilization of a plethora of reactionary forces without (that believe he has already tampered too much with the sacrosanct laicist tenets of Kemalism). The greater challenge comes from the so-called *état profond* or 'deep state', and from nationalist circles.[96] The deep state, the old order of military officers, secret service agents, public prosecutors and judges, fears that Erdoğan's efforts to pluralize Turkish national identity, formally recognize its cultural and linguistic diversity and, in the process, decentralize a traditionally republican state bureaucracy could have adverse ramifications for national unity.[97] 2005 registered a series of reactions to Erdoğan's course, from public prosecutors pressing charges against Turkish authors and publishers for insulting the state,[98] through a bizarre case of bombing a PKK-sympathetic bookstore allegedly involving military-affiliated *agents provocateurs*, to vociferous opposition by the CHP (Republican People's Party)[99] and a fervent public display of political strength by the nationalist MHP (Nationalist Movement Party).[100] Especially the increasingly volatile political antagonism, and the thinning line between what observers call healthy Turkish patriotism and virulent ethnic nationalism,[101] could result in polarizing and radicalizing Turkish politics along a new axis – nationalists and laicists versus pro-Islamists – with unpredictable consequences for the political scene.

The prospects of success for Erdoğan's ambitious plans are further complicated by a host of additional challenges. Among these are the renewed cycle of violence by a faction of Kurdish guerillas (whose terror campaign has left more than 150 dead in the two years after it declared an end to a truce); some inevitable reform fatigue; the need for promulgated legislation to be successfully enforced (for example despite laws banning torture, serious complains regarding human rights violations in Turkey still persist);[102] the outstanding Cyprus question; the drift towards complete independence of the *de facto* state of Kurdistan in Iraq's solidly Kurdish northern provinces; and finally, the deterioration due to the Iraq War and its aftermath of relations with Turkey's major ally, the United States. Together these compose a challenging picture, but if the popular support registered in strong showings during the 2004 local elections and in subsequent opinion polls endures, the AKP government appears likely to continue with this the most interesting of political experiments in modern Turkish times.

Conclusion

'Why have we been wavering for the last two hundred years?' ('*Ikiyuz yildir neden Bocaliyoruz?*'), asks a famous Turkish scholar; 'Where does Turkey belong? In the East? In the West?'[103]

At the core of the above questions rests the existential matter of defining 'Turkishness' and the raging cultural battle between staunch secularism and religion throughout the history of the Turkish Republic. In view of the renewed interest in this question after the electoral victory of the pro-Islamic Justice and Development Party of Tayyip Erdoğan, this chapter has sought to examine this issue by investigating the dialectic between competing secularist and religious identities throughout the course of modern Turkish political history. The process of democratization of the Turkish polity has been a major victim of this fierce competition, but democracy can also provide the remedy to this divisive malaise, by rejoining these two aspects of Turkish identity through the election and so far successful tenure of this openly practising Muslim prime minister and his pro-Islamic government. With Erdoğan's government, the stage has been set for the expansion of both the symbolic and the actual participation of Turks with different identities in the public discourse of the state – a significant departure, within a democratic framework, from the laicist conception of a culturally uniform, secularized national identity. Allowing for the coexistence, each in their own right, of secular and religious affinities as legitimate aspects of the Turkish state opens up the political space and further pluralizes the way of belonging, so as to include 'other' members of the Turkish society hitherto marginalized by artificially uniform, secularist national orthodoxy. In short, this process is about the transition from a narrow, ethnic nationalism to a civic, inclusive one under a supra-ethnic identity; it is about the enormous task of reconceptualizing Turkishness. As Erdoğan stated in late 2005, it can take the form of an inclusive citizenship to accommodate the diversity of the Turkish state: 'The Identity of a Turkish *Citizen* [emphasis added] is the security for the 73 million of the population ... A supra-ethnic identity to connect Kurds, Lazs, Turks, believers and non-believers.'[104]

In the end, if successful, such a reconceptualization would significantly enhance the quality of Turkish democracy and, eventually of Turkish public life, bringing the country closer to the democratic core values of the European Union. It would also finally provide the perennially agonizing question – on Turkey's orientation and allegiance to East or West – with a sound answer: that, in fact, a *truly democratic, Muslim* Turkey is possible and that it can belong to both.

Notes

1. Earlier versions of this work were presented at the 5th Annual Kokkalis Program graduate student workshop, Kennedy School of Government, Harvard University, and at the 8th Annual ASN Convention at the Harriman Institute, Columbia University. I would like to thank Müge Aknur, Tassos Giannitsis, John A. Hall, Barbara Haskel, Juliet Johnson, Charles King, Neophytos Loizides, Elaine Papoulias, Alan Patten, Efe Postalci, Blema Steinberg, Berna Turam, and Devrim Yavuz for their help and insightful comments. I remain solely responsible for this work's shortcomings.
2. The issue of a new identity (for example an Islamic versus a Turkic-based one) had been seriously argued before the collapse of the Ottoman Empire in World War I. Together with the outcome of the war and the delegitimizing of one side as a result, that debate was influential for the course of modern Turkish nation-building. See, for example, the influence of Gökalp's writings. This chapter focuses on the unfolding of the Kemalist project after the establishment of the republic, as the clearest confrontation between Turkish nationalism and Islam.

3. Bernard Lewis, *The Emergence of Modern Turkey*, 2nd edn (London: Oxford University Press, 1968), pp. 482–3. The new political entity was modelled on the French Jacobinist model of *laïcité*, of staunch secularism to create and preserve a unified state.
4. Elizabeth Özdalga, *The Veiling Issue: Official Secularism and Popular Islam in Modern Turkey* (Richmond, Surrey, UK: Curzon Press, 1998), p. 19. See also Lewis, *The Emergence of Modern Turkey*, pp. 262–78.
5. Binnaz Sayari, *Religion and Political Development in Turkey*. PhD dissertation, City University of New York (Ann Arbor, MI: Xerox University Microfilms, 1976), p. 116–25.
6. For an extensive discussion on religious reforms, see Lewis, *The Emergence of Modern Turkey*, pp. 401–24.
7. Ozay Mehmet, *Islamic Identity and Development: Studies of the Islamic Periphery* (London: Routledge, 1990), p. 126. Etatism was one of the six 'arrows' (or tenets) of the formal doctrine that came to be known, and subsequently taught to schoolchildren across Turkey, as Kemalism. The others were nationalism, secularism, republicanism, reformism and populism. In N. Sydney Fischer, *The Middle East, A History* (New York: Knopf, 1979), pp. 426–33.
8. See Ernest Gellner, *Nations and Nationalism* (Ithaca, NY: Cornell University Press, 1983), p. 142.
9. Ilkay Sunar, 'State, Society and Democracy in Turkey', in Vojtech Mastny and R. Craig Nation, eds, *Turkey Between East and West: New Challenges for a Rising Regional Power* (Boulder, CO: Westview Press, 1996), pp. 141–6.
10. Sayari, *Religion and Political Development in Turkey*, p. 119.
11. Max Weber, the main authority in legitimacy theory, offers three ways in which an authority can gain legitimacy: (1) traditional – based on inheritance; (2) charismatic – resting upon a leader's talents, and (3) rational-legal – based on popular acceptance of a set of governing rules. See Weber, *Staatssoziologie* (Berlin: Dunkert & Humbolt, 1956), p. 28, in Seymour M. Lipset, 'The Social Requisites of Democracy Revisited', *American Sociological Review* 59 (1994), 1: 1–22, p. 8.
12. Dietrich Jung with Wolfango Piccoli, *Turkey at the Crossroads: Ottoman Legacies and a Greater Middle East* (London: Zed Books, 2001), p. 118.
13. Ibid, p. 119.
14. Wendy Kristianasen, 'Un Défi aux élites laiques turques', *Le Monde Diplomatique-Manière de Voir* 64, Special Issue: Islam Contre Islam (Paris: Juliet-Août 2002), p. 70.
15. Mehmet, *Islamic Identity and Development: Studies of the Islamic Periphery*, pp. 133–9.
16. Gellner, *Nations and Nationalism*, p. 122.
17. Mehmet, *Islamic Identity and Development: Studies of the Islamic Periphery*, pp. 44–5.
18. Ibid., p. 102.
19. Ibid., p. 146.
20. The bankruptcy of 1978 and the negotiated aid with the IMF the following year heralded the official end of etatism and shocked that part of the Kemalist identity.
21. Resat Kasaba, *The Ottoman Empire and the World Economy in the Nineteenth Century* (Albany, NY: SUNY Press, 1988), pp. 57 and 110). Also, Canan Aslan,

Party-Building and Democratization: The Case of Turkey, 1983–1995 (Montreal: McGill University, Doctoral dissertation (unpublished), 2001), p. 88.
22. Ibid., p. 110.
23. Clement H. Dodd, 'Developments in Turkish Democracy', in Mastny and Nation, *Turkey Between East and West: New Challenges for a Rising Regional Power*, p. 132.
24. Mehmet, *Islamic Identity and Development: Studies of the Islamic Periphery*. See also 'Turkey in Trouble: Special Report', *Economist*, 20 July 2002, p. 20.
25. Aslan, *Party-Building and Democratization: The Case of Turkey, 1983–1995*, p. 115.
26. Sunar, 'State, Society and Democracy in Turkey', p. 148.
27. Ergun Ozbudun, *Contemporary Turkish Politics: Challenges to Democratic Consolidation* (Boulder, CO: Lynne Rienner, 2000).
28. Çigdem Balim, Ersin Kalaycioğlu, Cevat Karataş, Gareth Winrow and Feroz Yasamee, eds, *Turkey: Political, Social and Economic Challenges in the 1990s* (New York: Brill, 1995), p. 91.
29. Jung and Piccoli, *Turkey at the Crossroads: Ottoman Legacies and a Greater Middle East*, p. 121.
30. Ibid., pp. 119–20.
31. Ozbudun, *Contemporary Turkish Politics: Challenges to Democratic Consolidation*, pp. 131–5.
32. Ibid., p.128.
33. His brother held a high position in the *Nakşibendi* order; see Erik Cornell, *Turkey in the 21st Century: Opportunities, Challenges, Threats* (Richmond, Surrey: Curzon Press, 2001), p. 97.
34. Ozbudun, *Contemporary Turkish Politics: Challenges to Democratic Consolidation*, p. 136.
35. BBC News Special on Turkey, *Timeline Turkey: A Chronology of Key Events*, http://news.bbc.co.uk/2/hi/europe/1023189.stm
36. Ozbudun, *Contemporary Turkish Politics: Challenges to Democratic Consolidation*, p. 141.
37. For Turkish national election results since 1950, see the website of the Turkish Grand National Assembly at www.tbmm.gov.tr/develop/owa/secim_sorgu.genel_secimler
38. Jung and Piccoli, *Turkey at the Crossroads: Ottoman Legacies and a Greater Middle East*, p. 118.
39. Haldun Gülalp, 'Political Islam in Turkey: The Rise and Fall of the Refah Party', *Muslim World* 89 (1999), 1: 22–41, p. 35.
40. James Pettifer, *The Turkish Labyrinth: Atatürk and the New Islam* (London: Viking Press, 1997), p. 134.
41. Ibid., p. 35.
42. Since 1964, Turkey has an association agreement with the EU (then the EEC), and is actively seeking membership in the Union. For key dates and events in modern Turkish history and Turkey–EU relations, see http://news.bbc.co.uk/1/hi/world/europe/1023189.stm
43. Jung and Piccoli, *Turkey at the Crossroads: Ottoman Legacies and a Greater Middle East*, p. 118.
44. Ibid.
45. *Economist*, 20 August 2002.

46. The peculiarities of Turkish electoral law and the fragmentation of its politics meant that only the staunchly Kemalist Republican People's Party of veteran politician Deniz Baykal made it to the Parliament, with 19.4 per cent of the vote. All other parties fell below the 10 per cent threshold to gain representation in the legislative body (Ian Fisher, 'Turkish Voters Expel Leadership', *New York Times*, 4 November 2002).

47. Joseph Schumpeter, *Capitalism, Socialism and Democracy* (London: Allen & Unwin, 1943), p. 269.

48. For example, Huntington calls 'elections, open free and fair' essential for democracy, the inescapable *sine qua non* (Samuel Huntington, 'Democracy's Third Wave', *Journal of Democracy* 2 (1991), 2: 12–34. Equally focused, Przeworski's definition is of a 'regime in which some governmental offices are filled as a consequence of contested elections'. Adam Przeworski and Fernando Limongi, 'Modernization: Theories and Facts', *World Politics* 49 (1997), 2: 155–83, p. 178.

49. See, for example, Juan Linz and Alfred Stepan, *'Problems of Democratic Transition and Consolidation: Southern Europe, South America and Post-Communist Europe'* (Baltimore, MD: Johns Hopkins University Press, 1996).

50. Philippe Schmitter and Terry Lynne Karl, 'What Democracy Is … and Is Not', *Journal of Democracy* 2 (1991), 3: 75–88, p. 78. Diamond classifies this minimalist definition as a type of 'electoral' democracy; see Larry Diamond, 'Is the Third Wave Over?', *Journal of Democracy* 7 (1996), 2: 20–37, p. 21.

51. Robert Dahl, *Dilemmas of Pluralist Democracy* (New Haven, CT: Yale University Press, 1982), p. 11; derived from his classic *Polyarchy: Participation and Opposition* (New Haven, CT: Yale University Press, 1971).

52. Schmitter and Karl, 'What Democracy Is … and Is Not', p. 76.

53. Guillermo O'Donnell, 'Illusions About Consolidation', *Journal of Democracy* 7 (1996), 2: 34–51, p. 35.

54. Diamond, 'Is the Third Wave Over?', p. 21.

55. For example, what Diamond, calls pseudo-democracies, semi-democracies, proto-democracies and hegemonic party systems; ibid.

56. See Juan Linz and Alfred Stepan, 'Towards Consolidated Democracies', *Journal of Democracy* 7 (1996), 2: 14–33, pp. 18–19. Moreover, according to many democracy scholars, these constitutional requirements are the procedural minimum for democratic consolidation, since there also need to be present behavioural and attitudinal ones. These are spread out among five overlapping domains, or, societies, namely, *civil, political, constitutional/ procedural, bureaucratic* and *economic*. It is a set of criteria echoed by many scholars, among them Schmitter – when he writes of democracy being in essence 'a composite of partial regimes … which become institutionalized in a particular sequence, according to distinctive principles' – or Lipset, who discusses the political, cultural, constitutional, civil and economic requisites of democracy. Only after having fulfilled the above criteria is a democracy fully consolidated.

57. Diamond, 'Is the Third Wave Over?', p. 23.

58. See Alan Patten, 'Liberal Citizenship in Multinational Societies', in James Tully and Alain Gagnon, eds, *Multinational Democracies* (Cambridge University Press, 2001), pp. 279–98.

59. As late as 1996, then President Demirel declared the NSC an embodiment of the State (*Hurriyet*, 12 December 1996) in Aslan, *Party-Building and*

Democratization: The Case of Turkey, p. 148. On the 1980 coup's starkly evident legacy, see *The Financial Times*, 13 September 2005.

60. Ilkay Sunar, 'State, Society and Democracy in Turkey', p. 151.
61. The criteria used by Freedom House correspond closely to those discussed in the brief theoretical section on democracy, earlier in the chapter. See http://www.freedomhouse.org/template.cfm?page=15&year=2005 and http://65.110.85.181/uploads/FIWrank7305.xls for Freedom House definitions, criteria and world rankings since 1973.
62. 'Turkey Abolishes Death Penalty', *New York Times*, 3 August 2002.
63. His reciting of an Islamic poem in 1997 – 'the mosques are our barracks, the minarets are our bayonets, the domes are our helmets, the believers our soldiers' – led to his conviction for inciting religious hatred, and a four-month prison sentence; ibid. Another infamous quote of his from his more 'activist' days, often cited by his opponents, involves a vivid if alarming metaphor: 'Democracy is like a streetcar. When you come to your stop you get off'; Deborah Sontag, 'The Erdogan Experiment', *New York Times Magazine*, 11 May 2003.
64. 'I changed ... it was necessary to catch up with developments, the modern age'; Tayyip Erdoğan, quoted in Ian Fisher, 'Turkey Waits and Wonders How Closely Bound to Islam Is Election Victor?', *New York Times*, 7 November 2002.
65. See squabble with Council of Higher Education, which accused AKP as a fertile ground and philosophical foundations of Islamic terrorism (*Eleftherotypia*, Greek daily, 23 December 2002), and earlier warning from Army Chief of Staff, Gen. Himli Ozkok that while 'he respected the will of the nation ... the army will protect the secular state from the dangers of radical Islam', BBC online, 8 November 2002.
66. Metir Heper, quoted in *New York Times*, 11 November 2002.
67. Hough Poulton, *Top Hat, Grey Wolf and Crescent* (New York: New York University Press, 1997), p. 101, quoted in Aslan, *Party-Building and Democratization: The Case of Turkey*, p. 100.
68. Günter Verheugen, quoted in Ian Fisher, 'Turkey Waits and Wonders How Closely Bound to Islam is Election Victor?', *New York Times*, 7 November 2002.
69. See, for example, the ill-fated, bizarre attempt to criminalize adultery, the punitive duties successfully applied to the Turkish wine industry or the 'decriminalization of religious "clandestine" schools', in Christopher Caldwell, 'The East in the West', *New York Times*, 25 September 2005.
70. BBC online, October 2004.
71. Freedom House assesses political rights (PR) and civil liberties (CL) for each country on a scale from 1 (highest classification: Free) to 7 (lowest classification: Not Free). From the scores of 4 (PR) and 5 (CL) in 2002, Turkey's rankings have improved to 3 (PR) and 4 (CL) during 2003 and 2004, and to 3 (PR) and 3 (CL) for the years 2005 and 2006, respectively (classification: Partly Free).
72. Sontag, 'The Erdogan Experiment'.
73. Erdoğan, quoted in Ian Fisher, 'Turkey Waits and Wonders How Closely Bound to Islam is Election Victor?'.
74. In Robin Wright, 'Islam and Liberal Democracy: Two Visions of Reformation', *Journal of Democracy* 7 (1996), 2: 64–75.

75. It also represents a large segment of what Nancy Tapper and Richard Tapper call 'Middle Turkey' – an 'unselfconscious blend of Kemalist Republicans and urban Islam'; Nancy Tapper and Richard Tapper, 'The Birth of the Prophet: Ritual and Gender in Turkish Islam', *Man* 22 (1987), 1: 69–92; and 'Thank God We are Secular!: Aspects of Fundamentalism in a Turkish Town', in Lionel Caplan, ed., *Studies in Religious Fundamentalism* (London: Macmillan, 1987).
76. In its first two years in power, the liberal, measured fiscal policies of the AKP government have achieved positive results reflected by steady economic growth, lower inflation and a healthy surplus; see 'A Survey of Turkey', *Economist*, 19 March 2005.
77. Their application is evident in Erdoğan's successful bid to close down the money-losing, environmentally unfriendly public sector paper company, SEKA. See Caldwell, 'The East in the West'.
78. Ibid.
79. For an authoritative account of confessional party formation in early modern Europe and eventual secularization of politics, see Stathis Kalyvas, *The Rise of Christian Democracy in Europe* (Ithaca, NY: Cornell University Press, 1998).
80. Stephen Kinzer, 'Will Turkey Make It?', *New York Review of Books*, 15 July 2004.
81. BBC online text from BBC Radio 4, *From Our Own Correspondent*, 30 September 2004. Some thorny freedom-of-expression issues survived the latest round of reforms to remain in a legal no-man's land, such as 'criticizing state institutions or publishing material deemed contrary to fundamental national interests' (*BBC News*, 27 May 2005). Such vestiges of the old penal code (for example, arti. 301, para. 2 and arti. 1/1, 2 law 5812) created legal troubles for the celebrated Turkish author Orhan Pamuk, until the charges brought against him – for stating during an interview with a Swiss magazine that '30,000 Kurds and 1,000,000 Armenians had died in Turkey and nobody could speak about it' – were stayed in early 2006.
82. The still closed Greek Orthodox Patriarchal Theological School of Chalki is such an example.
83. For example, witness the unsuccessful Kurdish uprisings in the early decades of the Republic (1925, 1937) and the ensuing state policy of cultural and linguistic homogenization, as well as the latest ultra-violent, terrorizing conflict between Kurdish Marxist guerillas (the PKK) and Turkish military forces that lasted from 1984 to 1999. See Ioannis N. Grigoriadis and Ali M. Ansari, 'Turkish and Iranian Nationalisms', in Youssef Choueiri, ed., *A Companion to the History of the Middle East* (London: Blackwell, 2005), and Nadire Mater (trans. by Ayse Gul Altinay), *Voices from the Front: Turkish Soldiers on the War with the Turkish Guerrillas* (London: Palgrave Macmillan, 2005).
84. Specifically, out of 104,734 applicants, 5239 cases were considered and only 1190 of them received any compensation; *Economist*, 18 August 2005.
85. In the summer of 2005, Erdoğan stated that 'the Kurdish, as well as other problems can be solved within the framework of democratization, principles of democracy and the constitution', *Eleftherotypia*, 17 August 2005.
86. Quoted in Stephen Kinzer, 'Kurds in Turkey: The Big Change', *New York Review of Books*, 12 January 2006.

87. *Eleftherotypia*, 17 August 2005.
88. Peter Beyer, *Globalization and Religion* (London: Sage 1994), p. 26.
89. Charles Taylor, 'Reconciling the Solitudes', in Amy Gutmann, ed., *Multiculturalism: Examining the Politics of Recognition* (Princeton University Press, 1994), pp. 181–90.
90. Opening up political space and offering a legitimate voice to such groups could offer a viable and realistic alternative to the prospect of exit. Besides Hirschman's seminal book *Exit, Voice, Loyalty: Responses to Declines in Firms, Organizations and States* (Cambridge, MA: Harvard University Press,1970), on the application of the voice-exit premise to ethno-political conflict and federal structures, among others see Michael Hechter, 'Nationalism and Rationality', *Journal of World-Systems Research* 6 (2000), 2: 308–29; Hudson Meadwell, 'The Politics of Nationalism in Quebec', *World Politics* 45 (2003), 2: 203–41, and Philip G. Roeder, 'Soviet Federalism and Ethnic Mobilization', *World Politics*, 43 (1991), 2: 196–232. On the Kurdish problem, many scholars concur that it is this lack of institutionalized opening to legitimate participation and voice which has left the field open for the PKK and its wide popular support in the southeastern Turkey; see, for example, Kinzer, 'Kurds in Turkey: The Big Change'.
91. Robert McDonald, 'Islamists to the Fore in Turkey's Pursuit of EU Membership', *Journal of Southern Europe and the Balkans* 7 (2005), 1: 103–08.
92. Quoted in Kinzer, 'Kurds in Turkey: The Big Change'.
93. Kinzer, 'Will Turkey Make It?'
94. 'A New Beginning for Cyprus', editorial, *New York Times*, 29 February 2004.
95. For a powerful rebuttal by the author himself, see 'On Trial' comment by Orhan Pamuk, *New Yorker*, 19 December 2005.
96. 'A Survey of Turkey', *Economist*, 19 March 2005.
97. Stephen Kinzer, 'Courting Europe, Turkey Tries Some Soul-Cleansing', *New York Times*, 4 December 2005. The anxieties of the military forces are also reflected in the statement by the chief of the Turkish Navy, Admiral Karahanoglu, after the October 2005 nail-biting round of EU membership negotiations: 'I am afraid that if we shake hands with the EU we will be forced to count our fingers afterwards;' quoted in *Eleftherotypia*-Enet online, 4 October 2005.
98. 'Publisher is Charged with Criticizing Turkey', *New York Times*, 19 November 2005.
99. *Cumhuriyet*, 5 October 2005.
100. See, for example, the early October 60,000-strong MHP rally in Ankara; *Eleftherotypia*-Enet online, 5 October 2005.
101. Caldwell, 'The East in the West'.
102. Data from the Turkish Human Rights Foundation (TIHV) indicate virtually no change in the number of claims and treated cases between 2003 and 2004; see 'Survey of Turkey', *Economist*.
103. Niyazi Berkes quoted in Mehmet, *Islamic Identity and Development: Studies of the Islamic Periphery*, p. 214.
104. *Eleftherotypia*-Enet online, 22 November 2005.

4
The EU Challenge: A View from the Turkish Grand National Assembly

Neophytos G. Loizides and Elif Ersin

Introduction

This is a study of the Turkish parliament in the crucial decade 1992–2002, which sheds light on important issues, dilemmas and obstacles facing Turkey in its path to the European Union (EU).[1] During this decade, Turkish parliamentarians raised and answered questions on the importance of the EU and on its policies towards Turkey and other countries, as well as whether Turkey should join the EU and under what circumstances. In its attempt to map and evaluate EU debates in the Turkish parliament, the chapter is divided into four sections. The first provides a justification for studying national parliaments and the Turkish Grand National Assembly (TBMM) in particular. The second explains why Turkish parliamentarians remained committed to Turkey's EU accession despite their serious concerns and grievances over European policies. Starting from the early 1990s and the wars in Bosnia and the Caucasus, we examine a number of issues Turkish parliamentarians debated publicly, including crises involving the PKK, Greece and the country's EU candidacy status. The third section provides a case-study from August 2002, when Turkish parliamentarians, acting in accordance with EU prescriptions, legislated in favour of minority broadcasting in the country. Finally, section four concludes the study by providing relevant policy prescriptions and future research directions.

The Turkish Grand National Assembly

Although not the only place to study discourse and policy-making, a country's parliament, in this case the Turkish Grand National Assembly, has several advantages over other sources, such as local newspapers, evening news reports, or interviews with experts. First, national parliaments and their archives provide accessible links between discourse and policy-making, with both constituting a representative sample of elite thinking and acting. Second, unlike interviews which might take place years after a given event, parliamentary debates, particularly those occurring at times of crisis, do not allow participants to reconstruct their positions. Parliamentary speeches are unrefined and unedited – unlike an editor's selection of news, whether for a local newspaper or a translated source, such as the FBIS (Foreign Broadcast Information Service). Moreover, parliaments are good reflections of what is said publicly in a country; even though, admittedly, they do not perfectly mirror a society, nevertheless national parliaments normally include a variety of voices from all sides of the domestic political scene. And for the decade in question, 1992–2002, at one time or another, every major political party in Turkey had enough parliamentary representatives to establish a parliamentary group. Arguably, an elected representative reflects his or her party's views regarding any debated issue, in this case EU accession. It could also be argued, then, that these views reflect popular opinion, while at the same time reiterating the dominant thinking of the country's elected elites. Next, in most countries, including Turkey, members of parliament (MPs) enjoy legal immunity. Therefore, they are relatively unrestricted in what they say publicly, thereby making parliamentary records a valuable source of information. Finally, as the records of the parliamentary debates are easily accessible at the website of the TBMM (since 1995) and most libraries in Turkey, findings can be confirmed and retested (unlike the information gleaned from interviews).

Europe and the Balkan/Caucasus wars

In the early 1990s, the wars in Bosnia and Nagorno-Karabakh were among the most important issues debated in the Turkish parliament. The fact that Europe proved itself incapable of stopping these wars marked a negative turn in its image in the Turkish parliament. The six-year (1987–93) Nagorno-Karabakh conflict resulted in approximately 10,000 deaths and created about 750,000 Azeri refugees, a tenth of the national population of Azerbaijan,[2] while in Bosnia more than 150,000 died and 2 million were expelled from their homes – mostly Bosnian Muslims.[3] At the end of the war, Armenians occupied nearly 20 per cent of Azerbaijan (four times the area of Nagorno-Karabakh, the original scene of conflict). The Bosnian war lasted from 1992 to 1995 when the Dayton agreement was signed and it included in its latest phase Europe's most extensive post- World-War-II massacre in Srebrenica after the Bosnian Serb Army entered the UN safe haven and assassinated approximately 8000 men and boys.

In the Turkish press, the military setbacks in Azerbaijan were often compared to the slaughter of Muslims in Bosnia-Herzegovina. 'We cannot and will not allow another Bosnia on our doorstep', was a common rallying-cry in Turkish newspapers, according to the *Financial Times*.[4] In the Turkish parliament, Deputy Prime Minister Erdal İnönü argued that 'the silence of the international organizations and the international community to the acts of Serbs in Bosnia-Herzegovina, has encouraged Armenians in the Caucasus as well'.[5] Another MP, İsmet Gür, made a connection to Turkish nationalism when he framed these conflicts in East–West terms and argued:

> You can stop all the *ezans* [calls to prayer] in the world if you wish, the West will still see you as a Muslim. The name of all Muslims in the Western world is 'Turk' and being a Muslim means being a Turk. That is why in Bosnia-Herzegovina there are genocides and that is why in Chechnya there is another one and that is why in Azerbaijan, northern Iraq, Western Thrace, Cyprus ... there is violence.[6]

Even so, it was highly unlikely that Turkey would take on a major unilateral expedition in the Balkans or the Caucasus: Bosnia was simply too far from Turkey. Moreover, Russia explicitly warned Turkey not to intervene in Azerbaijan-Armenia.[7]

Resentment, however, was inevitable, given the inability of outsiders, Europe in particular, to end these wars. In fact, Turkish parliamentarians used very strong words in their reactions against European policies. For example, conservative DYP MP Baki Tuğ blasted Europe for violating its own principles when it repeatedly stressed human rights issues (for Turkey) while watching the situation in Bosnia-Herzegovina with joy.[8] Another conservative parliamentarian, Esat Bütün, criticized the government for selling out the Azeris, their real brothers, in order to be seen as sympathetic to the Western community.[9] Anti-Western and anti-European rhetoric was repeated across the political spectrum, with leftist and former Prime Minister Bülent Ecevit emphasizing the failure of the West to deal with similar conflicts. As Ecevit argued:

> Turkey is doing nothing but asking help from the West. What happened when the West intervened in Yugoslavia? It accelerated

degeneration and collapse of Yugoslavia. What happened in Cyprus? The West made the agreement impossible. What happened in Middle East? When the West intervened, it complicated everything.[10]

Such criticisms, while openly voiced in the parliament, did not deter Turkey from its declared European orientation. For one thing, both conflicts were framed as being external or distant to Turkey. For instance, Foreign Minister Hikmet Çetin said: 'The issue of Azerbaijan shouldn't be seen as a part of domestic affairs,'[11] while even the leading campaigner in the Azerbaijan cause, President Turgut Özal, admitted: 'Actually, Azerbaijanis are closer to Iranian Azeris than Anatolian Turks; we speak the same languages but different dialects, and there is one more distinction; our confessions are different, they are Shiite and we are Sunni.'[12] For another thing, Turkish MPs did not concentrate exclusively on the European Union, but also accused the UN, NATO, OECD and the Islamic League of failing to protect Bosnia.[13] More importantly, while designing its policy towards state disintegration in USSR and the former Yugoslavia, Turkey was concerned with its own future. Making Bosnia the major issue in Turkish foreign policy would only undermine Turkish positions elsewhere. Thus, until early 1992, Turkey stopped short of supporting the independence of Bosnia, fearing that the problem might be replicated in its own Kurdish region.[14] This latter argument played a key role in subsequent decisions about Kosovo in 1998–9.

Eastern enlargement and the PKK

In the second half of the 1990s, two interrelated grievances dominated Turkish–EU relations: the EU preference for expansion into Eastern Europe rather than Turkey, and Europe's perceived sympathy for the PKK. Whether real or imagined, these grievances intensified after the Luxembourg Summit in December 1997, when Greece and other countries spearheaded a movement favouring the accession of Cyprus and Eastern European countries to the EU while excluding Turkey.[15] Subsequently, Ankara hardened its position on every issue including Cyprus, and a few months later in October 1998 issued a military ultimatum over Syria's support of the PKK and protection of its leader, Abdullah Öcalan.[16] Damascus gave in, and Öcalan left Syria for Russia and eventually for Italy, where he was arrested by the Italian authorities. The Italian government claimed that its constitution prohibited Öcalan's extradition, citing the possibility that Öcalan might face the death penalty.[17]

Not surprisingly, the handling of the Öcalan crisis produced a strong reaction from Turkish parliamentarians. Traditionally, Turkish parliamentarians attributed terrorism and political violence to factors external to Turkey and often resorted to a conspiracy rhetoric that cut across the parliament's Left–Right divide. Notably, the leader of the leftist party SHP, Erdal İnönü, saw both the UN and Europe as part of this conspiracy. Other MPs called for unity and asked the people to struggle against the external forces who were trying to divide the country.[18] In the case of Italy's handling of the Öcalan affair, reactions centred on the perceived support a 'terrorist' had received from a Western government and a NATO ally. Given Turkey's advantageous position in NATO, Turkish politicians had expected to receive some support from their allies and partners. When this was not forthcoming, MPs reacted against the policies of Italy and other European countries. Abdullah Gül, for instance, decried the fact that 'several countries formerly considered friendly by Turkey, appeared to have supported a terrorist organization'.[19]

Concerning the second major issue dividing Turkey and the European Union, preference for enlargement into Eastern Europe, Turkish MPs have been very critical as well. The EU was accused of favouring the Eastern European states over Turkey, even though these states were less developed.[20] Moreover, the leftist DSP MP Mümtaz Soysal argued that Europe could not depend on Turkey for soldiers (he was referring the various NATO military organizational plans) while at the same time rejecting its membership.[21] On the same subject, the conservative ANAP MP Kamran Inan argued that it was not fair for Turkey to be a half-member (partner) and wondered whether half-members would be shot with half-bullets in a war.[22] In another debate, the same MP used the word 'disloyalty' to describe EU policies towards Turkey.[23]

After Luxembourg (1997), Turkish discourse on the EU in general, and Greece in particular, worsened. To cite one of the more blatant examples, the MP Sedat Aloğlu said: 'Greece is a chronic problem for Turkey. Greece has an irrational obsession with Turkey and sees whatever is positive for Turkey as negative for itself.'[24] Not surprisingly, the Nationalist Action Party (MHP) benefited from the failure of Turkey's policy in Luxembourg as well as the handling of the Öcalan affair to reach its highest political performance ever and enter the parliament in April 1999 with an astonishing 18 per cent which made it the second largest party in the parliament.[25] Once in parliament, MHP members, along with other hard-line parliamentarians, targeted Greece and the EU over accession issues and the Öcalan incident.[26] Yet soon after the capture of the PKK leader in Kenya and the successful introduction of the 'earthquake diplomacy' by foreign ministers Papandreou and Cem, tension was replaced with rapprochement. For example, the leftist DSP MP Ali Tekin addressed the parliament, arguing that in international relations, friendship and enmity should not be strictly measured, and that the earthquake friendship provided the two nations with an opportunity to improve their relations.[27]

More interestingly, during the second half of the 1990s, the Turkish political system demonstrated a strong tendency towards self-criticism. Not all Turkish MPs blamed the EU exclusively for Turkey's failure to become a candidate member. For example, following the Luxembourg Summit, Abdullah Gül recalled how Turkey had started its relations with the EU and criticized the power elites of the county (including the military) for failing to develop the economy and democratize, even though they knew that these were prerequisites for accession. He addressed, for example, the parliament in the following manner:

> And 34 years ago Turkey was told 'Friend: (a) Go fix your economy, and (b) become a democratic, not a military democracy, in a real sense, a real democratic country.' They gave you 34 years of preparation and everything you did went in the opposite direction. You encountered at least three coups.[28]

Moreover, during the same session, DYP parliamentarian Nahit Menteşe emphasized the government's failure by arguing that Europe not only rejected Turkey but also rejected Ankara, meaning the Turkish government at the time. Specifically, ruling the ANAP and PM Mesut Yılmaz received criticism from the opposition over their own handling of the negotiations. Opposition MPs described how the government lacked coordination with the minister of foreign affairs contradicting the prime minister. They also pointed out that the prime minister misled the public following his meeting with Helmut Kohl two weeks before the Luxembourg Summit. Yılmaz boasted of support from Germany which in fact he failed to secure, and made unrealistic declarations to the press that unless the EU made Turkey a candidate member in six months, he would withdraw Turkey's application.[29]

These criticisms laid the groundwork for a subsequent compromise in the Helsinki European Council Summit of December 1999. Turkey's EU candidacy status came with two conditions for Turkey. For one thing, Turkey committed itself to accepting the jurisdiction of the International Court in The Hague concerning the Aegean disputes by 2004 at the latest. For another, Turkey did not prevent the accession of Cyprus to the EU. It could be argued that Helsinki was crafted around the principle of constructive ambiguity, a form of terminological acrobatism that avoided direct confrontation with the perceived interests and declarations of each side. With respect to the conditions of the Cypriot membership in the EU, Ecevit claimed that Turkey had received candidacy status, even though Europeans knew of Turkey's determination to protect Cyprus and oppose the island's accession.[30] More importantly, he argued, Turkey would be so powerful in the future that it would solve the Aegean problems on its own terms and not through the International Court in The Hague.[31] In this way, partners in the Ecevit leftist–nationalist coalition maintained their previous discourse, while at the same time, leaving their domestic cohesion untouched.[32]

Lifting restrictions against broadcasting minority languages

The compromise in Helsinki initiated a wave of domestic and foreign policy reforms in Turkey, including the aforementioned landmark decision to amend the law on broadcasting on 2 August 2002. This amendment, which included an additional article and made several changes in already existing articles, lifted the restrictions on broadcasting in local languages and dialects as long as such broadcasts were not against the main principles of the Turkish Republic and the unity of the state. At the same time, the state reserved the right to audit these broadcasts. All programs in local languages and dialects were to respect the secrecy of private life; they could not promote violence or prompt feelings of racist hatred. On the same day, the parliament issued another amendment in the law concerning the teaching of foreign languages; this amendment permitted the teaching and learning of the various dialects and languages traditionally used by Turkish citizens in their daily lives. The right to teach these dialects and languages was granted to private institutions. Again these institutions had to not serve purposes contrary to the main principles of the Turkish Republic and the unity of the state, and were subject to control by state institutions.

The main opposition to these amendments came from the Nationalist Action Party (MHP), which was part of the coalition government at that time, along with conservative ANAP and leftist DSP parliamentarians. MHP's arguments were based on the assumption that the new articles were prepared primarily because the European Union was now dictating Turkish reforms. In other words, the government could not say no to the EU, as this would represent a major misstep on the path to full membership. Interestingly enough, while speaking as the representative of MHP in the parliament, Kürşat Eser did not argue against broadcasting in minority languages. Rather, his arguments were related to what he described as unfair policies of the EU, specifically how the EU had always acted in favour of other candidate countries, and against the interests of Turkey. Having listed many occasions on which the EU acted unfairly against Turkey, he ended his speech without directly referring to the ostensible articles of debate, but by implying that he and his party were against the amendment.[33] Apparently, the main concern of MHP was not the law itself, but rather the fact that this law had, as they saw it, been imposed by the European Union.

Other MHP parliamentarians focused their critiques on the law and its consequences for the unity of the Turkish state. For instance, Sait Gönen contrasted Atatürk's Turkey with Tito's Yugoslavia by emphasizing the role of the Turkish language in unifying Turkish identity. He argued that recognizing the different cultural elements of Turkish citizens as rights would ultimately lead to the legal recognition of minorities, and this in turn would harm the unity and harmony of Turkey, and eventually those citizens who used different languages.[34] Gönen's point, an argument commonly voiced in debates on minority rights, was that the recognition of a group as a minority would worsen that group's situation. As he saw it, a minority group would be in a subordinate position to the majority group. He further argued that the definition of minorities in Turkey was determined by the Treaty of Lausanne, which recognized only the non-Muslim population in Turkey as a minority group. Accordingly, under this Treaty, groups such as the Kurds did not constitute a minority group. Yet if Kurds were given the right to use their own languages in the media, as the proposed amendment allowed, they would be recognized as a minority in Turkey and this would run counter to the Treaty. Gönen implied that the EU had tried to impose the recognition of a new minority group, even though every member of the EU had the right to define its own minorities.[35]

In contrast to MHP, most other parliamentary groups agreed that the ban on broadcasts in the various local languages and dialects of Turkish citizens should be lifted. Interestingly, some representatives tried to divert attention away from issues of nationalism and terrorism by introducing a new angle: the fact that liberties were necessary for increasing production. Some people reminded the parliament of a famous thinker, İbn-i Haldun, who had argued that there was a strong connection between restrictions in liberties and a diminishing ability to produce.[36] Therefore, lifting the language bans on broadcasts would increase production in Turkey.

Parliamentarians confronted MHP's arguments on several other grounds. To cite one example, Mehmet Bekaroğlu of the Islamist SP party asked the parliament, 'Do we do things in order to be a member of the EU, which are not beneficial for our nation or not beneficial for our country?' 'No,' he answered his own question.[37] He argued that the right to speak in one's mother tongue was a natural right. Thus, what they were trying to do with the amendment was a humane act, and the new laws would serve the good of the whole country. Even more interestingly, Nesrin Nas of ANAP stated that 'It should be known, that there is not any country, which was divided by liberties, however, history is full of countries that were divided because of suppression.'[38] In other words, giving more rights to Turkish citizens would have a unifying effect, rather than a dividing effect. Nas and later Ahmet Tan (from DSP) also mentioned that none of the other member states of the EU were divided because of their democratization reforms after joining the EU.[39] Even France, where the notion of the unitary state was very strongly expressed, could preserve its national unity, even though it permitted media broadcasts in local languages. Nas also pointed out that there were no laws in Germany, Spain, Italy or Denmark which prevented broadcasts in mother tongues. Moreover, other candidate countries, which had until recently been under communist rule, such as Bulgaria, Romania, Lithuania and Latvia, had taken significant steps towards enabling broadcasts in mother tongues.

Another argument was the presence of Kurdish-language broadcasts by illegal channels situated outside Turkey. Through satellite, even in the small villages in Anatolia, people could receive broadcasts from several TV channels, including MED-TV (a communication channel affiliated to PKK).[40] Many of these broadcasts contained anti-state propaganda and were not subject to state control. Accordingly, Nesrin Nas argued that it was impossible to control all means of communication because of the current high level of technology, and ignoring them was not the right position to take.[41] In order to open the lines of communication with people who might be exposed to and misinformed by external broadcasts, it was necessary to allow broadcasts in mother tongues, albeit under state control. Işın Çelebi, from ANAP, argued that when there are too many restrictions in a country, conflicts could emerge and that these restrictions could became a tool to facilitate exploitation by divisive powers. On the other hand, he argued, cultural richness constitutes the beginning of unity and the beginning of development, and it lays down the basis for the creation of a common future.[42] Finally, the representative of SP, Mukadder Başegmĕz stated

that Kurdish language should not be identified with PKK or Abdullah
Öcalan as Kurdish is the language of many Kurds who feel themselves to
be 'more Turkish than a Turk'.[43]

Conclusion

The voices of Turkish parliamentarians, speaking in the decade
1992–2002, shed ample light on a number of questions about Turkey's
contentious path to EU accession. Looking at parliamentary debates, we
can dismiss a stereotype of Turkish political discourse as monolithic or
lacking self-criticism and compromising voices. The examples cited
above highlight areas of increasing diversity in the views of Turkish
parliamentarians. Parliamentary speeches constitute a representative
sample of elite thinking and acting, and they are, therefore, mapping the
political discourse of Turkey. To some degree, they also identify common
ground with EU perspectives and could be of interest to policy-makers,
especially after the commencement of accession negotiations in October
2005. EU negotiators and officials, as well as members of the European
Parliament and national parliaments, can also find it beneficial to know
about the positions, sensitivities, assumptions, beliefs and debating
styles of their Turkish counterparts.

Concerning future research directions, formal quantified measure-
ments of parliamentary discourse can provide an even more accurate
picture of how major issues are framed and debated in the Turkish parliament, providing a refined list of Turkey's priorities in the accession
negotiations.[44] On this issue, TBMM demonstrates a vivid political culture which encourages critical views able to absorb both positive and
negative signals from the EU. Even during the wars in Bosnia and
Nagorno-Karabakh parliamentarians tried to draw and to maintain a
fine line between national feelings and state interest, including the need
for a functioning relationship with the EU. As demonstrated in the
broadcasting study, opponents of EU accession framed their reactions to
minority languages using the traditional nationalist discourse on the
Kurds aligning it to suspicions and accusations against the EU. Whether
this is an early warning that the EU may have a reverse effect on Turkey's
democratization is still uncertain and very much conditional on MHP's
future electoral performance, emphasis on ethnic nationalism and role
in government. It is, however, demonstrated that there is a desire among
reformist Turkish elites to defend EU standards not merely as conditions
for accession but primarily as necessary reforms for the future of a
democratic Turkey. Thus, rather than defending an externally imposed

programme, Turkish parliamentarians have tried to synthesize European standards with the interests of their own country.

Finally, critics might highlight the incompatibility of EU standards with Turkey's domestic conditions. Synthesizing EU standards with Turkey's domestic needs might threaten the quality and positive effects of those reforms. On the other hand, it is important to emphasize that the uncertainty of Turkey's EU accession and the demonstrated idiosyncrasies of the Turkish elite's thinking might well prevent a too intrusive EU involvement in Turkey's reform processes. Nonetheless, the reforms should be judged not only by their similarity to European standards – where those exist and they are clearly defined – but also by the positive effects and opportunities they provide for the millions of ordinary citizens affected, in Turkey and the Eastern Mediterranean.

Notes

1. We are grateful to Senan Mirzayev, Gözde Kücük, Birikim Özgür, Hayriye Kavfeci, Banu Cinkoz, Yasemin Ipek and Ayşe Üskül for providing valuable research support in preparation of this chapter, which is part of a larger project, as well as to the Hellenic Studies at Princeton and Belfer Center at Harvard for their generous financial support.
2. Dilip Hiro, 'Azerbaijan: Turkish Troops Build-Up Fuels', *Inter Press Service*, 7 September 1993.
3. Noel Malcolm, *Bosnia: A Short History* (London: Papermac, 1996), p. 252.
4. Andrew Borowiec, 'Turkey's Female Prime Minister Turns to Military for Support', *Washington Times*, 4 September 1993, p. A7.
5. Erdal Inönü, Turkish Parliament Debates, 6 April 1993.
6. Turkish Parliament Debates, 18 December 1994, p. 985.
7. Hiro, 'Azerbaijan: Turkish Troops Build-Up Fuels'; Sami Kohen, 'Turkey Avoids Force in Armenia Strife', *Christian Science Monitor*, 8 June 1992, p. 6.
8. Turkish Parliament Debates, 21 December 1994, p. 405.
9. Esat Bütün, Turkish Parliament Debates, 6 April 1993.
10. Bülent Ecevit, Turkish Parliament Debates, 4 March 1992.
11. Hikmet Çetin, Turkish Parliament Debates, 6 April 1993.
12. Turkish Parliament Debates, 24 January 1990, pp. 14–16.
13. Turkish Parliament Debates, 19 July 1995.
14. Lan Cowell, 'Turkey Faces Moral Crisis over Bosnia', *New York Times*, 11 July 1992, p. 4.
15. Edward Mortimer, 'Last Week's EU Summit May Look Like a Greek Triumph, but the Price Could Be Permanent Partition of Cyprus', *Financial Times*, 17 December 1997, p. 20.
16. Christopher de Bellaigue, 'Turkey's Generals Spoiling for a Fight with Kurds' "Protector": Ankara Is Desperate to Finish off Kurdish Guerrillas, Even if It Takes a War with Syria', *Financial Times*, 10 October 1998, p. 3.
17. Rana Dogar, Mark Dennis, Sami Kohen, Joseph Contreras, Stefan Theil, Barbie Nadeau, Carla Power and Amanda Bernard, 'Turkey vs. Europe', *Newsweek*, 30 November 1998, p. 9.

18. Turkish Parliament Debates, 18 December 1994, pp. 960–1; also 21 December 1994, pp. 396, 406, 416.
19. Islamist FP MP Abdullah Gül, Turkish Parliament Debates, 18 November 1998, p. 11.
20. See, for instance, speech by conservative ANAP MP Gurhan Çelenican, Turkish Parliament Debates, 21 December 1994, p. 398.
21. Turkish Parliament Debates, 12 June 1996, p. 18.
22. Ibid., p. 27.
23. Turkish Parliamentary Debates, 18 December 1994, p. 971.
24. Turkish Parliament Debates, 6 January 1998, p. 13.
25. *Turkish Daily News*, 'All about MHP', 27 April 1999.
26. MHP MP Oktay Vural, Turkish Parliament Debates, 12 October 1999, pp. 14–15; Conservative ANAP MP Kamran Inan, Turkish Parliament Debates, 12 October 1999, p. 13.
27. Turkish Parliament Debates, 12 October 1999, p. 17.
28. Turkish Parliament Debates, 20 December 1997, p. 53.
29. See Nahit Menteşe from DYP, Abdullah Gül from RP and Altan Öymen from CHP; Turkish Parliament Debates, 20 December 1997.
30. Turkish Parliament Debates, 14 December 1999, pp. 10–11.
31. Ibid.
32. 'Ecevit, Yilmaz Deny Turkey Made Concessions', *Turkish Daily News*, 15 December 1999.
33. Turkish Parliament Debates, 2 August 2002, pp. 99–101.
34. Ibid., pp. 103–4.
35. Ibid., p. 104.
36. Ibid., p. 97.
37. Ibid., p. 98.
38. Ibid., p. 97.
39. Ibid., pp. 100–1.
40. Ibid., p. 102.
41. Ibid., p. 97.
42. Ibid., p. 117.
43. Ibid., p. 118.
44. Neophytos G. Loizides, 'Communication and Framing Strategies in Conflict Management and Escalation', unpublished manuscript under review.

5
Relations Between the State and Civil Society in Turkey: Does the EU Make a Difference?[1]

Wendy Weber

Introduction

In December 1999, at the European Union's Helsinki summit, the European Council agreed to recognize Turkey as a candidate for European Union (EU) membership. The Council's expectation was that Turkey, like other candidate states, would benefit from a pre-accession strategy that would stimulate and support reforms in both the political and the economic realm.[2] With respect to the political realm, it was expected that Turkey's association with the European Union and, more importantly, its aspiration to full membership would lead to greater democratization in Turkey as it had in other candidate countries. This was understood to be necessary because, while multi-party elections had been taking place in Turkey since 1946 (with the first victory for the opposition over the government in 1950), there remained serious concerns about the condition of Turkish democracy – concerns regarding the role of the military in Turkish politics, the treatment of ethnic minorities and especially with respect to cultural rights, the use of torture and ill-treatment by the police and security forces, and the limitations on the rights of political parties and civil associations.

With its December 2004 decision to open accession negotiations with Turkey on 3 October 2005, the European Council confirmed that the Turkish government had met the European Union's basic expectations for political reform. However, in its revised Accession Partnership for Turkey, the Council also identified a number of priority areas where progress was still thought to be needed. These developments raise a number of questions about the current status of Turkish democracy.

Although there are many aspects of Turkish democracy that could be examined, this chapter will focus on the relationship between the state and civil society in contemporary Turkey. Of particular interest is the role of the European Union in shaping this relationship, especially in the area of human rights. The main questions that will be addressed are: How have Ankara's efforts to meet the political criteria for EU membership affected state–civil society relations in Turkey? And what specifically have these efforts meant for Turkish civil society organizations working to advance human rights?

In answering these questions, the chapter begins with a brief overview of the relationship between the state and civil society in Turkey. The second section looks at the post-Helsinki process of political reform, highlighting some key developments in the areas of freedom of expression, association and peaceful assembly. The third section of the chapter analyses the implications of these developments for state–civil society relations and for the advancement of human rights in Turkey. The main focus of this section is on civil and political rights. A final section considers the issue of economic rights. This analysis uses as an example the Helsinki Citizens' Assembly (HCA) in Istanbul. The HCA is a non-governmental organization (NGO) that works to advance human rights, strengthen civil society, create a more pluralistic and democratic political order, and promote peaceful processes of conflict resolution. It was founded in 1990 (registered in 1993) as part of an international coalition of civic organizations working for the democratic integration of Europe. Recent initiatives undertaken by HCA Turkey include training sessions for human rights practitioners, discussions on language rights in the context of European integration, and meetings to promote dialogue between Turkish and Armenian academics.

From this analysis it is clear that the European Union has played an important role in transforming the relationship between the state and civil society in contemporary Turkey. In order to meet the requirements for Turkey's accession to the EU, Ankara has eased or lifted a number of constitutional and legal restrictions on the freedoms of expression, association and peaceful assembly. Although some restrictions remain, the overall effect of recent reforms has been to broaden the legal framework within which civil society organizations operate. There are also signs that the attitudes of state officials toward civil society have recently begun to change. One particularly promising sign has been the decision to transfer the responsibility for associations from the police to civilian authorities. For human rights groups in particular, the reform process has contributed in important ways to their efforts to advance fundamental civil and political rights. Most notably, by enhancing both the legal and constitutional guarantees of these rights, the reform process has strengthened the hand of human rights organizations on a range of issues. At the same time, however, the nature of the economic reforms that have been undertaken as part of Ankara's efforts to meet the criteria for EU membership raises questions about the ability of these organizations to advance economic rights now and in the future.

Before proceeding with this argument, two additional points should be noted. First, while recognizing the central role of the European Union in transforming state–civil society relations in Turkey, it is important to acknowledge that change is not being driven by external forces alone. Civil society organizations in Turkey have also played a critical role, building support for EU membership and pushing for the required legal and political reforms. Business associations – most notably the Turkish Industrialists' and Businessmen's Association (TUSIAD) – have been particularly active in reform efforts. Second, it is important to note the significance of the November 2002 elections in Turkey which gave the Justice and Development Party (AKP), led by Recep Tayyip Erdogan, a majority of seats in parliament. The AKP entered office committed to achieving Turkey's accession to the European Union and to undertaking the reforms necessary to make this happen.

The state and civil society in Turkey

In most contemporary usage, the term 'civil society' refers to the space between the private realm of the family and the public realm of the state where individuals join together to 'influence the conditions in which they live both directly through self-organization and through political pressure'.[3] Although civil society emerged in Turkey with the drive to democratize the political system in the 1950s, it has remained relatively weak. Even today, and despite considerable gains in recent years, the number of voluntary associations in Turkey is lower than in the post-industrial liberal democracies of the West. Moreover, membership in voluntary associations (especially *active* membership) does not extend to much of Turkish society.[4] While there are several reasons for this, the most commonly noted impediment to the development of civil society is Turkey's state-centric political culture and, related to this, the popular image of the Turkish state. This image, which is captured by the Turkish word *devlet* (sometimes *baba devlet* or 'papa state'), is of 'an omnipotent entity that stands above every citizen and every institution'.[5]

It is not only this image of the state that has impeded the development of civil society in Turkey; it is also the attitude of state officials. This attitude is rooted in a number of long-standing beliefs. First, it is believed that Turkish citizens 'cannot yet be trusted with the fate of their nation, that an elite must continue to make all important decisions because the people are not mature enough to do so'.[6] This belief has allowed state officials to see their role as one that legitimately includes dominating every aspect of the country's social and political life. It is interesting to note that this view of the role of state officials is shared by some in the Turkish public. As Stephen Kinzer notes, 'In Turkey, it is not hard to find thoughtful worldly people who believe their country is not ready for full democracy'.[7] Second, it is also believed that Turkey is a state under constant threat and, consequently, it is necessary to restrict certain freedoms. In the early days of the Republic, the threat was perceived to come from those opposed to Ataturk's reforms. However, once this threat faded, state officials began to perceive new threats: first communism then Kurdish separatism and most recently Islamic fundamentalism.[8] The result has been a tendency for state officials to view civil society organizations as enemies of the state and to act to suppress civic activism.

Having said this, though, it is important to note that state officials have not held the same attitude towards all civil associations. Different types of associations have had different relationships with the Turkish state. Business associations, for example, have been tolerated and even encouraged by state officials. Associations that provide social services, such as those that responded to the 1999 earthquakes, have also received the support of the state.[9] In contrast, human rights organizations, which are often highly critical of the state, have had a much more antagonistic relationship with state officials.

In more concrete terms, state officials have impeded the development of civil society through the use of various constitutional and legal provisions that limit the civil and political rights of Turkish citizens. The Turkish constitution states that everyone has the right to freedom of thought and opinion as well as the right to disseminate thoughts and opinions. It also confirms the right to form associations and hold peaceful meetings and demonstrations without prior permission. However, the actual exercise of these rights has been subject to severe restrictions.[10] The activities of associations, for example, have been restricted by a complex array of laws and regulations including the law on associations, the law on foundations, the law on public meetings and demonstration marches, and the law on gathering of donations. The overall effect of these and other laws has been to limit the space within which civil society organizations can operate. Yet it is not only the existence of provisions restricting the rights of Turkish citizens that has impeded the development of civil society; it is also that these provisions have been enforced arbitrarily by state officials in order to intimidate and harass civil society activists. This has served not only to obstruct the activities of associations, but also to discourage other individuals from becoming involved in civic life. For organizations like the Helsinki Citizens' Assembly, the laws and regulations governing associations, as well as their selective enforcement, have had a number of practical effects. They have, for example, prevented these organizations from joining international bodies or engaging in international activities. They have also enabled the Turkish authorities to restrict some of their activities. As recently as 2000, the government prevented an HCA summer school programme from taking place owing to concerns about certain invited participants. These incidents have led to a sense of alienation from the state – a view that there is no point in investing in relations with the state when these relations can be wiped away at any time.[11] Despite these impediments, there have been changes in state–civil society relations in Turkey, most recently in the context of Ankara's efforts to meet the political criteria for EU membership. It is to this context that this chapter will now turn.

The post-Helsinki reform process

Although Turkey's relations with the European Union date back to the Ankara Agreement of 1963 and feature many important milestones, the European Council's decision to recognize Turkey as a candidate for EU membership at the 1999 Helsinki summit marked a fundamental turning-point in the relationship.[12] The reason is that it created both the conditions and the incentives needed to bring about major reforms in Turkey's domestic politics. During the 1980s and 1990s, Europe had begun to place increasing emphasis on human rights and democracy as part of its emerging identity.[13] This emphasis was formalized at the European Union's 1993 Copenhagen summit with the articulation of what have come to be known as the Copenhagen political criteria. The European Council stated that 'membership requires that the candidate country has achieved stability of institutions guaranteeing democracy, rule of law, human rights, and respect for the protection of minorities'.[14] This statement was followed by a 1997 decision that 'compliance with the Copenhagen political criteria is a prerequisite for opening accession negotiations'.[15] Consequently, when Turkey was recognized as a candidate for EU membership it was clear that major reforms would need to take place before accession negotiations could begin.

Following the Helsinki summit, the European Commission published an Accession Partnership Document (APD) that outlined the short- and medium-term reforms Turkey would be required to undertake in order to meet the Copenhagen criteria and to align Turkish law with the European acquis. Included in these reforms, and of particular significance for state-civil society relations, was a call for Turkey to strengthen its legal and constitutional guarantees of the rights to freedom of expression, association and peaceful assembly and to encourage the development of civil society. In March 2001, the Turkish government responded to the APD by adopting a 'National Programme for the Adoption of the Acquis' (a revised programme was adopted in 2003). The first step in implementing this programme was taken in October 2001 when the Turkish parliament adopted a package of 34 amendments to the constitution. This was followed by eight legislative reform packages, known as the 'harmonization laws,' that were adopted between February 2002 and July 2004, and a second major constitutional reform in May 2004. Also significant were the adoption of a new press law in June 2004, a new law on associations in July 2004, and a new penal code in September 2004. Although a detailed discussion of these constitutional and legal reforms is beyond the scope of this chapter, the following section will highlight a number of reforms that have significant implications for civil society organizations in Turkey, particularly those working in the area of human rights.

First, with respect to the right to freedom of expression, several reforms have been undertaken in recent years, the most notable of which pertain to three statutes: arts 159 and 312 of the penal code and art. 8 of the law for the struggle against terrorism (1991). These three statutes are the ones that have been used most frequently by Turkish courts to restrict what critics have long argued is legitimate freedom of expression, and to prosecute journalists, intellectuals, politicians and human rights activists, particularly those with dissenting views on Kurdish or Islamic issues.[16] Art. 159 of the penal code (insulting the state and state institutions) has been amended so that the expression of opinions intended only to 'criticize' rather than to 'insult' or 'deride' state institutions will no longer face criminal sanction.[17] In addition, the maximum sentence under art. 159 has been reduced from six years to three years while the minimum sentence has been reduced from one year to six months. Art. 312 of the penal code (incitement to racial, ethnic, or religious enmity and hatred) has been amended so that only statements delivered 'in a manner which could be dangerous for public order' will now be considered a crime.[18] The maximum sentence under art. 312 has also been reduced from three years to two years and the minimum sentence reduced from one year to six months. Finally, art. 8 of the law for the struggle against terrorism (separatist propaganda) was amended and later repealed. The new penal code, and subsequent amendments thereof, further narrow the scope of some articles used to restrict the freedom of expression, including art. 312 (art. 216 in the new penal code) which now states that individuals can only be convicted if their 'incitement to enmity and hatred' constitutes a 'clear and close danger'.[19] Other articles, including art. 159 (art. 301 in the new penal code) remain virtually unchanged.

Post-Helsinki reforms have also eased or lifted some of the existing restrictions on the right to freedom of association and peaceful assembly. With respect to the freedom of association, the new law on associations which entered into force in November 2004 reduces the possibility for state interference in the activities of associations.[20] For example, it allows for the establishment of associations on the basis of race, religion, ethnicity or any other minority group. It also removes restrictions on the ability of associations to open branches abroad, join foreign bodies, or hold meetings with foreigners. In addition, it allows associations to receive financial support from other organizations and removes the requirement that they seek prior permission to receive funds from abroad.[21] Other important developments that relate to associations include the establishment in August 2003 of the Department of Associations in the Ministry of the Interior to take over various functions and authorities from the Directorate-General of Security, and the decision to transfer the responsibility for inspecting associations from local police headquarters to a structure attached to the local governor's office in provinces or to another junior state official in districts.[22] With respect to peaceful assembly, the law on public meetings and demonstration marches has also been amended, easing a variety of restrictions. For example, the minimum time required to request permission to hold a demonstration has been reduced from 72 to 48 hours and the ability of governors to restrict public activities has been, to some extent, limited. In addition, a June 2004 circular issued by the Ministry of the Interior instructed local authorities to deal with demonstrations, marches and press conferences in a way that does not impinge upon the right to peaceful assembly.[23]

Also of relevance to state–civil society relations in Turkey and in particular to human rights organizations, Turkey has, as part of the post-Helsinki process of political reform, signed and/or ratified several major European and international human rights conventions. These include, *inter alia*, the International Covenants on Civil and Political Rights and on Economic, Social and Cultural Rights; the International Convention on the Elimination of All Forms of Racial Discrimination, the Optional Protocol to the UN Convention against Torture; and Protocol 13 of the European Convention on Human Rights which concerns the abolition of the death penalty in all circumstances. The Turkish government has also amended the constitution to establish the supremacy of European and international conventions over Turkish domestic law. In addition, Turkey has established a number of bodies at the national, provincial and sub-provincial levels to raise awareness about human rights and to investigate complaints of human rights violations. Finally, the European Commission has noted that since 2002 the Turkish government has strengthened its efforts to comply with decisions of the European Court of Human Rights.[24]

Implications for civil society and for the advancement of human rights

Although it is too early to determine the full effects of these and other reforms on state–civil society relations in Turkey, it is nevertheless possible to make several preliminary observations. First, progress has clearly been made in the area of freedom of expression. Both the European Commission and human rights organizations have noted a reduction in the number of prosecutions and particularly convictions for non-violent speech. However, restrictions on the freedom of expression still exist and Turkish citizens remain imprisoned – or threatened with imprisonment – for expressing their non-violent opinions. Writers, publishers, politicians and human rights activists continue to be prosecuted under art. 301 of the new penal code for insulting the government, insulting the armed forces, and insulting 'Turkishness'.[25] Perhaps the most notable recent case was the August 2005 arrest and subsequent trial of the Turkish author Orhan Pamuk who was charged with violating the Turkish constitution after an interview with a Swiss newspaper in which he spoke about Turkey's treatment of its Armenian and Kurdish populations. Although an Istanbul court dropped the charges against Pamuk in January 2006, thus ending his trial, the absence of a strong statement by the court affirming the right to the freedom of expression raised concerns for many. A key issue for human rights groups and others is the vague wording of articles such as art. 301 which allows them to be interpreted in such a way as to restrict unduly the freedom of expression. Another concern is that with certain articles of the penal code having been amended or repealed as part of the reform process, there has emerged a tendency for prosecutors to use alternative legal provisions to limit the freedom of expression.[26]

Progress has also been made in the areas of freedom of association and peaceful assembly. With the transfer of responsibility for associations from the Directorate-General of Security to the Department of Associations, civil society organizations have reported that dialogue with the authorities is more open than in the past.[27] Some have also observed a change in the attitudes of state officials in that they appear less inclined to view civil society as a threat.[28] This observation is supported by the government's September 2005 decision to invite a number of civil society organizations to a consultation about the reform process.[29] Continuing concerns with respect to the freedom of association focus mainly on the implementation of the new Law on Associations. One issue is that while some associations established on the basis of race, religion, ethnicity and so on have been allowed to register, a March 2005 regulation setting out rules for implementing the new law imposes restrictions on the registration of associations 'whose name and/or objectives are considered to be contrary to the Turkish Constitution'.[30] Also, despite the lifting of restrictions, civil society organizations continue to experience difficulties working with foreign and international organizations and especially receiving funds from abroad. For civil society organizations working in the area of human rights, operations continue to be hampered by judicial investigations and prosecutions, the closure of offices and the suspension of activities. With respect to peaceful assembly, recent years have seen a steady decline in the number of demonstrations that have been prohibited or postponed; however, the use of disproportionate force by the police as occurred during an international women's day demonstration in Istanbul in March 2005 have raised continuing concerns.[31]

Overall, it can be argued that although there is a need for further reform, Ankara's efforts to meet the political criteria for EU membership have had a positive effect on state–civil society relations in Turkey. What these efforts have done is to open up what was previously a very limited space for civil society organizations and their operations. In so doing, they have built upon the economic liberalization of the mid 1980s, which led to the abolition of state control over communications, as well as an earlier round of constitutional amendments in 1995.[32] One result is that the number of associations has increased in recent years as has the membership of these associations.[33] The role of the European Union has been to catalyze the reform process by providing the conditions and incentives necessary to bring about changes in areas such as freedom of expression, association and peaceful assembly. Put simply, the 1999 Helsinki summit made it clear that Turkey's bid for EU membership required major legal and political reforms. The EU has also supported Turkish civil society in other ways, for example, by working to create and reinforce links between civil society in the European Union and civil society in Turkey.[34] In these and other ways, the EU has acted as an agent of socialization, where socialization is understood as the 'induction of new members ... into the ways of behavior that are preferred in a society'.[35] It should be emphasized again, however, that the process of socialization is both top-down and bottom-up. As one human rights activist put it, in some areas the European Union has led the way while in others the pre-accession process has supported work already being done by civil society organizations.[36]

For human rights organizations specifically, the reform process has enhanced both the legal and constitutional guarantees of fundamental civil and political rights. In so doing, it has strengthened the hand of these organizations on a range of issues including freedom of expression and association, cultural rights, the prevention of torture and the improvement of prison conditions. Although there continue to be problems with the implementation of new laws, and in some areas further legal reform is still needed, human rights organizations are now operating in a new legal and political framework as they fight to protect and advance the human rights of Turkish citizens. The reform process has also helped to bring about changes in the attitudes of government officials with respect to human rights. It will, as the European Commission notes, 'take time before the spirit of the reforms is fully reflected in the attitudes of executive and judicial bodies, at all levels and throughout the country,' but progress has clearly been made.[37] Finally, the pre-accession process has placed Turkey's human rights practices on the European agenda, adding pressure 'from above' to pressure 'from below' on the Turkish government to meet its obligations under national and international law. This pressure comes in a variety of forms ranging from the decisions of the European Court of Human Rights to the public statements of EU officials.

Advancing economic rights

While the focus of this chapter has been on Turkey's efforts to meet the political criteria for EU membership and the effects of these efforts on civil and political rights, it is also necessary to discuss briefly the implications of the pre-accession process for the ability of human rights organizations to advance economic rights in Turkey. This is particularly important given the increasing prominence of economic rights on the agendas of many human rights organizations. The pre-accession process initiated at Helsinki has required Turkey to meet not only political criteria, but economic criteria as well. Although progress in some areas is still at an early stage, meeting these criteria will lead to major structural reforms in Turkey involving, *inter alia*, the privatization of state enterprises, the strengthening of fiscal discipline, enabling the provision cross-border services, and the removal of restrictions on the movement of capital. While reforms are expected to provide economic benefits to Turkey in the form of increased foreign direct investment, for example, they also create significant challenges for human rights organizations in their efforts to protect and advance economic rights. This is because the main function of the EU's economic criteria is to 'lock in' political commitments to neo-liberal policies that are thought to increase government credibility in the eyes of investors.[38] This process, which Stephen Gill refers to as 'new constitutionalism', separates 'economic policies from broad political accountability in order to make governments more responsive to the discipline of market forces and correspondingly less responsive to popular-democratic forces and processes'.[39] In so doing, it changes the relationship between the state and civil society, for example through the privatization of government services, making it more difficult for human rights organizations to work for the advancement of economic rights.

Conclusion

In conclusion, the pre-accession process has played an important role in transforming the relationship between state and civil society in contemporary Turkey. While the legal and political reforms undertaken as part of Ankara's efforts to meet the Copenhagen political criteria have contributed significantly to the efforts of human rights organizations to advance civil and political rights, the nature of the economic reforms undertaken raises questions about the ability of these organizations to advance economic rights now and in the future.

Notes

1. I would like to thank Macalester College for the opportunity to conduct research in Turkey; Bogazici University for hosting me; and the staff at the Helsinki Citizens' Assembly in Istanbul for welcoming me into their busy

offices and helping me to learn about their work. An earlier version of this chapter was published under the title 'State–Civil Society Relations in Turkey: Change in the Context of Regional Integration', in *Hybrid Geographies in the Eastern Mediterranean: Views from the Bosphorous, Macalester International*, vol. 15 (2005), pp. 289–97.

2. Özgül Erdemli, 'Chronology: Turkey's Relations with the EU', in Ali Çarkoğlu and Barry Rubin, eds, *Turkey and the European Union: Domestic Politics, Economic Integration and International Dynamics* (London: Frank Cass, 2003), p. 6.
3. Mary Kaldor, *Global Civil Society: An Answer to War* (Cambridge: Polity Press, 2003), p. 8.
4. Ersin Kalaycioğlu, 'State and Civil Society in Turkey: Democracy, Development and Protest', in Amyn B. Sajoo, ed., *Civil Society in the Muslim World: Contemporary Perspectives* (London: Tauris, 2002), pp. 253–66.
5. Stephen Kinzer, *Crescent & Star: Turkey between Two Worlds* (New York: Farrar, Straus & Giroux, 2001), p. 26.
6. Ibid., p. 10.
7. Ibid., p. 17.
8. Ibid., p. 146.
9. Kalaycioğlu, 'State and Civil Society in Turkey: Democracy, Development and Protest', p. 260.
10. William Hale, 'Human Rights, the European Union and the Turkish Accession Process', in Çarkoğlu and Rubin, *Turkey and the European Union: Domestic Politics, Economic Integration and International Dynamics*, p. 110.
11. Interview, Helsinki Citizens' Assembly, Turkey, June 2004.
12. Ziya Öniş, 'Domestic Politics, International Norms and Challenges to the State: Turkey–EU Relations in the Post-Helsinki Era', in Çarkoğlu and Rubin, *Turkey and the European Union: Domestic Politics, Economic Integration and International Dynamics*, p. 9.
13. Ibid., p. 10.
14. Cited in Hale, 'Human Rights, the European Union and the Turkish Accession Process', p. 108.
15. Ibid.
16. Ibid, p. 111.
17. European Commission, *2003 Regular Report on Turkey's Progress Toward Accession* (Brussels), p. 29.
18. Hale, 'Human Rights, the European Union and the Turkish Accession Process', p. 114.
19. European Commission, *2004 Regular Report on Turkey's Progress Toward Accession* (Brussels), p. 38.
20. Ibid., p. 40.
21. Ibid., pp. 40–1.
22. Amnesty International, *Turkey: Restrictive Laws, Arbitrary Application: the Pressure on Human Rights Defenders* (12 December 2002), p. 7, http://web.amnesty.org/library/index/EGNEUR440022004?open&of=ENG-TUR
23. European Commission, *2004 Regular Report on Turkey's Progress Toward Accession* (Brussels), p. 41.
24. Ibid., p. 16.
25. Human Rights Watch, *Turkey: Pamuk Trial Tests Commitment to Free Speech* (8 December 2005), http://hrw.org/english/docs/2005/12/08/turkey12174 txt.htm

26. European Commission, *2003 Regular Report on Turkey's Progress Toward Accession* (Brussels), p. 30.
27. European Commission, *2004 Regular Report on Turkey's Progress Toward Accession* (Brussels), p. 41.
28. Interview, Helsinki Citizens' Assembly, Turkey, June 2004.
29. Human Rights Watch, *Overview of Human Rights Issues in Turkey* (18 January 2006), http://hrw.org/english/docs/2006/01/18/turkey12220 txt.htm
30. European Commission, *2005 Regular Report on Turkey's Progress Toward Accession* (Brussels), p. 27.
31. European Commission, *2004 Regular Report on Turkey's Progress Toward Accession* (Brussels), p. 42.
32. See Fatma Muge Gocek, 'Contemporary Turkey: A Country of Tense Coexistence', in *Hybrid Geographies in the Eastern Mediterranean: Views from the Bosphorous*, Macalester International, vol. 15 (2005), pp. 17–18.
33. Kalaycioğlu, 'State and Civil Society in Turkey: Democracy, Development and Protest,' pp. 253–4.
34. See the European Commission's Communication on the Civil Society Dialogue between the EU and Candidate Countries (29 June 2005).
35. James Barnes, Marshall Carter and Max Skidmore as cited in Thomas Risse and Kathryn Sikkink, 'Introduction', in Thomas Risse, Stephen C. Ropp and Kathryn Sikkink, eds, *The Power of Human Rights: International Norms and Domestic Change* (Cambridge University Press, 1999), p. 11.
36. Interview, Helsinki Citizens' Assembly, Turkey, June 2004.
37. European Commission, *2005 Regular Report on Turkey's Progress Toward Accession* (Brussels), p. 9.
38. Stephen Gill, 'European Governance and New Constitutionalism: Economic and Monetary Union and Alternatives to Disciplinary Neoliberalism in Europe', *New Political Economy* 3 (1998), 1: 5–26, p. 5.
39. Ibid.

6
The Kurdish Problem in International Politics
Michael M. Gunter

Introduction

Although they are a large majority within the mountainous Middle East where Turkey, Iran, Iraq and Syria meet, the Kurds have been gerrymandered into being mere minorities within the existing states they inhabit. Thus, the approximately 25–28 million Kurds constitute the largest nation in the world without its own state. The desire of many Kurds for statehood or at least cultural autonomy within the states they now inhabit and the refusal of these states to grant such demands for fear they would lead to their own breakup have resulted in an almost continuous series of Kurdish revolts since the creation of the modern Middle East following World War I and constitute the Kurdish problem.[1]

The three wars (1980–8, 1991 and 2003) involving Iraq and the Kurds living in Iraq have greatly internationalized the Kurdish problem and led to the existence of a *de facto* state of Kurdistan in northern Iraq. This *de facto* state of Kurdistan has greatly influenced the international situation for Turkey and Iraq in particular, while also significantly impacting the policies of the United States, the Middle East and the European Union (EU), among others. Moreover, in Turkey, the insurgency begun by the Kurdistan Workers' Party (PKK) in 1984 and Turkey's candidacy for admission to the European Union (EU) have also served to make the Kurdish issue more significant in international politics. As the Arab–Israeli dispute slowly winds down, the Kurdish problem will bid to replace it as the leading factor of instability in the geostrategically important Middle East. Furthermore, since the Kurds sit on a great deal of the Middle East's oil and possibly even more considerable water resources, the Kurdish issue will become even more momentous in the twenty-first century. The purpose of this chapter is to analyse this situation.

Population

The Kurds are a largely Sunni Muslim, Indo-European-speaking people. Thus, they are quite distinct ethnically from the Turks and Arabs, but related to the Iranians with whom they share the Newroz (new year) holiday at the beginning of spring. No precise figures for the Kurdish population exist because most Kurds tend to exaggerate their numbers, while the states in which they live undercount them for political reasons.[2] In addition, a significant number of Kurds have been partially or fully assimilated into the larger Arab, Turkish or Iranian populations surrounding them. Furthermore, debate continues whether such groups as the Lurs, Bakhtiyaris and others are Kurds or not. Thus, there is not even complete agreement on who is a Kurd.

Nevertheless, a reasonable estimate is that there may be as many as 12 to 15 million Kurds in Turkey (18 to 23 per cent of the population), 6.5 million in Iran (11 per cent), 3.5 to 4 million in Iraq (17 to 20 per cent), and 1 million in Syria (9 per cent). At least 200,000 Kurds also live in parts of the former Soviet Union (some claim as many as 1 million largely assimilated Kurds live there) and recently a Kurdish diaspora of more than 1 million has risen in Western Europe. More than half of this diaspora is concentrated in Germany. Some 20,000 Kurds live in the United States. (Again it must be stated however that these figures are simply estimates given the lack of accurate demographic statistics.) Finally, it should be noted that numerous minorities also live in Kurdistan. These include Christian groups such as the Armenians and Assyrians, Turkomans and Turks, Arabs, and Iranians, among others.

The Kurds themselves are notoriously divided geographically, politically, linguistically, tribally and ideologically. Their mountains and valleys divide the Kurds as much as they stamp them ethnically. Whatever their exact origin, it is clear that racially the Kurds today constitute a mixture of various groupings, the result of earlier invasions and migrations.

The Kurdish language too (which is related to Iranian) has two main variants, Kurmanji (or Bahdinani) spoken mainly in the northwest of Kurdistan (Turkey and the Bahdinan or Barzani area of northwest Iraqi Kurdistan) and Sorani spoken mainly in the southeast of Kurdistan. In addition, Dimili (Zaza) is also spoken in parts of Turkish Kurdistan, while Gurani is spoken in sections of Iraqi and Iranian Kurdistan. Finally, there are numerous subdialects of each one of these four main dialects. These Kurdish language variants are only partly mutually understandable, a situation that adds to the many divisions in Kurdish society.[3]

Tribalism too has prevented Kurdish unity. Indeed, it is probably true that the tribe has received more loyalty than any sense of Kurdish nationalism. In all of the Kurdish revolts of the twentieth century, for example, significant numbers of Kurds have supported the government because of their tribal antipathies for those rebelling. In Iraq, these pro-government Kurds have been derisively referred to as *josh* (little donkeys), while in recent years the Turkish government created a pro-government militia of Kurds called village guards. Similarly, the aghas (feudal landlords or tribal chieftains) and sheikhs (religious leaders) continue to command allegiances inconsistent with the full development of a modern sense of nationalism.

Historical background

The origin of the Kurds is uncertain, although some scholars believe them to be the descendants of various Indo-European tribes which settled in the area as many as 4000 years ago. The Kurds themselves claim to be the descendants of the Medes who helped overthrow the Assyrian Empire in 612 BCE, and also recite interesting myths about their origins involving King Solomon, jinn, and other magical agents. Many believe that the Kardouchoi, mentioned in his *Anabasis* by Xenophon as having given his 10,000 such a mauling as they retreated from Persia in 401 BCE, were the ancestors of the Kurds. In the seventh century CE, the conquering Arabs applied the name 'Kurds' to the mountainous people they Islamicized in the region, and history also records that the famous Saladin (Salah al-Din), who fought so chivalrously and successfully against the Christian Crusaders and Richard Coeur de Lion, was a Kurd.

Early in the sixteenth century, most of the Kurds loosely fell under Ottoman Turkish rule, while the remainder were placed under the Persians. In 1597, Sharaf Khan Bitlisi completed the Sharafnama, a very erudite history of the ruling families of the Kurdish emirates. During the following century, Ahmad-i Khani wrote *Mem u Zin*, the Kurdish national epic, and was seen by some as an early advocate of Kurdish nationalism. Badr Khan Beg, the ruler of the last semi-independent Kurdish emirate of Botan, surrendered to the Ottomans in 1847. Some scholars argue that Sheikh Ubeydullah's unsuccessful revolt in 1880 represented the first indication of modern Kurdish nationalism, while others consider it little more than a tribal–religious disturbance.

Turkey

Background

In 1891, Ottoman Sultan Abdul Hamid II created the Hamidiye, a modern pro-government Kurdish cavalry that proved to be an important stage in the emergence of modern Kurdish nationalism. Nevertheless, the Kurds supported the Ottomans in World War I and Mustafa Kemal (Ataturk) during the Turkish War of Independence following that conflict.

During World War I, one of US President Woodrow Wilson's Fourteen Points (no. 12) declared that the non-Turkish minorities of the Ottoman Empire should be granted the right of 'autonomous development'. The stillborn Treaty of Sèvres signed between the Ottoman Empire and the Allies on 10 August 1920 provided for 'local autonomy for the predominantly Kurdish areas' (art. 62) and in art. 64 even looked forward to the possibility that 'the Kurdish peoples' might be granted 'independence from Turkey'. Turkey's quick revival under Ataturk – ironically enough with considerable Kurdish help as the Turks played well on the theme of Islamic unity – altered the entire situation. The subsequent and definitive Treaty of Lausanne in July 1923 recognized the modern Republic of Turkey without any special provisions for the Turkish Kurds.

Ataturk's creation of a secular and purely Turkish state led to the first of three great Kurdish revolts, the rising in 1925 of Sheikh Said, the hereditary chief of the powerful Naqshbandi Sufic Islamic order. Sheikh Said's rebellion was both nationalistic and religious as it also favoured the reinstatement of the caliphate. After some initial successes, Sheikh Said was crushed and hanged.[4] In 1927, Khoyboun (Independence), a transnational Kurdish party that had been founded that year in Lebanon, helped to launch another major uprising under General Ihsan Nuri Pasha in the Ararat area that also was completely crushed, this time with Iranian cooperation. Finally, the Dersim (now called Tunceli) rebellion from 1936 to the end of 1938, and led by Sheikh Sayyid Riza until his death in 1937, also ended in a total Kurdish defeat.

Although many Kurdish tribes either supported the Turkish government or were at least neutral in these rebellions, the Turkish authorities decided to eliminate anything that might suggest a separate Kurdish nation. A broad battery of social and constitutional devices was employed to achieve this goal. In some cases what can only be termed pseudo-theoretical justifications were offered to defend what was being done. Thus, the so-called Sun Theory taught that all languages derived from one original primeval Turkic language in central Asia, and that isolated in the mountain fastnesses of eastern Anatolia the Kurds had simply forgotten their mother tongue. The much-abused and criticized appellation 'Mountain Turks' when referring to the Turkish Kurds served as a code term for these actions. Everything that recalled a separate Kurdish identity was to be abolished: language, clothing, names and so on.[5]

The present constitution (1982) contained a number of specific provisions that sought to limit even speaking or writing in Kurdish. Its preamble, for example, declared: 'The determination that no protection shall be afforded to thoughts or opinions contrary to Turkish national interests, the principle of the existence of Turkey as an indivisible entity'. Two articles banned the spoken and written usage of the Kurdish language without specifically naming it.

Although restrictions on the usage of the Kurdish language were eased following the Gulf War in 1991, art. 8 of the anti-terrorism law that entered into force in April 1991, made it possible to consider academics, intellectuals, and journalists speaking up peacefully for Kurdish rights to be engaging in terrorist acts. Similarly, under art. 312 of the Turkish penal code, mere verbal or written support for Kurdish rights could lead one to be charged with 'provoking hatred or animosity between groups of different race, religion, region, or social class'. Yasar Kemal, one of Turkey's most famous novelists and an ethnic Kurd, was indicted in 1995 for violating these provisions of what some have termed 'thought crime'.

PKK (Partiya Karkaren Kurdistan)

Beginning in the 1970s, an increasingly significant portion of Turkey's population of ethnic Kurds has actively demanded cultural, linguistic and political rights as Kurds. Until recently, however, the government ruthlessly suppressed these demands for fear they would lead to the breakup of the state itself. This official refusal to brook any moderate Kurdish opposition helped encourage extremism and the creation of the PKK (Kurdistan Workers' Party) headed by Abdullah (Apo) Ocalan on 27 November 1978. In August 1984, the PKK officially launched its insurgency that by the beginning of 2000 had resulted in more than 37,000 deaths, as many as 3000 villages being partially or completely destroyed, and some 3 million people being internally displaced.

For a short period in the early 1990s, Ocalan actually seemed close to achieving a certain degree of military success. In the end, however, he overextended himself, while the Turkish military spared no excesses in containing him. Slowly but steadily, the Turks marginalized the PKK's military threat. Ocalan's ill-advised decision in August 1995 to also attack Massoud Barzani's Kurdistan Democratic Party (KDP) in northern Iraq because of its support for Turkey further sapped his strength. The final blow came when Turkey threatened to go to war against Syria in October 1998 unless Damascus expelled Ocalan from his longtime sanctuary in that country.

Ocalan fled to Italy where US pressure on behalf of its NATO ally Turkey forced Italy and others to reject Ocalan as a terrorist undeserving of political asylum or negotiation. Indeed, for years the United States had given Turkey intelligence training and weapons to battle against what it saw as the 'bad' Kurds of Turkey, while ironically supporting the 'good' Kurds of Iraq against Saddam Hussein. With US and possibly Israeli aid, Ocalan was finally captured in Kenya on 16 February 1999, flown back to Turkey for a sensational trial, and sentenced to death for treason.

Recent events

Instead of making a hard-line appeal for renewed struggle during his trial, however, Ocalan issued a remarkable statement that called for the implementation of true democracy to solve the Kurdish problem within the existing borders of a unitary Turkey. He also ordered his guerrillas to evacuate Turkey to demonstrate his sincerity. Thus, far from ending Turkey's Kurdish problem, Ocalan's capture began a process of implicit bargaining between the state and many of its citizens of Kurdish ethnic heritage as represented by the PKK and the People's Democracy Party (HADEP). HADEP had been founded in 1994 as a legal Kurdish party and had had numerous of its representatives elected as mayors in the Kurdish areas during the local elections held shortly after Ocalan's capture.

At the same time (August 1999), Harold Hongju Koh, the US assistant secretary of state for democracy, human rights and labour, visited Turkey and met with a wide variety of people. Although recognizing Turkey's right to defend itself against the PKK, he also argued that one could oppose terrorism and still support human rights. He further maintained that far from hurting Turkey's territorial integrity, now that the PKK's military threat had been defeated, an inclusive policy that acknowledged human rights would strengthen the Turkish state by giving its Kurdish ethnic community a genuine stake in their country's future.

At this point, Turkish candidacy for membership in the EU entered the picture when in December 1999 the EU finally accepted Turkey as a candidate member. If implemented, EU membership would fulfil Ataturk's ultimate hope for a strong, united and democratic Turkey joined to the West. Until Turkey successfully implemented the so-called

Copenhagen criteria of minority rights for its Kurdish ethnic population and suspended Ocalan's death sentence to conform with EU standards which banned capital punishment, however, it was clear that Turkey's long-treasured candidacy would be only a pipedream. As some have noted, Turkey's road to the EU lies through Diyarbakir (the unofficial capital of Turkish Kurdistan).

Although the election of Ahmet Necdet Sezer, a reform-minded judge, as Turkey's new president in May 2000, demonstrated a willingness to seek new, bolder approaches, there are unfortunately still powerful elements in Turkey which do not want further democratization because they fear it would threaten their privileged positions as well as Turkey's territorial integrity. The military's privileged position in Turkey has been a prime example of this continuing situation. Thus, Turkey's passage of reform legislation beginning in August 2002 to harmonize its laws with EU norms and allow significant Kurdish cultural rights in theory, as well as the commutation of Ocalan's death sentence to life imprisonment in October 2002, did not solve the continuing Kurdish problem in practice.

The tremendous electoral victory of the moderate Islamist AK Party (AKP) on 3 November 2002 brought an even stronger Turkish determination to implement the necessary reforms for the EU, resulting in Turkey finally being given 3 October 2005 as a specific date for its candidacy talks with the EU to begin. Although HADEP was finally closed down in 2003, the Democratic People's Party (DEHAP) had already taken its place. Leyla Zana – a Kurdish leader elected to the Turkish parliament in 1991 but imprisoned in 1994 for her non-violent support of the Kurdish cause – was finally released in 2004 after her case had become a *cause célèbre* for Kurdish human rights. In August 2005, Prime Minster Recep Tayyip Erdogan became the first Turkish leader to admit that Turkey had a 'Kurdish problem'. In a dramatic speech in Diyarbakir, he added that Turkey had made 'grave mistakes' in the past and called for more democracy to solve the problem.[6] As of November 2005, however, much work had to be done both on the part of Turkey and by the EU if Turkey is ever going to enter the EU and in so doing help solve the Kurdish problem in Turkey.[7]

Arguing that Turkey has not implemented the necessary reforms, for example, the PKK ended its cease-fire implemented after Ocalan's capture and renewed low-level fighting in June 2004. In addition, opposition to Turkish membership in the EU seems to be growing in such EU members as France, Germany and Austria, among others. New EU members must be approved unanimously, so any one member of the EU could veto Turkey's membership, which many now see as not possible until sometime in the distant future.

US alliance

Turkey's opposition to the Kurdish identity and Turkey's strong strategic alliance with the United States since the days of the Truman Doctrine, guaranteeing aid to any 'free nation' resisting communism, first promulgated in 1947, have arguably been two of the main reasons for the inability of the Kurds to create any type of an independent state in the modern Middle East that began to develop after World War I. Although the United States paid lip-service to the idea of Kurdish rights, when the chips were down, again and again the United States backed its strategic NATO ally Turkey when it came to the Kurdish issue.

Only when the United States perceived the Iraqi Kurds to be a useful foil against Saddam Hussein did the United States begin to take a partly pro-Kurdish position, at least towards the Iraqi Kurds. Although this US support for the Iraqi Kurds did not prohibit Turkey from unilaterally intervening in northern Iraq in pursuit of the PKK during the 1990s, US support for the *de facto* state of Kurdistan in northern Iraq, and disagreements over sanctions against Saddam Hussein's Iraq and the future of Iraq itself, helped to begin to fray the long-standing US–Turkish alliance.

The US war to remove Saddam Hussein from power in 2003 furthered this process and even partially reversed alliance partners. For the first time since the creation of Iraq, the Iraqi Kurds now – at least for the present – have a powerful ally in the United States. This ironic situation was brought about by Turkey refusing to allow the United States to use its territory as a base for a northern front to attack Saddam Hussein's forces in March 2003. Courtesy of Turkey, the Iraqi Kurds were thrust suddenly into the role of US ally, a novel position they eagerly and successfully assumed. Quickly, the Iraqi Kurds occupied the oil-rich Kirkuk and Mosul areas, which would have been unthinkable encroachments upon Turkish 'red lines' had Turkey anchored the northern front. What is more, Turkey had no choice but to acquiesce in the Iraqi Kurdish moves.

The new situation was further illustrated in July 2003 when the United States apprehended 11 Turkish commandos in the Iraqi Kurdish city of Sulaymaniya who were apparently seeking to carry out acts intended to destabilize the *de facto* Kurdish government and state in northern Iraq. Previously, as the strategic ally of the United States, Turkey had carte blanche to do practically anything it wanted to in northern Iraq. No longer is this true. The 'Sulaymaniya incident' caused what one high-ranking Turkish general call the 'worst crisis of confidence'[8] in US–Turkish relations since the creation of the NATO alliance. It also illustrated how the United States was willing to protect the Iraqi Kurds from unwanted Turkish interference. What is more, the same US principle of non-interference now began to apply to Turkish proposals that either the United States eliminate the PKK guerrillas holed up in northern Iraq or permit the Turkish army to do so. Previously, the Turkish army had entered northern Iraq any time it desired in pursuit of the PKK.

Powerful Iraqi Kurdish opposition to the deployment of 10,000 Turkish troops to even areas in Iraq south of the Kurdish area – a decision the Turkish parliament took in October 2003 in an effort to revive its failing fortunes with the United States and control over evolving events in Iraq – helped force Turkey to rescind its offer shortly after it was issued. Osman Faruk Logoglu, the Turkish ambassador to the United States, complained that the United States was giving 'excessive favours' to the Iraqi Kurds and thus encouraging future civil war and Kurdish secession.[9]

Iraq

Background

The Kurds in Iraq have been in an almost constant state of revolt ever since Great Britain artificially created Iraq – according to the Sykes–Picot Agreement of World War I – out of the former Ottoman *vilayets* (provinces) of Mosul, Baghdad and Basra. There are three major reasons for this rebellious situation.[10]

First, the Kurds in Iraq long constituted a greater proportion of the population than they did in any other state they inhabited. Consequently, despite their smaller absolute numbers, they represented a larger critical mass in Iraq than elsewhere, a situation that enabled them to play a more important role there than they did in Turkey and Iran. Second, as an artificial, new state, Iraq had less legitimacy as a political entity than Turkey and Iran, two states that had existed in one form or another for many centuries despite their large Kurdish minorities. Thus, discontent and rebellion came easier for the Iraqi Kurds. Third, Iraq was further divided by a Sunni–Shiite Muslim division not present in Turkey or Iran. This predicament further called into question Iraq's future.

For its part, the Iraqi government has always feared the possibility of Kurdish separatism. Kurdish secession would not only deplete the Iraqi population; it would also set a precedent that the Shiites, some 60 per cent of the population, might follow and thus threaten the very future of the Iraqi state. In addition, since for many years approximately two-thirds of the oil production and reserves as well as much of the fertile land were located in the Kurdish area, the government felt that Kurdish secession would strike at the economic heart of the state. Thus were sown the seeds of a seemingly irreconcilable struggle between Iraq and its Kurdish minority.

To further their goals, the British, who held Iraq as a mandate from the League of Nations, invited a local Kurdish leader, Sheikh Mahmud Barzinji of Sulaymaniya, to act as their governor in the Kurdish *vilayet* of Mosul. Despite his inability to overcome the division among the Kurds, Sheikh Mahmud almost immediately proclaimed himself 'King of Kurdistan', revolted against British rule, and began secret dealings with the Turks. In a precursor to subsequent defeats at the hands of the Iraqi government in Baghdad, the British Royal Air Force (RAF) successfully bombed the sheikh's forces, putting down several of his uprisings during the 1920s.

Although the Treaty of Sèvres (1920) held out the possibility of Kurdish independence, as mentioned above, the definitive Treaty of Lausanne (1923) made no mention of the Kurds. What is more, the British already had decided to attach the largely Kurdish *vilayet* of Mosul to Iraq because of its vast oil resources. The British felt that this was the only way Iraq could be made viable.

With the final defeat of Sheikh Mahmud in 1931, Mulla Mustafa Barzani began to emerge as the leader almost synonymous with the Kurdish movement in Iraq. Although the Barzanis' power was originally founded on their religious authority as Naqshbandi sheikhs, they also became noted for their fighting abilities and still wear a distinctive turban with red stripes. For more than half a century, Barzani fought the Iraqi government in one way or another. Despite his inherent conservatism and tribal mentality, he was the guiding spirit of the Kurdistan Democratic Party (KDP) founded on 16 August 1946, spent a decade of exile in the Soviet Union (1947–58) and at the height of his power in the early 1970s negotiated the March Manifesto of 1970 which theoretically provided for Kurdish autonomy under his rule. Kurdish infighting against such other leaders as Ibrahim Ahmad and his son-in-law Jalal Talabani and continuing government opposition, however, finally helped to lead to Barzani's ultimate defeat in 1975. Barzani's defeat also occurred because the United States and Iran withdrew their support in return for Iraqi concessions, an action US National Security Advisor Henry Kissinger cynically explained as necessary covert action not to be confused with missionary work.[11]

Following Barzani's collapse in March 1975, his son Massoud Barzani eventually emerged as the new leader of the KDP, while Talabani established his Patriotic Union of Kurdistan (PUK) on 1 June 1975. Divided by philosophy, geography, dialect and ambition, Barzani's KDP and Talabani's PUK have alternated between cooperation and bloody conflict ever since. They also have suffered grievously from such horrific repression as Saddam Hussein's genocidal Anfal campaigns of 1987–8, and the chemical attack against the city of Halabja on 16 March 1988.

After the Gulf War and failure of the ensuing Kurdish uprising in March 1991, the mass flight of Kurdish refugees to the mountains reluctantly forced the United States to create a safe haven and no-fly zone in which a *de facto* Kurdish state began to develop in northern Iraq. In addition, the unprecedented United Nations Security Council Resolution 688 of 5 April 1991 condemned 'the repression of the Iraqi civilian population ... in Kurdish populated areas' and demanded 'that Iraq – immediately end this repression'. Symbolic though this may have been, never before had the Kurds received such official international mention and protection.

Despite the *de facto* Kurdish state that emerged in northern Iraq following Saddam Hussein's defeat in the Gulf War, the KDP and PUK actually fought a civil war against each other from 1994 to 1998. As a result of this internal Kurdish fighting, there were two separate rump governments in Iraqi Kurdistan after 1994: the KDP's in Irbil and the PUK's in Sulaymaniya. Inevitably, the resulting instability and power vacuum drew in neighbouring Turkey and Iran, among others including the United States, Syria and of course Iraq, since for reasons of state none of the powers wanted to see a Kurdish state established in northern Iraq.

The United States finally brokered a cease-fire by bringing Barzani and Talabani together in Washington in September 1998. The Kurds also began to receive 13 per cent of the receipts from the oil Iraq was allowed to sell after 1995. Peace, relative prosperity and democracy began to grow in the *de facto* state of Kurdistan in northern Iraq. In October 2002, the reunified parliament of the *de facto* Kurdish state met for the first time since 1994 and declared that Iraqi Kurdistan would be a federal state in a post-Saddam-Hussein Iraq.

The 2003 war

On 19 March 2003 the United States finally launched a war against Iraq that quickly overthrew Saddam Hussein's regime. Establishing a stable new government has proven much more difficult. As Peter W. Galbraith recently explained: 'The fundamental problem of Iraq is an absence of Iraqis.'[12] The interim constitution – known as the Transitional Administrative Law (TAL)[13] – promulgated on 8 March 2004 for a demo-cratic federal Iraq proved only a temporary compromise given the majority Shiites' insistence on what they saw as their right to unfettered majority rule. Thus, United Nations Security Council Resolution 1546 of 8 June 2004, which authorized Iraq's new interim government, failed even to mention the TAL and federalism as a solution for the Kurdish problem in Iraq. Grand Ayatollah Ali al-Sistani, the *de facto* Shiite leader and spokesman, in general felt that the TAL should not tie the hands of the Iraqi parliament elected on 30 January 2005 and specifically objected to art. 61(c) in the TAL which gave the Kurds an effective veto[14] over the final constitution which was eventually adopted in October 2005.

Many Arabs consider the Kurds traitors for having supported the United States in the 2003 War. On the other hand, many Kurds see the Arabs as chauvinistic nationalists who oppose Kurdish rights because they would end up detaching territory from the Arab world. The future of Iraq, of course, has become even more uncertain given the virulent insurgency against the interim Iraqi government and its US ally.

Moreover, Turkey fears the demonstration effect on its own restless Kurds of any Kurdish entity on the Turkish border. Indeed, General Ilker Basbug, Turkey's deputy chief of staff, declared that 'if there is a federal structure in Iraq on an ethnic basis, the future will be very difficult and bloody'.[15] Turkish Prime Minister Recep Tayyip Erdogan accused the Iraqi Kurds of 'playing with fire'[16] by trying to annex the oil-rich Kirkuk area to their prospective federal state. Turkish opposition to ethnic or multinational federalism in Iraq reflects its long-standing security fears that any decentralization there – especially in favour of the Kurds – will inevitably encourage the Kurds in Turkey to seek autonomy and eventu-ally separation. Thus, in the name of stability, Turkey remains an inveterate opponent of an ethnically based or multinational federal system in post-Saddam-Hussein Iraq.

The most Turkey seems willing to grant is some type of geographical federalism. Such an arrangement would tend to dilute Kurdish ethnic strength and its perceived challenge to Turkey. Turkey also has argued that geographical federalism would dampen ethnic animosities that might be aroused by ethnic federalism by encouraging multi-ethnic and multi-sectarian civic nationalism.[17] Some, of course, have noted the inconsistencies of this Turkish aversion to ethnic federalism in Iraq with Turkey's demand for ethnic-based federalism in Cyprus. When the present author brought this inconsistency up at a scholarly conference held at the Eastern Mediterranean University in northern (Turkish) Cyprus in April 2003, he was sharply informed by his Turkish interlocutors what there was no inconsistency. This was because the Turkish position in Cyprus had been guaranteed by the international treaty that had originally established a binational Cypriot state in 1960. No such treaty, of course, existed on behalf of the Iraqi Kurds.

Will federalism work?

Iraq lacks a democratic tradition. For one to develop requires the existence of an implicit consensus on the legitimacy of the underlying order and trust on the part of the minority that the majority will not abuse its power. These, however, are the very ingredients that have 'mostly been in pitifully short supply' in modern Iraq.[18] Moreover, federalism is a sophisticated division and sharing of powers between a central government and its constituent parts that would probably demand, as a prerequisite for its successful implementation, a democratic ethos. Trying to establish federalism in Iraq before that state is able to imbue a democratic tradition may be placing the cart before the horse.

Elections

A number of other problems face a prospective Kurdish federal state. Unofficial referenda held in February 2004 and again in January 2005 almost unanimously called for independence despite the opposition of the KDP and PUK leaders who argued that independence would not be practical.[19] In maintaining this position, Massoud Barzani and Jalal Talabani ran the risk of losing control of the Kurdish 'street' and thus their long-term grip on power. For the present, however, the two leaders seem secure in their positions.

In the immediate aftermath of the national elections held on 30 January 2005 for an interim parliament that then chose a new interim government and began to write a new permanent constitution for Iraq, the Kurds held the balance of power. To form the necessary two-thirds majority coalition government, the majority Shiite coalition had to accept the Kurdish demands for strong Kurdish rights in a democratic federal Iraq. These demands included one of the two main Kurdish leaders, Jalal Talabani, as the interim president of Iraq, while the Shiites would gain the leading office of prime minister. Other Kurdish demands included the so-called Kurdish veto over approving or amending any future Iraqi constitution, the limited role of Islam, the rights of women, no Arab troops in Kurdistan, and Kirkuk, among others. The Kurds also decided that the other Kurdish leader, Massoud Barzani, should become president of the unified Kurdistan regional government. Should these demands not be met, the Kurds could simply wait until they were while maintaining their *de facto* independence. On paper, it seemed a win–win situation.

After a great deal of debate and against strong Sunni Arab opposition, the permanent constitution finally was concluded at the end of August 2005 and then approved by nearly 79 per cent of those who voted in a referendum held on 15 October 2005. Sunni Arab opposition almost derailed the document, however, as the Sunnis achieved a two-thirds negative note against the constitution in two governorates and fell just short of doing so in a third.[20] (As noted above, a two-thirds negative vote in any three governorates would have scuttled the constitution.) Thus, the future of a democratic, federal post-Saddam-Hussein Iraq looked problematic by the end of 2005. Only time would reveal whether the strong theoretical Kurdish position could be maintained in practice.

Kirkuk

Kirkuk is on the cusp where most of Iraq's Arab, Kurdish and Turkmen ethnic factions and Sunni, Shiite and Christian sectarian divisions meet. It also possesses vast oil reserves. Thus, the Iraqi government and the Kurds have never been able to agree on whether Kirkuk should be included in a Kurdish autonomous region. The uncompromising position Barzani and Talabani seem to be taking on Kirkuk being part of Kurdistan is probably at least in part a result of their fear of losing control of the Kurdish area which is considered to be the Kurdish 'Jerusalem'.

Kirkuk voted against Faisal becoming king of Iraq during the referendum of 1921. Turkey also claimed it until the League of Nations finally handed it over to Iraq as part of the former Ottoman *vilayet* of Mosul, in 1926. Indeed, the 1957 census indicated that Kirkuk city (as distinguished from Kirkuk province or governorate) had a slightly larger Turkman (39.8 per cent) than Kurdish (35.1 per cent) population. The Arabs (23.8 per cent) constituted only the third largest group. The 1957 census, however, also showed that Kirkuk province had a Kurdish majority of 55 per cent, while the Arabs numbered only 30.8 per cent and the Turkmans 14.2 per cent.[21]

During the 1960s and 1970s, Kirkuk was perhaps the most important point of disagreement between Mulla Mustafa Barzani (Massoud Barzani's legendary father who died in 1979) and the Iraqi government. Illustrating how strongly he felt about the issue, the elder Barzani reputedly declared that even if a census showed that the Kurds were only a minority in Kirkuk, he would still claim it. Showing his ultimately poor judgment on the matter, Barzani also stated that he would allow the United States to exploit its rich oil fields if the United States would support him.[22] Thus, the Iraqi government had reason to believe that – given the Kurdish links to the United States, Israel and then pro-Western Iran – handing Kirkuk to the Kurds, in effect, would be giving it and its rich oil reserves back to the West.

Given its oil and geostrategic location, Kirkuk's Kurdish majority was diluted over the decades by Saddam Hussein's Arabization policies so that when the dictator fell from power in 2003, the city had roughly equal populations of Kurds, Arabs and Turkmans, as well as a considerable number of Christians. Indeed, the census that had been taken in 1977 even showed that Kirkuk province had an Arab plurality of 44.41 per cent, while the Kurds numbered 37.53 per cent and the Turkmans 16.31 per cent.[23] Saddam Hussein accomplished this demographic legerdemain by expelling and killing many Kurds, replacing them with Arab settlers and gerrymandering the province's boundaries. The Iraqi government even officially renamed Kirkuk as Tamim (Nationalization), supposedly in honor of the nationalization of the oil fields in 1972. In a theoretical victory for the Kurdish position, art. 58 of the TAL declared that

> the Iraqi Transitional Government ... shall act expeditiously to take measures to remedy the injustice caused by the previous regime's practices in altering the demographic character of certain regions, including Kirkuk, by deporting and expelling individuals from their places of residence, forcing migration in and out of the region, settling individuals alien to the region, depriving the inhabitants of work, and correcting nationality.

The TAL, however, was not able to settle on a time schedule to implement these decisions, speaking only of 'a reasonable period of time' and declaring 'the permanent resolution of disputed territories, including Kirkuk, shall be deferred until ... a fair and transparent census has been conducted and the permanent constitution has been ratified'.

Although tens of thousands of Kurds have returned to Kirkuk and filed claims for homes and property lost when they were expelled, no claims have been settled by the end of 2005. Indeed, Jalal Talabani, now the interim president of Iraq, has complained formally to Ibrahim Al-Jafari, the (Shiite) interim prime minister of Iraq, about the situation.[24] As for taking a census, the Kurds, of course, argued that one should only be taken after all the expelled Kurds have been allowed to return to Kirkuk and the Arab newcomers returned to their original homes. To summarily oust the new Arab population after it has lived in Kirkuk for some thirty years, however, would simply create new injustices. In addition, what would it say about the future of Iraqi unity if most Iraqi Arabs were not allowed even to live in Kirkuk? Furthermore, the Turkish military has suggested that it would take it only 18 hours to reach Kirkuk if the Kurds insisted on tampering with the city's population to their own benefit and to the detriment of the Turkmans.[25]

In a partial victory for the Kurds, the Independent Electoral Commission of Iraq authorized some 100,000 Kurds to return to Kirkuk and vote in the elections held on 30 January 2005. The result was a resounding Kurdish electoral victory in the Kirkuk municipal elections. As noted above, however, this victory has not yet been translated into the Kurds regaining their lost property in Kirkuk. Clearly, Kirkuk constitutes one of the main stumbling blocks in the effort to create a successful post-Saddam-Hussein Iraq, especially given the lack of any group manifesting a willingness to compromise on their maximal demands.

Independence?

On the above analysis, it would be very difficult for the Kurds to obtain the type of ethnic federalism that would satisfy their demands. Moreover, even were the Kurds able to achieve some type of federalism in theory in the final version of the new constitution, Iraq's lack of a democratic culture would make actual federalism very difficult to implement.

Therefore, if a federal Iraq proves impossible to construct, why not an independent Iraqi Kurdish state? What would be so sacred about the territorial integrity of a failed state like Iraq that was becoming increasingly unstable?[26] Indeed, within the past fifteen years, both the Soviet Union and Yugoslavia have broken up into numerous new states. Earlier, Singapore split off from Malaysia, Bangladesh from Pakistan and, more recently, Eritrea broke away from Ethiopia and East Timor from Indonesia. The United Nations also has in the past officially approved self-determination for the Palestinians[27] and the black South African majority.[28]

Why do the Arabs so rightfully demand a state for the Palestinians, but so hypocritically deny one for the Iraqi Kurds? Why do the Turks demand self-determination for the Turkish Cypriots, but deny the same for the Iraqi Kurds? For the Kurds and their supporters, the current situation is neither fair nor logical. Indeed, a strong case can be made that the injustice done to the Kurds contributes to the instability in the Middle East.

The Iraqi Kurds, however, would be well advised to proceed with the consent of the United States, Turkey and the other involved regional neighbours because without their consent an independent Iraqi Kurdistan would prove impossible to sustain for obvious geopolitical reasons. The first step to achieve this seemingly impossible task is for the Iraqi Kurds to be seen giving their all in trying to make a democratic federal Iraq work. If such an Iraq proves impossible to achieve, the Iraqi Kurds then would be seen as having the right, in the name of stability that also would benefit the United States, Turkey and other neighbouring states, to move towards independence.

At that point, the Iraqi Kurds must convince these states that in return for their support for Iraqi Kurdish independence, an independent Iraqi Kurdistan would not foment rebellion among the Kurds in neighbouring states either directly or indirectly. These states' guarantee of an independent Iraqi Kurdish state would be a powerful incentive for the Iraqi Kurds to satisfy them on this point. Furthermore, the Iraqi Kurds must proceed in a manner that their neighbours including the Iraqi Arabs would perceive to be fair to them. This will probably mean compromise on the Kurdish demands for complete control of oil-rich Kirkuk.

In addition, the Iraqi Kurds should encourage Turkey's begrudging democratic reforms that will help lead to eventual Turkish membership in the EU and thus help solve the Kurdish problem in Turkey without secession, as discussed above. If Turkey joins the EU, its fears about an independent Iraqi Kurdish state would most likely abate gradually since EU membership would guarantee Turkish territorial integrity. Furthermore, once Turkey joins the EU, the influence of the Turkish military on political decisions regarding such issues as the Iraqi Kurds would diminish, a process already underway as Turkey's candidacy proceeds. A more civilian-directed Turkish government within the EU would be less likely to fear an independent Iraqi Kurdish state. The late Turkish president Turgut Ozal's imaginative initiatives towards the Kurds during the early 1990s illustrate that these arguments concerning Turkish–Kurdish cooperation are not divorced from reality.[29]

On the other hand, were Turkey kept out of the EU, it would be more likely to continue to view the Kurdish issue through tradition national security issues hostile to an independent Iraqi Kurdish state. Cast adrift from both the EU and the United States, Turkey would be more likely to seek succour from Syria and Iran, which both remain very hostile to any concept of an independent Iraqi Kurdish state. On 19 July 2005, for example, Turkish officials suggested at a meeting of the foreign ministers of Turkey, Iran and Syria that the three states join forces to help eliminate the PKK forces sheltering on the Iraqi-Kurdish–Iranian border given the US and Iraqi Kurdish hesitancy to do so.[30] The United States responded that such operations could have 'unintended consequences' and denied that it had issued orders to capture PKK leaders sheltering in northern Iraq.[31]

Iran

Although twice as many Kurds live in Iran as do in Iraq, the Kurdish national movement in Iran has enjoyed much less success owing in part to the relatively greater long-term strength of the Iranian governments. This, however, did not prevent Ismail Agha Simko from leading major Kurdish revolts in the 1920s that ended only when the Iranian government treacherously assassinated him under false pretences of negotiation in 1930.[32]

This Iranian technique of solving its Kurdish problem was used again on 13 July 1989 when Iranian agents assassinated the leader of the Kurdistan Democratic Party of Iran (KDPI) Abdul Rahman Ghassemlou in Vienna while supposedly negotiating with him. On 17 September 1992, Iranian agents also assassinated Ghassemlou's successor, Sadegh Sharafkandi, while he was dining at a restaurant in Berlin. Earlier, the KDPI's revolt against the Ayatollah Ruhollah Khomeini's new government had been completely smashed by 1981. Armed KDPI remnants, however, continued to shelter in northern Iraq. Their goal remained 'autonomy for Kurdistan, democracy for Iran'. Fighting, however, broke out between the more moderate KDPI and the more radical, Marxist Komala in 1985. Hundreds died in this intra-Kurdish bloodletting.

Despite these failures, the Iranian Kurds are famous among their Kurdish brethren for having established the only Kurdish state in the twentieth century, the short-lived Mahabad Republic of Kurdistan (January–December 1946). When this rump Kurdish state was destroyed, however, its president, Qazi Muhammad, was summarily hanged on 31 March 1947, a blow from which the Iranian Kurds still have not completely recovered.[33]

Unlike the Arabs and the Turks, the Persians are closely related to the Kurds. This ethnic affinity at times has probably served to moderate Kurdish national demands in Iran. Iran also received large numbers of Kurdish refugees from Iraq after the failed Iraqi Kurdish revolts in 1975 and 1991. Unlike the Azeris, however, the Kurds have been barred from high levels of power in Iran.

Many Iranian Kurds supported the reformist Mohammad Khatami when he was elected president of Iran in May 1997.[34] Khatami appointed

Abdollah Ramazanzadeh, a Shiite Kurd, as the first governor general of Iranian Kurdistan. In turn, Ramazanzadeh appointed a number of Sunni Kurds to important governmental positions. Khatami's reformist movement, however, proved too weak to stand up against the hard-liners. In April 2001, Ramazanzadeh was accused of libellous statements against the powerful watchdog body, the Council of Guardians, for objecting to the nullification of the Majlis votes in two Kurdish cities. A non-Kurd succeeded him. During the same year, several legislators from the Kurdish provinces resigned from the Majlis, accusing the government of discrimination. The situation continued to deteriorate when over half of the Kurdish members of the Majlis were prevented from participating in the February 2004 elections. As a result, more than 70 per cent of the Kurds boycotted the elections and civil unrest occurred in several Kurdish cities.

Many Kurds also boycotted the election of the hard-line Mahmoud Ahmadinejad, who was elected president of Iran in June 2005. Only 25 per cent of those eligible voted in the decisive second round of the June 2005 presidential elections in Kordestan province. Even fewer Kurds voted in other provinces. This compared with a national turnout of more than 60 per cent and would seemingly be indicative of Kurdish alienation from the current Iranian political system.[35] Ahmadinejad immediately rebuked Kurdish appeals to place qualified Kurds in his new administration. Indeed, some Kurdish sources claimed that Ahmadinejad had been behind the assassination of Ghassemlou in 1989.[36]

The creation of a *de facto* state of Kurdistan in northern Iraq and the inauguration of Massoud Barzani in June 2005 as its president have also influenced the neighbouring Iranian Kurds to demand changes. On 9 July 2005, Iranian troops killed Shivan Qadiri, a young Kurdish leader, and dragged his body through the streets. The government claimed that Qadiri had organized the destruction of ballots in three voting centres in the recent elections that had resulted in Mahmoud Ahmadinejad winning the presidency. Thousands of Iranian Kurds launched protests in Mahabad, the unofficial capital of Iranian Kurdistan, as well as in Sanandaj, Sardasht, Oshnavieh, Divandareh, Baneh, Sinne, Bokan and Saqqez, among others.[37] The Iranian government had to respond with a state of *de facto* martial law and deploy large numbers of security forces. A number of deaths were reported on both sides. Further Kurdish demonstrations in protest against a death sentence handed down for the July unrest occurred in Mahabad at the end of October 2005. Moreover, during 2005, the Kurdistan Independent Life Party (PJAK), apparently cooperating with the PKK, was reported to be engaging in various military operations against government troops in the Merivan region along the border with Iraq. These events served as a reminder to the Iranian authorities that they still had a volatile Kurdish problem.

Syria

Approximately a million Kurds live in Syria, a much smaller number than in Turkey, Iraq and Iran.[38] Although the largest minority in Syria, the Kurds there live in three non-contiguous areas and have been much less successfully organized and developed than in the other three states. For many years the repressive Syrian government of Hafez Assad sought to maintain an Arab belt between its Kurds and those in Turkey and Iraq. This Arab belt uprooted many Syrian Kurds and deprived them of their livelihoods.

Many Kurds in Syria have even been denied Syrian citizenship. In 1962, Law 93 classified some 160,000 Kurds as *ajanib* or foreigners, who could not vote, own property or work in government jobs.[39] Some 75,000 other Syrian Kurds are known as *maktoumeen* or concealed. As such, they have virtually no civil rights. A government decree in September 1992 prohibited the registration of children with Kurdish first names. Kurdish cultural centres, bookshops and similar establishments have also been banned. Indeed, some have suspected that in return for giving the Kurdistan Workers Party (PKK) sanctuary in Syria for many years, the PKK kept the lid on Syrian Kurdish unrest. For all these reasons, therefore, little was heard about the Kurds in Syria.

Events in Kurdistan of Iraq, however, helped begin to change this situation. In March 2004 Kurdish rioting broke out at a football match in Qamishli. Since then, the atmosphere has remained tense. Renewed rioting occurred a year later in Aleppo following the killing of Maashouq al-Haznawi, an outspoken Kurdish cleric critical of the regime. Within days of becoming the president of Kurdistan in Iraq in June 2005, Massoud Barzani demanded that the Syrian Kurds be granted their rights peacefully. On 16 October 2005 an emboldened domestic opposition consisting of such disparate groups as the Muslim Brotherhood and the communists issued a 'Damascus Declaration for Democratic National Change'. Among many other points, this called for 'a just democratic solution to the Kurdish issue in Syria, in a manner that guarantees the complete equality of Syrian Kurdish citizens, with regard to nationality rights, culture, learning the national language, and other constitutional … rights'.[40]

The forced Syrian troop withdrawal from Lebanon following the assassination of the former Lebanese prime minister, Rafiq Hariri, in

February 2005, a strong UN Security Council response to apparent Syrian involvement in the affair, and the US occupation of neighbouring Iraq have also presented grave international challenges to the Syrian regime. Bashar Assad – who had succeeded his father when he died in 2000 – indicated that he was willing to entertain reforms, but has not offered any specific timetable.

Israel

Because of its precarious position in the Arab world, and in particular the threat formerly posed by Iraq and now an Iran reputed to be attempting to build nuclear weapons, Israel has long taken an interest in Iraqi Kurdistan. Even before the creation of the state of Israel, the Jewish Agency planted an operative in Baghdad.[41] From there, under journalistic cover, Reuven Shiloah, who later became the founder of the Israeli intelligence community, trekked through the mountains of Kurdistan and, as early as 1931, worked with the Kurds in pursuit of a 'peripheral concept' to promote Jewish and later Israeli security.

Most Jewish Kurds immigrated to Israel after its establishment in 1948. Yitzhak Mordechai, the Israeli defence minister in one of the Likud governments of the mid-1990s, was one of them. Nevertheless, as recently as 1994, the present author, in company with several Muslim Kurds from Iraq, visited a Jewish Kurdish cooperative near Jerusalem. The two Kurdish groups greeted each other like long-lost brothers.

During the 1960s, Israeli military advisers trained Kurdish guerrillas as a way to reduce the potential military threat Iraq presented to the Jewish state and also to help Iraqi Jews to escape to Israel. This training operation was code-named Marvad (Carpet). The important defection of an Iraqi air force MIG pilot with his plane to Israel in August 1966 was effected with Kurdish help, while Israeli officers apparently assisted Mulla Mustafa Barzani in his major victory over Baghdad at Mt Hindarin in May 1966. In September 1967, Barzani visited Israel and met with Moshe Dayan, the famous Israeli defence minister. Both the Israeli Mossad and the Iranian Savak of the Shah helped Barzani establish a Kurdish intelligence apparatus called Parastin (Security).[42] These intelligence contacts between Israel and the Iraqi Kurds continued into the 1990s. In 1996, however, Israel and Turkey began to develop a significant alliance that partially reversed the pro-Kurdish sympathies of Israel. Many Kurds believe, for example, that Israeli intelligence agents helped Turkey capture Abdullah Ocalan, the leader of the PKK, in February 1999.

The 2003 war in Iraq has apparently help create a new era of Israeli interest in Iraqi Kurdistan, while causing problems to arise between Israel and Turkey.[43] Although Turkey feared the emergence of an independent Kurdish state in northern Iraq, Israel looked favourably upon such a possibility given the potential nuclear threat posed by Iran and the uncertainty of continued cooperation on the matter from Islamic Turkey. Israel came to see Kurdistan in Iraq as offering a golden opportunity to monitor events in Iran and preempt them if necessary. Reports indicated that Israeli agents were operating in northern Iraq much to the displeasure of Turkey.[44]

Conclusion

Despite the seemingly endless conflicts of the past century, most Kurds in Turkey would probably still be satisfied with meaningful cultural rights and real democracy. In Iran and Syria, the less-developed Kurdish movements would also be more than pleased with such a result. In Iraq, on the other hand – owing to the incredible incompetence of Saddam Hussein in calling forth the Gulf Wars of 1991 and 2003 upon himself and thus the resulting institution of a *de facto* state of Kurdistan in northern Iraq – the Iraqi Kurds will probably be satisfied with nothing less than a federal solution in any post-Saddam-Hussein Iraq. Now that Saddam Hussein has been removed from power, it remains to be seen what the precise arrangements will be.

The further development of Kurdistan in Iraq has played a major role in the furthering of Kurdish assertion throughout all those other states with Kurdish populations. Until the election of Mahmoud Ahmadinejad as president in Iran in June 2005, the fledgling democracy in Iran seemed to offer cautious hopes for greater Kurdish cultural rights in that state too. Even Syria has demonstrated a modicum of hope for modest Kurdish rights now that its longtime strongman Hafez Assad has died and his possibly more progressive son Bashar Assad has succeeded him. As indicated above, the Syrian Kurds have recently begun to assert themselves and the Syrian government has indicated that it would respond favourably to these demands. Only time will tell, however, whether this occurs.

Any Kurdish independence and even more pan-Kurdish unity remains unlikely, however, because all the neighbourring states bitterly oppose it as a threat to their own territorial integrity. The United States, although protecting the *de facto* state of Kurdistan in northern Iraq with a no-fly zone until Saddam Hussein's removal from power in 2003, opposed independence for the Iraqi Kurds because of Turkey's attitude and the US fear that Kurdish independence would destabilize the geostrategically important Middle East. Officially, both the United States and the Iraqi Kurds have accepted that the Kurds will remain as part of a post-Saddam-Hussein, democratic and federal Iraq which will allow the Kurds to exercise a great deal of self-government. Given the current uncertain situation regarding the future of a post-Saddam-Hussein Iraq, however, the Kurdish situation there remains highly uncertain. What is certain, however, is the increasing importance of the Kurds for the future of regional Middle East and international politics.[45]

Notes

1. Possibly the two best recent studies of the Kurds in English are Martin van Bruinessen, *Agha, Shaikh and State: The Social and Political Structures of Kurdistan* (London: Zed, 1992); and David McDowall, *A Modern History of the Kurds* (London: I.B. Tauris, 1996). Also see Mehrdad Izady, *The Kurds: A Concise Handbook* (Washington: Crane Russak, 1992); Thomas Bois and Vladimir Minorsky, 'Kurds, Kurdistan', *The Encyclopedia of Islam*, new edition (1981), pp. 438–86; Gerard Chaliand, ed., *People without a Country: The Kurds and Kurdistan* (New York: Olive Branch Press, 1993); Philip G. Kreyenbroek and Stefan Sperl, eds, *The Kurds: A Contemporary Overview* (London: Routledge, 1992); and Nader Entessar, *Kurdish Ethnonationalism* (Boulder: Lynne Rienner, 1992). All of the above sources, of course, may be consulted along with the additional works listed below. For a wealth of further studies, see Lokman I. Meho, compiler., *The Kurds and Kurdistan: A Selective and Annotated Bibliography* (Westport, CT: Greenwood, 1997); and Lokman I. Meho and Kelly L. Maglaughlin, compilers, *Kurdish Culture and Society: An Annotated Bibliography* (Westport, CT: Greenwood, 2001).
2. For further discussions on the size of the Kurdish population, see McDowall, *Modern History of the Kurds*, pp. 3–5; Bruinessen, *Agha, Shaikh and State*, pp. 14–15; and Izady, *Kurds: Concise Handbook*, pp. 111–20. For a detailed analysis that lists smaller figures, see Servet Mutlu, 'Ethnic Kurds in Turkey: A Demographic Study', *International Journal of Middle East Studies* 28 (November 1996), pp. 517–41.
3. On the Kurdish language, see Amir Hassanpour, *Nationalism and Language in Kurdistan, 1918–1985* (San Francisco, CA: Mellen Research University Press, 1992); and Philip G. Kreyenbroek, 'On the Kurdish Language', in Kreyenbroek and Sperl, *The Kurds: A Contemporary Overview*, pp. 68–83.
4. For a solid study of the Sheikh Said revolt, see Robert Olson, *The Emergence of Kurdish Nationalism and the Sheikh Said Rebellion 1880–1925* (Austin: University of Texas Press, 1989).
5. For detailed analyses of the Kurdish problem in Turkey, see Henri J. Barkey and Graham E. Fuller, *Turkey's Kurdish Question* (New York: Rowman & Littlefield, 1998); Michael M. Gunter, *The Kurds and the Future of Turkey* (New York: St Martin's Press, 1997); Kemal Kirisci and Gareth M. Winrow, *The Kurdish Question and Turkey: An Example of a Trans-State Ethnic Conflict* (London: Frank

Cass, 1997); and Paul White, *Primitive Rebels or Revolutionary Modernizers? The Kurdish National Movement in Turkey* (London: Zed Books, 2001).

6. 'The Sun Also Rises in the South East', *Briefing* (Ankara), 15 August 2005, pp. 1–2.

7. For a meticulous analysis of the many problems involved, see Kerim Yildiz, *The Kurds in Turkey: EU Accession and Human Rights* (London: Pluto Press, 2005), as well as the chapter in this collection by Nathalie Tocci.

8. 'Ozkok: Biggest Crisis of Trust with US', *Turkish Daily News*, 7 July 2003; and Nicholas Kralev, 'U.S. Warns Turkey Against Operations in Northern Iraq', *Washington Times*, 8 July 2003.

9. Jonathan Wright, 'Turkey Accuses U.S. of "Favoritism" in Iraq', Reuters, 4 November 2003.

10. For detailed analyses of the Kurdish problem in Iraq, see Kerim Yildiz, *The Kurds in Iraq: The Past, Present and Future* (London: Pluto Press, 2004); Michael M. Gunter, *The Kurdish Predicament in Iraq: A Political Analysis* (New York: St Martin's Press, 1999); and Gareth Stansfield, *Iraqi Kurdistan: Political Development and Emergent Democracy* (New York: Routledge Curzon, 2003). For earlier events, see Edmund Ghareeb, *The Kurdish Question in Iraq* (Syracuse, NY: Syracuse University Press, 1981). In addition, see C. J. Edmonds, *Kurds, Turks and Arabs: Politics, Travel and Research in North-Eastern Iraq, 1919–1925* (London: Oxford University Press, 1957); Edgar O'Ballance, *The Kurdish Revolt, 1961–1970* (Hamden, CT: Archon, 1973); Sa'ad Jawad, *Iraq and the Kurdish Question, 1958–1970* (London: Ithaca, 1981); Michael M. Gunter, *The Kurds of Iraq: Tragedy and Hope* (New York: St Martin's Press, 1992); and Ismet Sheriff Vanly, 'Kurdistan in Iraq', in Chaliand, *People Without a Country*, pp. 139–93.

11. For Henry Kissinger's exact words, see 'the CIA Report the President Doesn't Want You to Read', *Village Voice*, 16 February 1976, pp. 70–92. This article contains the US Congress House of Representatives Pike Committee Report, which investigated the CIA in the mid 1970s. The part dealing with the Kurds is entitled 'Case 2: Arms Support', and appears on pp. 85 and 87–8. Many years latter, Kissinger explained his position more thoroughly in *Years of Renewal* (New York: Simon & Schuster, 1999), pp. 576–96.

12. Peter W. Galbraith, 'What Went Wrong', in Brendan O'Leary, John McGarry and Khaled Salih, eds, *The Future of Kurdistan in Iraq* (Philadelphia: University of Pennsylvania Press, 2005), p. 242. In other words, given that Iraq has proven to be a failed state, its inhabitants simply reject further identification with it, identifying instead with their ethnic and/or sectarian groups. In addition to the series of articles in the O'Leary collection cited here, see Mohammed M.A. Ahmed and Michael M. Gunter, *The Kurdish Question and the 2003 Iraqi War* (Costa Mesa, CA: Mazda, 2005), for background analysis of the results of the 2003 War in Kurdistan in Iraq.

13. For a copy of the TAL, see http://www.cpa-iraq.org/government/TAL.html

14. Art. 61 (c) of the TAL – the so called 'Kurdish veto' – declares that 'the general referendum will be successful and the draft constitution ratified if a majority of the voters in Iraq approve and if two-thirds of the voters in three or more governorates do not reject it'. Since Iraqi Kurdistan consists of three governorates, this provision gives the Kurds an effective veto over the final constitution. Iraq's Sunni Arabs also came close to using it successfully to

block approval of the permanent constitution in the referendum held on 15 October 2005.

15. Cited in Daniel Williams, 'Iraqi Kurdish Leader Demands Guarantees: Minority Seeks Autonomous Region, Expulsion of Arabs under New Government', *Washington Post*, 18 January 2004.

16. Cited in 'Turkey's Growing Uneasiness over Iraqi Kurds' Federalist Aspirations', *Briefing* (Ankara), 19 January 2004.

17. For further analysis, see M. Hakan Yavuz, '*Provincial* not *Ethnic* Federalism in Iraq', *Middle East Policy*, 11 (Spring 2004), 1: 126–31.

18. Liam Anderson and Gareth Stansfield, *The Future of Iraq: Dictatorship, Democracy or Division?* (New York: Palgrave Macmillan, 2004), p. 10.

19. What Barzani and Talabani probably really meant was that to declare independence now would be premature.

20. For details, see Richard Boudreaux, 'Iraq Charter Ratified by Big Margin in Final Tally', *Los Angeles Times*, 26 October 2005.

21. Directorate of Population, Ministry of Interior, *Iraq's General Statistical Census for 1957*.

22. On these points, see Gunter, *Kurds of Iraq*, pp. 17 and 28.

23. Nouri Talabani, *Mantikat Kirkuk Wa Muhawalat Taghyeer Wakiiha Al-Kawmy* (The Kirkuk District and Attempts at Changing Its National Reality) (London, monograph, 1999), p. 81.

24. 'Talabani Accuses Al-Ja'fari of Assaulting the Kurds' Rights', *Al-Hayat*, 11 July 2005. Ominously, Talabani also accused Al-Jafari of 'converting the Prime Minister's [Kurdish] deputies to ministers without a job or work. ... You act as if the government is only you.'

25. 'Military Issues Dire Warning on Iraq', *Briefing* (Ankara), 8 November 2004, p. 11.

26. See, for example, Ralph Peters, 'Break Up Iraq Now!', *New York Post*, 10 July 2003; Leslie H. Gelb, 'The Three-State Solution', *New York Times*, 25 November 2003; Peter W. Galbraith, 'Iraq: The Bungled Transition', *New York Review of Books*, 23 September 2004; and Christopher Catherwood, 'Everything about Iraq Says: Chop It in Three', 26 December 2004.

27. See, for example, U.N. General Assembly Resolutions 2672 C (XXV), in *UN Chronicle*, 1971, no. 1, p. 46; 3236 (XXIX), in *UN Chronicle*, 1974, no. 11, pp. 36–74; and 33/23, in *UN Chronicle*, 1978, no. 11, p. 80.

28. See, for example, U.N. General Assembly Resolutions 2396 (XXIII), in *UN Chronicle*, 1969, no. 1, p. 94; and 31/61, in *UN Chronicle*, 1976, no. 1, p. 79.

29. For an analysis of Ozal's initiatives, see Gunter, *Kurds and the Future of Turkey*, pp. 61–79.

30. Kathleen Ridolfo, 'Iraq: Turkey Proposes Cross-Border Action To Rein in Kurdish Fighters', Radio Free Europe, 20 July 2005.

31. Mark Landler, 'U.S. Orders Arrest of Kurdish Militants, Turkey Says', *New York Times*, 19 July 2005.

32. For further background on the Kurds in Iran, see Farideh Koohi-Kamali, *The Political Development of the Kurds in Iran: Pastoral Nationalism* (New York: Palgrave Macmillan, 2003); and A.R. Ghassemlou, 'Kurdistan in Iran', in Chaliand, *People without a Country*, pp. 95–121.

33. On the Mahabad Republic of Kurdistan, see William Eagleton, Jr, *The Kurdish Republic of 1946* (London: Oxford University Press, 1963); Archie Roosevelt, Jr,

'The Kurdish Republic of Mahabad', *Middle East Journal* 1 (July 1947), pp. 247–69; and the special issue of *International Journal of Kurdish Studies* 11, nos. 1–2 (1997), entitled 'The Republic of Kurdistan: Fifty Years Later'.

34. For further analysis, see Nader Entessar, 'The Impact of the Iraq War on the Future of the Kurds in Iran', in Ahmed and Gunter, *Kurdish Question and the 2003 Iraqi War*, pp. 174–91.

35. These figures were taken from Bill Samii, 'Iran: Country Faces Agitated Kurdish Population', Radio Free Europe/RL, 23 July 2005.

36. These data and the following were taken from 'Iran Puts Pressure on Kurdish Cities in East Kurdistan', KurdishMedia.com, 15 July 2005.

37. Michael Howard, 'Iran Sends In Troops To Crush Border Unrest', *Guardian*, 5 August 2005.

38. For further background on the Kurds in Syria, see Kerim Yildiz, *The Kurds in Syria: The Forgotten People* (London: Pluto, 2005); Amnesty International, *Amnesty International Report: Kurds in the Syrian Arab Republic One Year after the March 2004 Events*, 2005; Ismet Sheriff Vanly, 'The Oppression of the Kurdish People in Syria', in Mohammed M.A. Ahmed and Michael M. Gunter, eds, *Kurdish Exodus: From Internal Displacement to Diaspora* (Sharon, MA: Ahmed Foundation for Kurdish Studies, 2002), pp. 49–61; and David McDowall, *The Kurds of Syria* (London: Kurdish Human Rights Project, 1998).

39. Some of the following information is based on Bashdar Ismaeel, 'Kurdish Expectations Will Test Assad', *Daily Star* (Beirut), 11 July 2005.

40. Cited in 'Politics & Policies: Pressure for Change Mounts in Syria', United Press International, 3 October 2005.

41. The following information was largely taken from Dan Raviv and Yossi Melman, *Every Spy a Prince: The Complete History of Israel's Intelligence Community* (Boston, MA: Houghton Mifflin, 1990), pp. 21 and 82; Ian Black and Benny Morris, *Israel's Secret Wars: A History of Israel's Intelligence Services* (New York: Grove Weidenfeld, 1991), pp. 184–5 and 327–30; and Andrew Cockburn and Leslie Cockburn, *Dangerous Liaison: The Inside Story of the US–Israeli Covert Relationship* (New York: HarperCollins, 1991), pp. 104–5.

42. Ghareeb, *Kurdish Question in Iraq*, p. 133.

43. See Mustafa Kibaroglu, 'Clash of Interest over Northern Iraq Drives Turkish–Israeli Alliance to a Crossroads', *Middle East Journal* 59 (Spring 2005), 2: 246–64.

44. For background, see Seymour Hersh, *Chain of Command: The Road from 9/11 to Abu Ghraib* (New York: HarperCollins, 2004), pp. 351–60; and 'As June 30th Approaches Israel Looks to the Kurds', *New Yorker*, 28 June 2004.

45. Portions of this chapter originally appeared in other articles I have published before, including 'The Kurdish Question in Perspective', *World Affairs* 166 (2004), 4: 197–205; and (with M. Hakan Yavuz) 'The Continuing Crisis in Iraqi Kurdistan', *Middle East Policy* 12 (2005), 1: 122–33.

7
The Europeanization of Turkey's Kurdish Question

Nathalie Tocci

The EU's objectives in Turkey's Kurdish question

The EU's interests in Turkey's Kurdish question are motivated first and foremost by Turkey's geostrategic importance to Europe. This explains European concerns about Turkey's democracy and human rights, its internal stability and its foreign policy orientation, that is all issues influenced by the Kurdish question. The EU's specific concern with Turkey's Kurds has also been fed by the Kurdish Diaspora in Europe, by fears of rising immigration and by developments in neighbouring Iraq.

This is not to say that the Union has spelled out its preferred solution to Turkey's Kurdish question. Beginning with its 1998 Progress Report, the Commission has called for 'a political and non-military solution to the problem of the southeast', without specifying what such a solution entailed – it simply stated that 'a civil solution could include the recognition of certain forms of Kurdish cultural identity and greater tolerance of the ways of expressing that identity, provided it does not advocate separatism or terrorism'.[1] The 2004 and 2005 Reports went a tentative step further, discussing the Kurdish question in the context of minority rights and recommending an end of emergency rule, the return of internally displaced persons (IDPs), a socio-economic development strategy for the Kurdish populated southeast, a dissolution of the village guards[2] and the full enjoyment of rights and freedoms by the Kurds.[3]

The Union has instead spelled out far more precise guidelines on issues that are directly or indirectly relevant to Turkey's Kurds. On top of the EU's wish-list has been the imperative of respecting individual human rights. The Progress Reports and the Accession Partnership documents have repeatedly stressed the need to guarantee non-discrimination, and the freedoms of thought, expression, association, peaceful assembly and religion. The EU has called for the abolition of the death penalty, the eradication of torture and the respect for rights and standards in trials and detention periods. Beyond individual human rights, EU institutions have made specific demands on governance and on cultural and minority rights, affecting principally (but not exclusively) the Kurds. They have called upon Turkey to ensure effective, transparent and participatory local government. They have also called for the right to use Kurdish names and for the right to Kurdish broadcasting and education. Finally, they have insisted on effective Kurdish political participation, frowned upon the closure of pro-Kurdish parties and criticized the 10 per cent electoral threshold (which prevents parliamentary representation of pro-Kurdish parties, regionally concentrated in the southeast).

The evolution of the Kurdish question

Taking a step back to the region, let us assess whether, how and to what extent the evolution of Turkey's Kurdish question has been moving in line with the EU's interests and its accompanying recommendations. In what follows, the focus will be on the post-1999 period, when the EU became more actively engaged with Turkey.

By the late 1990s, encouraging developments had taken place, offering the prospects for a reconciliation between the Kurdish cause and the Turkish republican project through a rights-based approach. Indeed in its mildest and most articulate form, which developed at the turn of the century, the Kurdish challenge is about the respect for individual and collective rights in Turkey. From a Kurdish perspective, a 'rights-based' solution has been articulated in terms of:

- The freedom to publish and broadcast in Kurdish.
- Private and public education in and of Kurdish.
- The freedom to establish and operate Kurdish civil society associations, freedom of assembly and freedom of expressing non-violent political opinions.
- Freedom from torture and access to fair trial. The abolition of state security courts. The abolition of the death penalty.
- Compensation and IDP return.
- Lifting the state of emergency (OHAL) in law and practice and abolishing the village guard system.
- A general amnesty for all militants.
- Freedom to establish and operate political parties and a reduction of the 10 per cent electoral threshold.

- The reduction of regional disparities and promotion of socio-economic development in the southeast, including through local autonomy.

The 'democratic Turkey' solution was ostensibly advocated by the PKK in 1999 following the capture of its leader Abdullah Ocalan.[4] However, this change appeared to be the tactical response to the PKK's progressive weakening at the time. What appears more genuine has been the rights-based platform of pro-Kurdish parties and NGOs. In the early and mid-1990s, the People's Democratic Party (HADEP) argued in favour of a phased approach to the Kurdish question, beginning with the respect for individual human rights and then engaging in a debate on the multicultural nature of the Turkish nation-state. One of its most recent reincarnations, the Democratic People's Party (DEHAP), in the early 2000s attempted to disassociate itself from an exclusively Kurdish cause, standing for human rights of all cultural minorities and socio-economic classes. DEHAP's successor, the Democratic Society Movement (DTH), has however in some respects moved a step backwards, calling for extensive territorial autonomy and failing to distance itself fully from the PKK.

Key actors within the Turkish establishment have also progressively warmed to the concept of a rights-based solution, making this the only route to reconciliation between the Kurdish cause and the Turkish republican project.[5] However, unlike Kurdish and pro-Kurdish voices, most Turks who support a rights-based approach have focused on the respect of individual and not of collective rights. It is through the exercise of individual rights that citizens would be free to express their communal identity while remaining committed to the Kemalist endeavour to create a civic nation. Collective rights are viewed by many both as a form of discrimination and as a trigger for the territorial disintegration of the country.

The first tentative steps towards a rights-based approach were taken in the early 1990s during Turgut Ozal's presidency. However, the tide decisively turned only by the end of the century. The cessation of large-scale violence in the southeast saw an end to the destruction of villages, to the evacuation of civilians, to mystery killings and to widespread torture. Moreover, Turkish authorities have undertaken fundamental constitutional and legal reforms, many of which have benefited (albeit not exclusively) the Kurds.

First, freedom of expression was enhanced through constitutional amendments easing restrictions on the use of languages other than Turkish. The legal harmonization packages that followed amended the anti-terror Law and introduced a new penal code. Collectively, these reforms enhanced the freedom of expression by reducing the criminalization of opinions allegedly threatening territorial integrity, manipulating ethnic, social or religious differences, or supporting terrorism. The amendments however left untouched restrictions attached to the exercise of these rights for the purposes of safeguarding 'the indivisible integrity of the State'. In turn, at the level of implementation, there has been a strong tendency within the judiciary either to rely on other provisions left untouched or to (mis)use the amended laws to restrict the freedom of expression. Although most of these ongoing prosecutions have resulted in acquittals, cases continue to be brought forward. The trial in 2005 of the novelist Orhan Pamuk, on the basis of his statements regarding the state's approach to the Kurds and Armenians, is a notable case in point.

Second, the reforms enhanced the right to fair trial by allowing for interpreters in courts and by providing for retrial of cases that have been found to be in violation of the European Convention on Human Rights. The amendments also abolished the death penalty and state security courts. The best-known beneficiaries of these reforms were former Kurdish deputies (Selim Sadak, Leyla Zana, Hatip Dicle and Orhan Doğan), whose cases were retried and who were released from detention in June 2004. In May 2005, the ECHR also ruled on the unfairness of Ocalan's trial. Beyond the certainty that Ocalan will not receive capital punishment, it remains to be seen whether and how the Turkish judiciary will allow for his retrial, especially considering that the reforms only provide for retrial of cases pending after February 2003 (that is, excluding the Ocalan case).

Third, freedom of association was enhanced, with an overhaul of the law on associations, which *inter alia*, opened the legal space for associations founded by and/or that seek to serve Kurds. However, important legal restrictions remain, particularly *vis-à-vis* associations advocating Kurdish rights. In addition, a March 2005 regulation imposed further restrictions by stating that associations which promote a particular cultural or religious identity cannot be registered. Indeed in May 2005, the Court of Cassation ruled to close the teachers' union (Eğtim Sen) because of its calls for education in languages other than Turkish.

Fourth, the reforms alleviated restrictions on political parties both by increasing the difficulty of banning a party and by allowing for alternative sanctions (that is, the denial of state aids). However, what was not altered were the substantive legal grounds for sanctioning a party (that is, an alleged violation of the state's indivisible integrity). In addition, the political parties law continues to restrict the use of languages other than Turkish in official meetings and programmes, and no attempt has been made to lower the 10 per cent electoral threshold. More problematic still have been the decisions of the Constitutional Court after these amendments. In March 2003, the Constitutional Court ruled permanently to dissolve HADEP, because of its threat to the state's indivisible integrity. The choice of dissolution rather than financial sanctions was motivated by the fact that HADEP had not reached the 10 per cent threshold required to benefit from state funding.

Fifth, cultural rights have been extended. The restriction on parents' freedom to name their children with names deemed 'politically offensive' was removed. However, an ensuing circular restricted the scope of the amended law to names containing letters of the Turkish alphabet only (thus banning names involving the letters *q*, *w* and *x*, commonly used in Kurdish). Legal amendments also narrowed the scope for suspending or banning works of art. However, the legal grounds for such bans remained the alleged violation of the state's indivisible integrity (potentially restricting the production of artwork in Kurdish). Local police has in fact often attempted to prevent concerts, cultural events and conferences in Kurdish. On most occasions, events have ultimately taken place through the intervention of the upper echelons in the administration or the judiciary.

Moving to the far more controversial subject of collective rights, it is imperative to note, that despite marginal steps forward, these have arguably been the most significant features of the reform process. This is not because of their concrete impact on the Kurds. To date, the constitution continues to deem Turkish as the only 'mother tongue' in the republic, thus prohibiting public education in languages other than Turkish, retaining Turkish as 'the language of the State' and providing for the exclusive protection of and financial support for the Turkish language, history, and culture. However the importance of these reforms regards their impact on the nature and evolution of the Turkish republican project. The debate on collective rights has only just begun in Turkey. An interesting example of this was the publication in November 2004 of a 'minorities report' by the Human Rights Advisory Board set up by the Prime Minister's Office. The report, calling for constitutional revisions to fully respect language rights, as well as for the signature of the Framework Convention on National Minorities, created much disdain within conservative circles. The government also reacted strongly against it, disowning the report. But the very fact that such a report was published says much about the process of change in Turkey.[6]

Within strict legal confines, collective rights reforms have entrusted linguistic minorities with broadcasting and education rights. The broadcasting law was amended to allow radio and television broadcasting in languages other than Turkish. However, these rights were restricted by subsequent implementing regulations, which have limited regional or local broadcasts, required state authorization and state control over content, and restricted the nature and timing of programmes. The reform packages also amended the law on the teaching of foreign languages, allowing for private courses teaching Kurdish. These education rights do not allow for public education in Kurdish. Neither do they amount to the same opportunities available for education in foreign languages. Most critically, the amendments only allow education *of* rather than *in* Kurdish. In addition, the amendments have faced important hurdles in implementation, by precluding state funding and specifying strict conditions on the curricula, the appointment of teachers, timetables and student requirements. Unsurprisingly, by August 2005 the few remaining Kurdish private schools were closed because of to financial difficulties linked to the above-mentioned restrictions.

Turning more specifically to the southeast, since late 2002 the state of emergency has gradually been lifted in all provinces. However, tensions have remained high owing to the 2003 war in Iraq, the deployment of Turkish military units in border regions, the reinstatement of several roadblocks and checkpoints, and the resumption of PKK attacks following the end of the five-year cease-fire in June 2004. In an effort to remedy the legacy of the state of emergency regime, the parliament has passed laws allowing for IDP return, compensation and a partial amnesty for former militants. However, implementation proceeds at a slow and uneven pace. Regarding compensation, eligibility criteria are excessively strict, the burden of proof is high, the threshold for maximum compensation is low and there is limited capacity to process claims and provide legal support for applicants. Regarding return, the need for state authorization, the presence of village guards, the absence of basic infrastructure and poor socio-economic prospects have all circumscribed the prospects for return.

Finally, the first steps were made in the field of governance, beginning to modify the highly centralized Turkish state. A framework law on public administration was adopted in 2004, but subsequently vetoed by the president. Notwithstanding, the Turkish parliament approved a set of laws aimed at redistributing competences, rationalizing the administration and raising transparency and accountability. The government has also established 26 new regions and is in the process of preparing a national development plan as well as the legislation for the establishment of regional development agencies.[7] Much remains to be done however. Little progress has been made in the establishment of regional development agencies and powers remain concentrated in the central State Planning Organization.

Assessing the EU's impact on Turkey's Kurdish question

A rights-based approach offers the only feasible means to reconcile the (nonetheless diverging) positions of moderate Kurdish actors and the Turkish state. In fact, as and when the Turkish state has engaged in political reforms, Kurdish public opinion has become increasingly sympathetic to a rights-based solution.[8] A rights-based approach also approximates best to the EU's recommendations. When comparing across these three sets of wants, it is clear that since late 2001 the Turkish establishment has moved towards meeting the Union's recommendations as well as the wishes of its Kurdish citizens. It has sought a political solution by extending the protection of individual human rights, by enhancing the rule of law, by making the first steps towards the recognition of Kurdish cultural and collective rights, and finally by lifting the infamous OHAL regime. Particularly under the AKP government, Turkey has moved a long way towards recognizing the Kurdish question as such, and openly advocating a political and democratic solution to it.[9]

When cross-checked with the EU's recommendations, the most visible omissions relate to the need for an effective socio-economic development in the southeast, tangible steps towards decentralization, the need to abolish village guards and to ensure IDP return and/or compensation. Equally important is the need to encourage Kurdish political participation, not least by lowering the 10 per cent threshold and inducing governance reform in Turkey. Turning instead to the actual reforms passed, two sets of problems remain pending. First, several omissions in the amended laws have preserved important constraints on the exercise of these rights. Second and most important, the tensions inherent in some of the new laws render the legal system susceptible to abuse in implementation, as indeed has been the case.

Hence, while up until the turn of the century, realities on the ground were far removed from the EU's wishes, since then Turkey has taken unprecedented steps forward. While much remains to be done, an important and unprecedented process of progressive and democratic change is in the making. But what exactly has the role of the EU been, both in encouraging the reforms and in explaining the pending gaps and problems?

Before proceeding it is important to clarify that the EU has not and could not act as the principal, let alone the only, determinant of the transformation of the Kurdish question. Domestic factors have represented the key determinants of change. More specifically, the end of large-scale violence in the southeast with the capture of Ocalan in 1999 both set the context and provided the momentum to embark on a non-military solution to the Kurdish question. Had the war not ended, the reforms would not have been possible.[10] The ongoing self-reassessment within the Turkish military, following four military coups in the republic's history, is another key factor. The November 2002 election of the AKP with a wide parliamentary majority has meant that for the first time since the Ozal years in the 1980s Turkey has had a strong government, which is also motivated to embark on a radical reform agenda. The ensuing strengthening of civil society as a result of the reforms in turn added to the reform momentum. On the negative side, the remaining tensions between progressive and nationalist forces in Turkey, and the relative re-empowerment of the nationalist front by the 2003 war in Iraq, the resurgence of PKK violence and the fears of northern Iraq's drift towards independence all explain the limits of Turkey's democratic transformation.

Based on these premises, the following sections assess the EU's impact by examining the manner in which three key variables determining the effectiveness of the Union's role have interacted with domestic and wider international factors.

The value of the EU benefit: from association to uncertain accession

A first determinant of the EU's impact is the objective and subjectively perceived value of the contractual tie on offer. Since its 1963 association agreement with the then EC, Turkey has had the prospect of enjoying the most valuable form of contractual engagement, namely that of full membership. Yet up until when membership was a remote possibility, the EU's influence on the Kurdish question was effectively nil (if not negative).

Between Turkey's 1987 application for membership and the December 1999 Helsinki European Council which accorded Turkey candidacy, EU actors refrained from giving the green light to Turkey's accession course. The nadir of EU–Turkey ties came at and after the 1997 Luxembourg European Council, in which the Union opened accession negotiations with the Central and East European Countries (CEECs), Cyprus and Malta, while not recognizing Turkey as a candidate for membership. In that period, in view of the mounting violence in the southeast, EU institutions became increasingly vocal on the Kurdish question. Yet EU calls and conditions largely fell on deaf ears. The absence of genuine reform was due largely to the instability of Turkish governing coalitions at the time, coupled with the PKK violence in the southeast. However, equally important in explaining the EU's limited impact was the fact that the association and the customs union agreements, confined to the economic sphere, were not viewed by Turkey as a sufficiently valuable prize to engage in difficult reforms.

The change in Turkey's approach since it was accorded EU candidacy in December 1999 could not be starker. The precise timing of the reforms is explained by domestic developments. In 2000, the overall attitude of Bülent Ecevit's cabinet towards reform became increasingly prudent owing to the dynamics within the coalition. The mounting divisions within the coalition were then pivotal in accelerating the reform drive by triggering the extensive August 2002 legal harmonization package and in leading the country to early elections in November 2002. The ensuing landslide victory of the AKP projected the reform process into a higher gear. This was partly due to the creation of a stable single-party government and largely due to the fact that the AKP based its political platform on the goals of modernization and democratization. Another domestic factor is the economy, which collapsed in the aftermath of the 2000–1 financial crises and triggered a national debate in Turkey on the structural illnesses of Turkey's political economy. But while the precise timing of the reforms (in late 2001–2 rather than early 2000) was due to domestic factors, the jump from association to accession acted as a key external determinant of the reform process. Indeed the reforms were undertaken with the stated intention of fulfilling the EU's Copenhagen political criteria (necessary to open accession negotiations).

The importance of the jump from association to accession is not purely objective in nature. It is also and indeed primarily due to the subjective value ascribed by Turkey to it. Turkey, collectively, has long viewed EU accession as the natural corollary of the Kemalist project. In turn, it is hardly surprising that for the sake of accession, authorities have been willing to go the extra mile in terms of the reforms undertaken. This willingness is explained primarily by the sense of security embedded in the EU, which explains the key difference between association and customs union on the one hand and accession on the other. When over the course of the 1990s, EU actors called on Turkey to undertake reforms, the authorities rebuffed the Union, viewing these as too risky for the country's security. The 'Sèvres syndrome' exacerbated these views. The 1920 Treaty of Sèvres, pushed forth by the Western victors of World War I, allowed for the possibility of Kurdish secession. Since then, Turkish policy-makers have often viewed foreign proposals in favour of the Kurds as an attempt, in the legacy of Sèvres, to dismember Turkey. Hence, it was only as and when 'Europe' made the qualitative choice to include Turkey in its club that it signalled its increased willingness to share the burden of Turkish security, thus easing Turkish suspicions.

Equally important is the prime value accorded to EU accession by Turkey's Kurds. Support for EU accession by Kurdish and pro-Kurdish groups, while deriving from an expectation of political and economic gains, appears genuine. A public manifesto signed by over 200 Kurdish politicians and intellectuals in December 2004 stated that 'the European process offers both Turks and Kurds new and promising prospects, and gives them a chance for reconciliation on the basis of a peaceful resolution of the Kurdish question, with due respect for existing borders'.[11] Kurdish public opinion conveys a similar message. While support for accession is well over 70 per cent on average in Turkey, the highest peaks of support come consistently from the southeastern provinces.[12]

But turning to an explanation of the remaining gaps in the reforms, it is important to note that key actors across the establishment have paid only lip-service to the goal of membership. More accurately, their support was high up until membership became a more realistic goal. When the accession process began, their effective support dwindled rapidly. The expected transformation that came with EU accession was viewed as too costly to enact for the 'sake of' membership. The mounting tensions within the 1999–2002 governing coalition were in fact due largely to disagreements over the first steps in Turkey's reform process. The accession process coupled with the rise to power of the AKP contributed to the relative weakening of the nationalist camp.

Yet this change cannot be considered irreversible. Indeed in 2005, there has been a slowdown in Turkey's reform drive. Much of the explanation derives from the resurgence of nationalist sentiment across society. This is due partly to insecurities stemming from events in neighbouring Iraq and PKK violence, and partly to high unemployment rates and the adjustment costs of structural economic reforms.[13] But the uncertainties in Turkey's accession process (paradoxically) following the December 2004 European Council's decision to open accession talks with Turkey have also contributed to the reform lull by reducing the value of the accession process. The fact that the European Council (over)emphasized the 'open-ended' nature of negotiations and the need to account for the EU's 'absorption capacity', the evident impact of the Republic of Cyprus's EU membership on the Union's stance on the conflict, and the possibility of permanent derogations in key areas such as free movement of persons, structural funds and agriculture, diluted the value of Turkey's accession drive.[14] Turkey's accession process is also plagued with a problem of timing. Despite the launch of negotiations in October 2005, membership itself is expected to occur at least a decade later. The uncertainty of the process due to its timeframe affects negatively Turkey's incentives to engage in reforms in the short and medium terms.

The credibility of EU obligations

Turning from EU benefits to obligations, a first key observation is that even in this respect, the jump from association to accession was pivotal. The 1963 agreement did not include any conditionality related to democracy and human rights, which could have been used by the Community to exert leverage on the Kurdish question. Although the European Parliament attempted to attach conditions related to the Kurdish question to its ratification of the customs union agreement in 1995, it largely failed in its intent.[15] The political influence of EU actors through more diffuse processes of social learning were also extremely limited. Contact between Turkish and EU bureaucrats and politicians, let alone civil society, was circumscribed and occasional. In addition, following the 1997 Luxembourg European Council's fiasco, Turkey froze its political dialogue with the Union. The Association Council did not meet between April 1997 and the post-Helsinki period, and Turkey refused to participate in the European Conferences held on the margins of European Council meetings.

As Turkey entered the accession process, EU obligations became more credible. More specifically the *ex ante* political conditionality embedded in the accession process could no longer be viewed as a matter for political bargaining, but rather became the *sine qua non* for entering the EU club. The most important period of leverage to date has been between 1999 and 2004. The Helsinki European Council accorded Turkey candidacy, but refrained from opening accession talks because Turkey did not comply with the Copenhagen political criteria. In light of the generality of these criteria, the Commission, beginning in 1998, has published annual 'progress reports' assessing 'progress' (or lack thereof) in Turkey's alignment with EU requirements. With the launch of the accession process, the progress reports became much more detailed. Beginning in 2001, the Union has also published Accession Partnership documents, pinpointing the specific short- and medium-term recommendations that Turkey should follow in its bid to fulfil the criteria. Since 1999, the six-monthly European Councils have regularly voiced their views on Turkey. Up until late 2001, the slow pace of Turkey's reforms meant that no additional expectations were raised. Yet as and when the reform process accelerated, the tune of the European Council meetings changed, building up to the momentum of the accession talks, which in turn contributed to Turkey's determination to pursue its human rights and democracy agenda.

The launch of Turkey's accession process also widened the scope for social learning. Contacts between Turkish and EU officials have increased at both political and bureaucratic levels. Institutional contacts have intensified under the Association Council, the Joint Parliamentary Committee, the subcommittees established to review progress in meeting the Accession Partnership priorities, working groups, technical assistance and twinning projects. Increased funding for Turkish civil society on the one hand and Turkish (and Kurdish) civil society's rising interest in EU accession on the other has triggered a social learning effect beyond elite officials. Important problems persist regarding the access of EU funds by NGOs in the southeast (owing to the lack of expertise to successfully compete for EU funds). However, an increased openness of Turkish civil society to its European counterparts has already had a positive impact on civil society's views and perceptions. Broadening out further still, the EU accession process has provided a new discourse, which has provided a common ground to discuss what were previously viewed as mutually exclusive positions. As put by one interlocutor, 'the EU effect has sparked an internal debate in the region; it has provided moderate Turkish and Kurdish actors with a new (EU) language, which in time could facilitate debate both within the two groups and between them'.[16] More precisely, the EU discourse has legitimized what were previously considered taboo subjects, providing the political space both for suppressed Kurdish demands to come to the fore and for these to be discussed (albeit not necessarily accepted) within the more liberal segments of the establishment.[17]

The opening of accession negotiations starts a new chapter in EU–Turkey relations. This adds credibility to EU conditionality on *acquis*-related matters. In fact, accession negotiations are not negotiations at all, but rather the candidate country's progressive adoption of EU laws and regulations. However, a question remains regarding the EU's effectiveness in exerting sustained positive influence on democracy and human rights reforms over the next decade. Turkey's Negotiation Framework states that the European Council will lay down benchmarks for the opening and provisional closure of each chapter of the *acquis*. But these benchmarks relate to the negotiation chapter in question, and apart from chapter 23 on the judiciary and fundamental rights, these are not strictly speaking related to political reforms. The Framework also states that the Union would strengthen its monitoring role in Turkey. But little information is provided as to how this would be done. The opening of negotiations does however raise the potential for social learning. The Turkish government will conduct negotiations through the involvement of a wide section of the bureaucracy. While this would probably be inefficient, Turkish officials have argued that this could provide a *de facto* training programme for the entire bureaucracy.[18] Finally, the Framework specifies that the EU and Turkey would engage in an intensive civil society dialogue. While the primary purpose of this is that of shifting European public opinion, a possible by-product is an increasing social learning effect within Turkey's civil society.

Finally, the credibility of the obligations also hinges on their degree of clarity. With respect to Turkey, individual human rights conditions have been defined relatively clearly, and increasingly so since the beginning of the accession process. The EU's reliance on the human rights standards set by other pan-European organizations such as the Council of Europe and the OSCE has also raised the clarity of EU conditions. This helps explain why individual rights and democratic standards have been the areas where most political reforms have taken place. But the same cannot be said for other conditions regarding more specifically the Kurds, the southeast, and decentralization, which possibly partly explains the pending problems in these areas. In the sphere of governance, the Union has been extremely vague in its recommendations.[19] This is not least because chapter 21 on regional policy consists only of general framework and implementing regulations, which are neither clear nor legally binding. In terms of Kurdish collective rights, Turkey's Accession Partnerships never even used the term 'Kurd'. Only the 2004 Progress Report referred to the Kurds as a 'community' when discussing minority rights, although it did not follow through with specific recommendations. This is not least because the EU legal framework does not include adequate minority rights protection clauses and in practice there is a significant discrepancy among the minority policies of different member states. This vagueness has had the merit of not antagonizing Turkey, entrusting the protagonists involved with the detailed task of peaceful reconciliation. However, the vagueness of EU conditions has generated problems of assessment. Without a detailed specification of expected reforms, standards and benchmarks, Turkish authorities could (and have) claimed that all conditions have been met, while EU institutions could (and have) come up with new requirements over the years.[20] The subsequent lack of clarity in the EU–Turkish relationship has hindered effective communication, eroding trust between the parties.

The political management of EU–Turkey relations

The uneven pace of the Europeanization of Turkey's Kurdish question can be largely explained by the political imperatives underpinning EU–Turkey ties. This has two distinct components.

First, compared with other minority issues in Europe, EU actors have paid only sporadic attention to the Kurdish question, turning to it mainly when the problem has become acute. While in the case of the Central and Eastern European Countries (CEECs), minority issues were viewed as a security issue for Western Europe itself, this has not been so in the case of Turkey's Kurds.[21] In addition, and particularly with the resumption of PKK violence and the EU's greater sensitivity towards global terrorism after the September 2001 attacks, EU actors have become far less outspoken on Kurdish collective and territorial rights.

Second, the EU's political influence on Turkey has been bedeviled by the Turkish suspicion, often corroborated by EU actions at different points in time, of Europe's reluctance to include Turkey in the EU club. Up until 2002–3, EU scepticism was rarely voiced openly, being hidden behind Turkey's shortcomings in the areas of democracy and human rights. Yet Turkey's suspicions were motivated by hard facts. When the 1997 Luxembourg European Council denied Turkey candidacy while opening accession talks with the CEECs, Cyprus and Malta, Turkey interpreted the decision as evidence of European double standards. As Turkey's reform process gained ground, other, non-Copenhagen-criteria-related reservations began to be aired in the open. These have included the fears that Turkey's accession would dilute the EU's loosely defined *'esprit communautaire'*, that Turkey's economic development would entail high levels of redistribution of EU funds to Anatolia and lead to an 'invasion of Turkish plumbers', and that that Turkey's geopolitical location would increase the EU's security risks.

This does not entail that the Union has secretly decided against Turkey's membership. On the contrary, accession negotiations were launched in October 2005. However, the very existence of a debate on the desirability of Turkey's membership has led to two spin-off effects. On the positive side, it has entailed that EU institutions have been relatively strict in their observance of Turkey's progress in meeting the Copenhagen criteria, adding to the credibility of the Union's calls for reform. On the negative side, the absence of a strong European commitment to Turkey's membership has fuelled Turkey's sense of insecurity, bolstering the argument of those nationalists who argue that Turkey should be cautious in passing potentially dangerous reforms given that 'Europe' will never accept Turkey into its club. At each and every instance in which EU decisions are (or are perceived as) evidence of rejection or double standards, Turkish euro-sceptics are bolstered by the 'we told you so' effect. In turn, the more EU–Turkey ties are politically managed, the less will the EU's impact be on a peaceful and democratic resolution of the Kurdish question.

Notes

1. European Commission, '1998 Regular Report on Turkey's Progress towards Accession', p. 20, http://www.europa.eu.int
2. The village guards are Kurdish civilians armed and paid by the state to fight the PKK. There are approximately 60,000 village guards in the region.
3. European Commission, '2004 Regular Report on Turkey's Progress towards Accession', p. 167, http://www.europa.eu.int
4. Abdullah Ocalan, 'Declaration of the domestic solution to the Kurdish Question', translated by the Kurdistan Information Centre (London: Mesopotamia Press, 1999), p.18.
5. The term 'establishment', here and in what follows, is used loosely. By establishment, I refer to all those actors within the executive and the administration, the judiciary, the military, the security services and intelligence community, political parties, the media and academia, which ascribe to the Kemalist republican values. There are wide variations within the establishment, with some actors supporting greater political liberalism and others promoting nationalist and conservative ideologies.
6. Prime Ministry Advisory Committee on Human Rights, Sub-Committee on Minority Rights and Cultural Rights, 'Report on Minority Rights and Cultural Rights', 1 October 2004.
7. Ebru Ertugal, 'Strategies for Regional Development: Challenges Facing Turkey on the Road to EU Membership', European Stability Initiative (2005), http://www.esiweb.org
8. Interview with lawyer, Diyarbakir, May 2004.
9. See, for example, the speech delivered by Prime Minister Erdoğan in Diyarbakir on 12 August 2005, which DEHAP Diyarbakir mayor Osman Baydemir acclaimed as a 'foundation for turning a new page in relations between Kurds and the government'. See Evren Balta-Paker, 'The Ceasefire This Time', *Middle East Report Online*, 31 August 2005.
10. This was a view supported by all Kurdish interlocutors during interviews conducted in Diyarbakir, May 2004.

11. 'Kurdish Demands Ahead of EU Summit', BIA News Center, 14 December 2004.
12. Presentation by Ali Çarkoğlu at a conference organized by the British Council and the Centre for European Reform, 14–15 October 2004, Istanbul.
13. Güven Sak, 'Turkey's Transformation Process and the Risk of an Anti-EU Backlash', presented at the Bosphorus Conference, 14–15 October 2005, Istanbul.
14. European Council, *Negotiating Framework for Turkey* (2005), http://www.europa.eu.int
15. Stefan Krauss, 'The European Parliament in EU External Relations: The Customs Union with Turkey', *European Foreign Affairs Review* 5 (2000), pp. 215–37.
16. Adviser to the mayor, Diyarbakir, May 2005.
17. Speech delivered at a seminar organized by the EUISS, 'The Kurdish Issue and the EU', Paris, 27 October 2005.
18. Debate at the Bosphorus Conference, Istanbul, 14–15 October 2005.
19. Commission of the EC, *Turkey 2005 Progress Report*, p. 103, http://www.europa.eu.int
20. Piotr Zalewski, 'Sticks, Carrots and Great Expectations: Human Rights Conditionality and Turkey's Path Towards Membership of the EU', *Centre for International Relations*, Report 09/04, Warsaw.
21. I would like to thank Ulli Sedelmeier for raising this point.

8
The Greek Variable in EU–Turkish Relations

Alexander Kazamias

Introduction

Since it became itself a member in 1981, Greece stood in Turkey's gateway to the EU like Kafka's enigmatic 'door-keeper'. In the first nineteen years of its membership, it followed a largely obstructionist approach, seeking to either block or severely slow down Ankara's path to Europe. Occasional departures from this norm, such as the 'Davos' *rapprochement* of 1988–93 or the acceptance of Turkey's customs union with the EU in 1995, were so often overshadowed by vetoes and condemnations about Ankara's 'un-European' behaviour[1] that few would have perceived them as a fore-taste of the policy to come. However, since the Helsinki European Council of 10–11 December 1999, Greece not only ceased to pose an obstacle on Turkey's closer attachement to the EU, but began to champion the cause of its accession. There, after a new bilateral *rapprochement*, it abrogated its previous veto on Turkey's nomination as an 'EU candidate state' and then demanded an early start of its accession talks with the Union. With these talks now under way since October 2005, it would appear that Greece, in a typical display of Kafkaesque absurdity, has stood in Turkey's gateway to Europe for nearly two decades, waiting to guard its entry.

This paradoxical volte-face has given rise to several conflicting inter-pretations about its policy towards EU–Turkish relations. One of them is the nationalist Turkish thesis which emphasizes the continuity between the old obstructionism and what it sees as Helsinki's tactical shift of turning Turkey into 'a demandeur from the EU ... so that [Greece] can have leverage on the country'.[2] A second interpretation, advanced by Turkish anti-nationalist scholars, also stresses the continuity of Greek policy, but only in so far as this is deemed to be uninfluential. Mehmet

Uğur, for example, seriously questions whether 'a "Greek factor" ever existed in EU–Turkish relations' and argues that this term 'allows not only Turkey, but also the EU, to conceal their mutual failures' on the pretext that 'EU policy makers have become increasingly receptive to Greek pressure'.[3] Similarly, Ziya Öniş also warns against 'overestimating [Greece's] importance' in posing a 'constraint on the smooth development of Turkey–EU relations'.[4] A third thesis, probably the most popular among Euro-Atlanticists across the Aegean and the Atlantic, stresses the sharp break between Greece's policy before and after Helsinki. According to MEP Pauline Green:

> the death of Andreas Papandreou ... in 1996 marked the end of an era in Greece. The election of Costas Simitis ... presented an absolute break with the past ... His appointment of George Papandreou as Foreign Minister ... had ... a major impact on the strategic shape of the region, and in particular [on] the nature of the relationship between Greece and Turkey.[5]

In a more theorized manner, Ayten Gundogdu also speaks about a 'transformation' in Greek policy after 1999, arguing that this was caused by a process of 'critical self-examination' which led its elites to 'perceive ... that it is not in her interests to define Turkey in alienating, hostile terms such as "Asiatic", "barbarian", and "uncivilised" '.[6] Her evidence draws mainly on official statements, including several by George Papandreou, who also presented Helsinki as 'a culmination of a new phase in Greek foreign policy'.[7]

Despite their value in projecting several aspects of Greece's role in EU–Turkish relations, in other respects these interpretations are both partial and mutually incompatible. First, their respective conclusions cannot provide us with clear answers about the level of Greece's influence on EU–Turkish relations: is there an overriding 'Greek factor' undermining these relations or is this term a meaningless invention of Turkish nationalist discourse? Second, there is little agreement among them on whether the substance of Greek policy changed after Helsinki or not. Despite their differences, both Turkish nationalists and anti-nationalists present Greece's role as fundamentally unchanged, while Euro-Atlanticists perceive a clear 'shift in the Greek position'.[8] Third, their respective assumptions about Greece's motives in supporting Turkey's EU candidacy are also mutually exclusive. The first interpretation considers these motives as firmly embedded in the revised tactics of Greece's old *realpolitik*, the second presents them as part of the EU's changing consensus about Turkey and the third attributes them to Simitis's desire to 'Europeanize' the conflict with Turkey in order to end it.

It is contended here that these analytical limitations arise from a failure common to all three approaches in situating Greek policy in its appropriate geopolitical and institutional context. The first adopts an ethnocentric perspective which accords the Greek state a degree of autonomy it never had, the second places it in a European context which virtually denies it any autonomy at all and the third overstates the importance of domestic ideological and political change, that is Simitis's 'modernization', over external forces. To overcome this analytical impasse, it is necessary to reinstate Greek policy in its appropriate setting, which is both more complex and less easily reducible to a single determining variable than hitherto assumed. At least since 1974, this policy has evolved within a multilayered geopolitical and institutional environment which operates simultaneously on three distinctive yet interconnected levels: the national Greek, the regional Southeast European and the systemic Euro-Atlantic. In this regard, if we are to make better sense of Greece's role in EU–Turkish relations with reference to (1) its level of influence (2) its possible change after 1999 and (3) its underlying motives, then we must examine it in relation to this broader, multilayered context.

In stressing what critical theory calls 'the historical framework of action'[9] surrounding Greece's handling of Turkey's EU application, the aim is to identify three major structural contraints which have been hitherto neglected in the relevant bibliography. The first is the role of the United States which, both through NATO and through direct pressure on the national governments of the EU, has had a major impact in guiding Greek policy towards facilitating Turkey's European path, especially since the mid 1990s. The second constraint is Turkey's own regional influence on Greece, exerted partly through the indirect impact of its domestic democratization and partly through its periodic initiatives to open direct dialogue with Athens, especially after president Özal applied for EU membership in April 1987. The third and rather paradoxical contraint is Greek nationalism itself which, in its determined support for Cyprus's EU membership as means to ending the island's partial occupation by Turkey, has opened the path of a more conciliatory policy towards Turkey's own EU bid. This analysis, of course, will not seek to present Greece's role in EU–Turkish relations as a passive reaction to these constraints. Its aim, rather, is to show how Greek policy began to actively modify its diplomacy through a process of functional adaptation in order to respond to the new historical context which these structural constraints began to build around it.

Greece as a 'permanent variable' in EU–Turkish relations

Irrespective of its content, Greek influence on EU–Turkish relations has often been reduced to a controversy over its ability to manipulate the institutions of the EU. On one hand, Kramer argues that 'Greece abuses its membership in the EU in order to spoil EU–Turkish relations', because 'the remaining EU member-states ... are bound by the ... need [for] unanimity in the EU Council'.[10] On the other hand, Uğur dismisses this thesis because 'it accords Greece a degree of influence on EU policy-making that is not confirmed by the evidence'.[11] Even in the limited context of Greece's role in the EU, both arguments are flawed. The former, for example, cannot explain opposition to Turkey's application from EU institutions that are not subject to the national veto, like that of the European Commission on 18 December 1989; and the latter does not acknowledge that EU decisions affecting Turkey, like those on Cyprus's accession, were taken under the explicit Greek threat of otherwise vetoing the entire 2004 enlargement.[12] Both, however, fail to recognize that Greek influence inside the EU – or the lack of it – is but one aspect of its wider role in EU–Turkish relations. Equally important in this respect are the extra-European constraints which started to condition Greek policy both inside and outside the EU as soon as Turkey applied to join the organization.

An early manifestation of these extra-European influences was prime minister Turgut Özal's bilateral dialogue with his Greek counterpart, Andreas Papandreou, shortly after the submission of Turkey's EC application. Until that point, Greek opposition to the revival of Turkey's 1964 Association Agreement with the EC followed the prevailing Community consensus which had decided to 'freeze' it when General Evren's military junta took power in 1980.[13] Contrary to widespread belief, Papandreou's first meeting with Özal on 30–31 January 1988 in the Swiss town of Davos was not caused by 'the near-war crisis of March 1987',[14] but by the latter's desire 'to pave the ground for [Turkey's] entry in the Community'.[15] The success of Özal's initiative led Papandreou at their second meeting in Brussels on 3–4 March 1988 to 'consent to the signing of the Additional Protocol of the Treaty of Ankara'.[16] With this decision, Greece emerged among the earlier supporters in the EC of a revived Association Agreement with Turkey, while Özal proved how effective bilateral engagement can be in curbing Greek obstructionism. Already by that time several Greek diplomats were publicly arguing that 'it is in our obvious interest, instead of opposing the Turkish application ... to deploy it as a means of exerting pressure', and criticized fiercely 'our boastful self-projection as a relentless opponent of Turkey's entry in the EEC, and the inopportune and thoughtless deployment of our right of veto'.[17]

While the Greek veto reappeared in June 1990 against the Commission's 'Matutes package', which proposed the revival and upgrading of Turkey's Association Agreement, by 1995 most of the proposals were adopted. This *de facto* implementation of the 'Matutes Package' still stands unacknowledged in Turkish nationalist discourse, but is duly stressed by Uğur who explains it, however, in terms of Greece's 'inability' to withstand EC pressure.[18] Nevertheless, both Turkey's return to the EC's Association Council in September 1991,[19] and the Lisbon European Council's decision of 27 June 1992 'to intensify and develop relations with Turkey ... including a political dialogue at the highest level',[20] were products of a revived Turkish–Greek dialogue. The first of these decisions followed the Yilmaz–Mitsotakis meetings in Paris on 11 September 1991 and the second came shortly after Demirel's meetings with Mitsotakis at Davos and Ankara on 2 February and 20 June 1992, respectively. According to the former Greek foreign minister, Theodoros Pangalos, 'the decision ... of the twelve ... to upgrade Turkish-EC relations to the highest level' was a product of Mitsotakis's support for a 'Friendship and Cooperation Agreement' with Turkey during his meeting with Demirel at Davos.[21] At that time, President George Bush also related Demirel's 'commitment to improve relations with Greece' to the issue of 'Turkey's importance to Europe',[22] although there is no evidence to suggest that US pressure was exerted on Greece over the Matutes package in 1991–2 at that point.

US involvement, however, did play a vital role in lifting the Greek veto from Turkey's Customs Union Agreement with the EU on 6 March 1995, which was the most substantive proposal contained of the Matutes package. After his re-election in October 1993, Papandreou began 'secret negotiations with Turkey proposing to accept [its] customs union with the EU in return for a firm timetable for making Cyprus a full EU member'.[23] The role of the US in this process was revealed by Undersecretary Richard Holbrooke when he announced discussing the matter with Prime Minister Tansu Çiller in September 1995.[24] A letter to her from President Clinton on 24 February 1996 also recalled that 'the US had supported the customs union between Turkey and the EU' and through it the US president also issued the virtual command that 'the EU should pay out its promised financial aid to Turkey – despite the dispute with fellow member Greece'.[25] Besides these interventions, the main check against the Greek veto was Cyprus's EU accession, which became a realistic prospect when the Commission issued its favourable *Opinion* in October 1993.[26] From that point onwards, Papandreou faced a dilemma between two conflicting strategies of Greek nationalism: either to block Turkey's European path and risk Turkish retaliation in Cyprus (for example the annexation of its occupied north) or to support Turkey's customs union in return for a clean Cypriot accession. What Suvarierol describes as 'the compromise of March 6, 1995, which guaranteed Cyprus ... accession negotiations ... in return for the lifting of the Greek veto on the customs union with Turkey'[27] was Papandreou's strategic choice, which then needed Washington's mediation to take effect.

Despite the new period of bilateral tension which erupted after the Imia/Kardak crisis of January 1996, the prospect of Cyprus's EU accession was bound ultimately to produce a new Greek–Turkish compromise. Although this took three years to achieve, in the course of which Greece, along with Germany and Luxembourg, vetoed Turkey's nomination as an EU 'candidate' in December 1997, a new round of triangular diplomacy would eventually reverse this decision. It is now established[28] that the outbreak of a popular wave of Greek–Turkish solidarity during the consecutive earthquakes of Marmara and Athens in August–September 1999 did not cause the new bilateral *rapprochement*, which had in fact already started under the auspices of the US Pentagon in June 1999,[29] when NATO's bombing campaign in Kosovo was coming to an end.[30] The lifting of the Greek veto on Turkey's EU candidacy six months later at Helsinki was agreed during President Clinton's visits to Athens and Ankara in mid November 1999.[31] This followed two months of intensive diplomacy which included meetings between Secretary of State Madeleine Albright and her Greek and Turkish counterparts in New York on 23 September 1999 and an official visit to Washington by Prime Minister Bulent Ecevit later that month. During this visit, Ecevit announced that 'it appears a dialogue has begun with Greece' while Clinton for the first time revealed that

there has been some progress ... some change of position in certain European capitals about the inclusion of Turkey in the EU ... The US, from the first day of my presidency ... has strongly supported Turkey's inclusion in the EU.[32]

After Helsinki, US–Turkish–Greek triangular diplomacy proved again decisive, especially over the thorny issues of setting a date for the start Turkey's accession talks and arranging its controversial inclusion in the

EU's European Security and Defence Policy (ESDP). Both were finally settled at the Copenhagen European Council of 12–13 December 2002, mainly around Washington's proposed formula.[33]

This brief historical review leaves little doubt that references to a 'Greek factor' in EU–Turkish relations are both simplistic and misleading. In so far as the term 'factor' refers not only to a 'force ... that actively ... influences the result of something',[34] but also to 'an agent'[35] acting on behalf of a greater interest, its analytical merits here are limited. The usage of this term aims to present Greece as an endemically suspect and conspiratorial actor with the aim of turning it, as Uğur says, into 'a scapegoat' for all the other problems in Turkey's relations with the EU.[36] Greece could be criticized for delaying Turkey's EU application in 1989–91 and 1997–9, for turning it into a bargaining tool in its efforts to bring Cyprus in the EU and for blocking the €600 million of Financial Protocol IV which was, as Papandreou put it, a purely 'symbolic matter'.[37] At the same time, Greece proved highly responsive to Turkish democratization in 1988, accepted the Matutes package and the customs union by the deadline of 1995, and championed Turkey's accession after 1999. This mixed record moreover demonstrates that far from being a mere follower of the prevailing EU consensus, Greece has maintained a continuous and felt presence at every step of Turkey's long accession path. While the influence of this presence never ceased to vary between moments of greater and lesser strength, at the same time it has shown an invariable and undeniable *permanency* throughout the course of EU–Turkish relations.

There is, however, a deeper dimension to this influence which goes beyond the quantitative controversy about its degree. This is the question of its quality and direction, where most Turkish scholars and Turcologists face their Greek counterparts on opposite ends of a long continuum. According to the former, whatever influence Greece might have on EU–Turkish relations, this is always deemed to be negative and divisive. Expressions ranging from 'downright hostility', 'persistent efforts to blacken',[38] 'stubborn attitude', 'abuses its membership',[39] to 'yet another hurdle',[40] 'used its membership to impede progress'[41] and so on have all been used by Turkish scholars and Turcologists to describe Greek involvement in EU–Turkish relations. By contrast, Greek scholars have also stereotypically assumed, mostly after 1999, that Greece's role is not only devoid of such negative attributes, but even imbued with a unifying and 'Europeanizing' mission, thereby echoing the 'orientalist' discourse of the European Enlightenment. 'Greece prefers a secular and European-oriented Turkey',[42] says Papanicolaou, while Heraclides argues that 'lifting the Greek veto on Turkey's candidacy' shows 'a case of enlightened civil society ... presenting a credible alternative to perennial antagonism'.[43] The popularity of these views among Greek academics was reported in a recent survey by Stavridis where 'most interviewees confirmed ... that there has been a Europeanisation of Greek foreign policy, especially with regards to Turkey/Cyprus'.[44]

Closer examination of the evidence, however, shows that historically, Greece has been neither monolithically hostile nor so clearly supportive towards the prospect of a 'European Turkey', but mainly frustrated and ambivalent about it. Papanicolaou identifies one manifestation of this dualist attitude when he says that 'Greeks are supportive of Turkey's entry ... in the hope of better bilateral relations', but are 'more concerned when it comes to thinking as Europeans'.[45] Ogutcu has also found through inteviews that in the early 1990s most Greek diplomats and scholars considered 'Turkey's full membership [to] be in the best interests of Greece' (a view which returns, as we saw, to the late 1980s), but the same individuals also told him that 'Athens will make the best use of its veto power in extracting Turkish concessions on Cyprus and the Aegean'.[46] A further confirmation of this dualist perception comes out of the research of Heraclides who found that

> the idea that the various Greek vetoes were the wrong policy had been in the air since the early 1990s and apparently had been adopted (in private at least) by many a major political figure. Yet no Greek government dared budge but moved along as if in a trance, dreading the political cost of appearing to appease aggressive-expansionist Turkey.[47]

Indeed, Papandreou's willingness to revive Turkey's Association Agreement in 1988, Mitsotakis's efforts to upgrade its political dialogue with the EC in 1991–2 and Karamanlis's approval for the start of its accession talks at the Brussels Council of December 2004 were all unconditional decisions reflecting a deeper Greek interest in stronger EU–Turkish relations. In other words, Greek policy always perceived clear benefits from Turkey's closer attachment to the EU. The question, however, is that more often than not, this policy has chosen to contravene this interest in favour of the electorally appealing and politically safer vetoes.

The constant presence of this dualism at the heart of Greek policy requires more than a passing reference in analyses intent on reaching uniform conclusions. Its centrality underlines the need for a greater flexibility of approach capable of grasping this policy's endemic instability and its historically proven changeability. For this reason, it is counterproductive to fix on this policy such a rigid label as 'the Greek factor' or even to seek to present it monolithically as either 'uninfluential' or 'Europeanizing'. In place of these reductionist simplifications it would be more appropriate to speak of an oscillating, yet *permanent Greek variable* in EU–Turkish relations.

The balance of continuity and change: Greek policy after Helsinki

The vacillations of Greek policy towards EU–Turkish relations, although by no means eliminated, have nevertheless significantly diminished since the Helsinki European Council of December 1999. The new regional dynamic generated by the decisions of this summit was founded on three limited but highly significant decisions. These were: (1) The nomination of Turkey as a 'candidate state', a decision which opened the prospect of its EU membership for the first time since 1987; (2) the disconnection of Cyprus's EU accession from any conditions about a prior solution of the Cyprus question; (3) the setting of a solution in Cyprus and the Aegean as preconditions of Turkey's EU accession under the codified words 'disputes' and 'outstanding border disputes'.[48]

The stabilizing effect of this complex piece of diplomatic architecture lay neither in its relegation of Turkey to the status of a 'demandeur', nor in its success in 'bringing the values of the EU to [the] region'.[49] If anything, Helsinki turned Turkey into less of a 'demandeur' than it used to be when its leaders strove to persuade their Greek counterparts to lift their veto, while the 'European values' claimed by exponents of 'Europeanization' theory, at least according to the text of the summit itself, were the *international* values of the United Nations and the International Court of Justice. This is how the Council put it:

> The European Council stresses the principle of peaceful settlement of disputes in accordance with the United Nations Charter and urges candidate States to make every effort to resolve any outstanding border disputes and other related issues. Failing this they should within a reasonable time bring the dispute to the International Court of Justice.[50]

Indeed, Helsinki's significance as the cathartic moment in the history of Greek–Turkish relations after 1974 lay in its success in producing the first comprehensive agenda of the major issues dividing the two states on a single document which proposed their settlement under the framework of international law. This is why Turkey's acceptance of Helsinki's terms was as important an event as the terms themselves, an approval which required a special visit to Ankara by the EU's High Representative for Common Foreign and Security Policy (CFSP), Xavier Solana, on the summit's first day. The stabilizing factor in Greece's subsequent policy towards Turkish–EU relations was Ecevit's grudging yet unambiguous 'yes'.[51]

In so far as Helsinki broke the cycles of Greece's vacillations between vetoes and deals, this in itself marked a considerable change from previous policy. Moreover, the breaking of these cycles with a comprehensive package, which included both Cyprus and the Aegean for the first time, triggered a qualitatively new phase in Greek policy whereby Turkey's attachment to the EU began to appear not only as a worthy cost, but also as the fittest strategy towards the attainment of national security. This second change also grew out of the rapid improvement in Greek–Turkish relations which, between January 2000 and November 2001, produced nine bilateral treaties in the areas of military cooperation, trade, energy, the environment, tourism, culture, drug trafficking, anti-terrorism and illegal migration.[52] Third, the long time-scales implied by Helsinki and affirmed at the Brussels Council of December 2004[53] practically removed the Greek veto ahead of several decisions because Helsinki had given sufficient guarantees on Cyprus and the Aegean. This meant that Greek policy, besides accepting Turkey's candidacy, was now expected to actively support it with an element of a priori trust.

Despite these changes, Helsinki did not mark a clearcut break with the policy of the past. Although it did reduce its previous vacillations, their underlying cause, that is the dualist perception of Turkey by Greek policymakers, was still left intact. This underlying dualism resurfaced at NATO's Prague Summit on 20–22 November 2002, when the Turkish president Ahmet Cezer demanded both a date for the start of accession talks and his country's membership in the EU's ESDP. Simitis initially protested that 'Turkey cannot have everything',[54] but a month later he quietly accepted both demands.[55] Another manifestation of this dualism occurred during the Bürgenstock negotiations on Cyprus in March–April 2004, when the Karamanlis government 'wrung its hands on the sidelines',[56] failing either to support or reject the UN-sponsored peace plan. Besides these vacillations, it is moreover questionable if Greek support for Turkey's candidacy in 1999 was anything more than a continuous progression from the policies of the Mitsotakis and last Papandreou governments who also encouraged Turkey's attachment to the EU. These continuities are even more apparent in view of the fact that neither Simitis nor Karamanlis has ever expressed support for Turkey's EU membership, but only for its candidacy. Moreover, the diplomatic groundwork which led to Helsinki was modelled on the same method which brought about Turkey's customs union with the EU in 1995: both were secret, extra-European package deals founded on Washington's formula of requesting Greece to lift its veto in return for Turkish compromises in Cyprus and the Aegean.

Finally, the new element of trust which Helsinki introduced was also much less authentic than it would first appear. As the Brussels Council of December 2004 reaffirmed, unanimous voting, and by implication the Greek veto, is always present in the process of Turkey's accession. As art. 23(1) of its Decisions provides, Turkey's accession negotiations will be conducted in an intergovernmental conference and

> where decisions require unanimity [these] will be broken down into a number of chapters, each covering a specific policy area. The Council, acting by unanimity on a proposal by the Commission, will lay down benchmarks for the provisional closure and, where appropriate, for the opening of each chapter.[57]

This means that Greece has never lost its power of veto on Turkey's accession, but rather has chosen to freeze it unilaterally for as long as it deems Ankara to be compliant with Helsinki's terms. Of course, six years into this process, no Greek government has shown any signs of retreat from this trust. At the same time, however, this is a trust devoid of risk, since Turkey's prolonged accession offers Greece ample opportunities to stall the entire process at any stage up to the final point of entry, which is currently not expected before 2014.

On balance, Greek policy after Helsinki has been a changed policy, yet bound by the chains of an unbroken continuity. In place of the old mistrust about Ankara's willingness to compromise on Cyprus and the Aegean, Greece was now trustful of Turkey, but only in so far as this amounted to giving it the benefit of an otherwise continuing doubt. This policy of doubting trust was reached through a new strategy of support for Turkey's EU candidacy that was not followed up by a full paradigmatic shift from *realpolitik* to institutional interdependence. Indeed, what has been described as a 'fragile and incomplete rapprochement'[58] between the two states since 1999 was the outcome of a Greek policy which never ceased to operate under the dualist mix of nationalist and

Euro-Atlanticist doctrines. What is usually seen as Andreas Papandreou's *realpolitik* in the 1980s and 1990s was essentially no more than an obstructionist nationalism which, far from contemplating military solutions, appealed to international law and manipulated institutions like NATO and the EU in the hope of extracting concessions from Turkey. Similarly, what goes by the name of Simitis's 'Europeanization' in the late 1990s and early 2000s was no more than a Euro-Atlantic diplomacy of selective engagement with Turkey which aimed to restore the Southeast European balance of power to its pre-1974 order. Both policies, in other words, were variations of the same inter-paradigmatic approach which sought to combine elements of *realpolitik* and institutional interdependence under a single doctrine. Where they did differ, however, was in the type of mix they adopted: while the former projected its nationalist/realist component more forcefully, the latter sought to conceal it behind a pronounced Euro-Atlantic institutionalism. These were the limited parameters of change which defined Greece's revised approach to Turkey's EU candidacy after 1999.

Beyond neo-realism and 'Europeanization' theory: the myth of a 'European Turkey'

Helsinki was neither a product of pure design, nor an accidental reaction to a series of accumulating circumstances, but rather a mixture of both. The new Greek policy inaugurated at this summit was an attempt by the Simitis government to respond strategically to a set of autonomous events which began to affect one another in highly unpredictable ways. These were: (1) the secret Greek–Turkish military liaison at the end of NATO's bombing campaign in Kosovo, (2) Turkey's decision to break off all contacts with the EU after the Luxembourg European Council's refusal to grant it candidate status in December 1997; (3) the fear that Cyprus's EU accession might be derailed at Helsinki following indications by Britain, Germany and France that they might demand stringent precoditions; (4) the removal of Greece's nationalist foreign minister Theodoros Pangalos over his blundering handling of the Oçalan Affair in February 1999; (5) the wave of popular solidarity which broke out during the Turkish and Greek earthquakes of August–September 1999. There is, in other words, a prominent historicity to Greece's policy change towards Turkey's EU candidacy in December 1999 which is bound as closely to the unique circumstances of that time as to Simitis's vision of 'modernizing' his country's foreign relations. For this reason, any attempt to explain it cannot substitute its historical context for readily available models, like neo-realism or 'Europeanization' theory, on the assumption that it was all a matter of changed perceptions in Simitis's mind.

Neo-realist scholars, however, have argued that Helsinki was caused by the realization that 'Greece's political and economic interests would be more easily served by a Turkey in the EU than a Turkey outside it'.[59] Besides the tautological basis of this proposition, its ahistorical approach fails moreover to explain why Greece was led to this realization only in 1999 and not before or after. Such models, however, confuse the expectation that Turkey's EU membership might be potentially in Greece's interest with the modest record of achievement of the post-Helsinki period. For instance, the UN-sponsored Annan Plan for Cyprus might have come closer than any previous plan to ending the island's division, but nearly two years after its rejection by the Greek Cypriots at the referendum of 24 April 2004, it remains a failed plan, leaving the Cyprus question as open as ever. Similarly, the secret Turkish–Greek talks on the status of the Aegean have yet to produce any results, despite Helsinki's '2004' deadline for taking the matter to the ICJ. Much to the contrary, Turkish violations of Greek air space have in reality increased since these talks began in 2002, forcing even the 'doveish' George Papandreou to report to the European Commission in May 2003 that 'over the last five months Turkish jets violated Greek air space more than 1,500 times'.[60] The only Greek interest served by this policy was Cyprus's accession to the EU in May 2004, but even this was overshadowed by its exclusion from ESDP, thanks to the 'Ankara Document' which Simitis had initially dismissed as 'unacceptable'.[61] With such a grim record of achievement, it is rather doubtful whether Greece continues to support Turkey's EU candidacy because this policy has proved to serve its interests more easily.

Similar limitations are apparent in the efforts of 'Europeanization' theory to explain Greek support for Turkey's candidacy as a reflection of the European norms and institutional logic which the country 'internalized' after two decades of EU membership.[62] In generic terms, this thesis is particularly problematic in so far as it attributes a 'Europeanness' to a policy that is opposed by most EU citizens. According to *Eurobarometer*, in July 2005 only 35 per cent of EU citizens supported Turkey's accession to the Union while 52 per cent opposed it.[63] If we disregard this problem and accept the assumption that support for Turkey's accession is a sign of 'Europeanization', then Greek opposition to this prospect by 76 per cent in 2002 and 70 per cent in 2005[64] suggests that, on this issue at least, the country has not 'Europeanized'. This, in turn, means that Greek 'Europeanization' may not be deployed as an argument to explain support for Turkey's EU candidacy. Furthermore, a central assumption of 'Europeanization' theory is that national decisions are motivated by the 'organizational traits, behavioural and regulatory patterns associated with European integration'.[65] Nevertheless, the three most decisive issues in Turkey's candidacy after Helsinki were handled by Greece in a manner which clearly defied either the EU's institutional logic or its behavioural patterns. In Copenhagen, the need to support Turkey's accession forced Simitis to accept what he had earlier descibed as 'an extra-institutional arrangement',[66] the US–British–Turkish proposal known as the 'Ankara Document', whereby Cyprus (a full EU member) would be excluded from ESDP and Turkey (a non-member) would be part of it.[67] In the second case, the Karamanlis government diverged from the prevailing EU consensus and avoided committing itself to the UN's Annan Plan for Cyprus, despite its centrality for Turkey's accession. The EU's intitutional logic was also disregarded in the failure to 'review'[68] or settle the Aegean dispute through the ICJ 'at the latest by the end of 2004' as S.4 of the Helsinki Council's 'Decisions' stipulated. Overall, this record suggests that Greek support for Turkey's candidacy is motivated by far more complex motives than a mere commitment to the norms of EU governance and their institutional logic.

To arrive at a more satisfactory explanation, a clearer distinction must be drawn between the strong sense of expectation among Greek elites that Turkey's candidacy might in time produce a solution in Cyprus and the Aegean, and the realization that neither the record of the last six years nor the insitutional logic of the EU can guarantee such an outcome. On the basis of this distinction, Greek support for Turkey's candidacy appears to be sustained initially by the unprecedented degree of movement which Helsinki generated between the two states. Beyond this rather self-evident conclusion, it is moreover apparent that this new mobility has been sufficiently dynamic as to forge among Greek elites a Sorelian 'political myth' regarding their ability to bring about a regional peace in line with the country's main national demands.[69] There is perhaps no better way of expressing this mythic view than the phrase 'a European Turkey will be a better neighbour', which Helsinki turned into a popular diplomatic cliché. Simitis's ministers uttered it frequently[70] and so did the then opposition leader, Costas Karamanlis, albeit with slight modifications: 'I wish to strongly and plainly repeat it. A European and democratic Turkey is in our interest.'[71] Because of its appeal to the promised land of good neighbourliness at the end of Turkey's accession path, this myth falls under the type described by Tudor as 'eschatological'.[72]

Most mythologists maintain that the ingredients of myth are drawn from their surrounding historical context. 'What the world supplies to myth is a historical reality', says Roland Barthes, and this reality, he adds, provides 'the motivation which causes the myth to be uttered'.[73] Myth, however, is strictly speaking not a lie but an inflection of an historical reality which hides inside it and transforms it into an artificial form.[74] In this respect, the mythic formula 'A European Turkey will be a better neighbour' serves to mobilize Greek foreign policy as a *transmission belt* which draws its original movement from the more complex historical reality which hides inside it. This is precisely how it operates: first, the adjectival complement, 'European Turkey', blurs the distinction between Turkey's candidacy and its membership and drains at once all the political, economic and cultural tensions between Turkey and Europe as if these do not exist. Then, the second adjectival complement, 'better neighbour', de-essentializes Greek–Turkish relations from all the thorny disputes associated with Cyprus and the Aegean and promises instead their abstract and indefinite 'improvement'. Finally, the verb 'will be' presents the complex relationship between Turkey's 'Europeanization' and 'better' bilateral relations as if bound up by a direct, automatic and absolute causality.

Beneath this mythic formulation lies, of course, a more complex historical reality which motivates and sustains it. If we were to give it a name, this would be 'NATO's Balkan Peace and Stability Pact', the security agreement signed on 30 July 1999 between the OSCE and nine of the peninsula's states at the end of the Kosovo conflict to 'promote the integration of Southeastern Europe' on the basis of 'good neighbourly relations'.[75] The centrality of this pact in changing Greek policy towards Turkey, while kept in the background because of the United States's vital role in promoting it, was nevertheless occasionally acknowledged. In February 2000, George Papandreou made it plain that the Greek–Turkish *rapprochement* came about because 'Kosovo changed our image and gave us a new identity',[76] while a year later he confirmed that

> the Balkan Stability Pact and the Decisions taken at the EU Helsinki Summit in December 1999 have created a new reality: a framework of principles and a roadmap for the Balkans, in the course towards European integration. This is why Greece strenuously supported a meaningful candidacy for Turkey.[77]

As late as April 2003, Simitis would again recall the Stability Pact to promote his policy of supporting EU membership for the states of

Southeastern Europe:

> We do believe that the Stability Pact will have an important role to play
> also in the future as a catalyst to strengthen regional cooperation ...
> The countries and the peoples of South Eastern Europe have a com-
> mon European future.[78]

These statements, however, confirm only one aspect of the United
States's role in guiding Greek policy towards Turkey's relations with the
EU. After Helsinki, secret US involvement in the Cyprus question, at
least during the preparations for the Annan Plan in 2001–2, was recently
revealed by the British representative for Cyprus, David Hannay.[79]
Intensive US pressure also appeared at NATO's Prague Summit on
20 November 2002, where State Department non-papers urged the
Alliance's EU members to 'send a signal for the possible receipt by
Turkey of a date for the start of accession talks from Copenhagen'.[80] On
the same day, President Bush also discussed the matter with the EU
Council's president, Prime Minister Rasmussen, and then announced
that they had 'agreed on the historic and strategic importance of
advancing Turkey's evolution towards the EU and the importance of the
Copenhagen Summit in that regard'.[81] These are among several other
cases of direct intervention which, together with Washington's decisive
role in influencing the outcome of Helsinki, confirm that the United
States's hegemony in the region has been the single most important
factor behind Greece's continuing support for Turkey's EU candidacy.

The Greek myth of a 'European Turkey' is moreover sustained by a
second historical reality which also lies hidden under its glossier exte-
rior. This is the powerful regional dynamic generated by Turkey's own
determination to become an 'EU' member since 1987. While this is usually claimed by both Greek and non-Greek advocates of 'Europeanization'
theory as a response to the 'environmental inputs ... originating from
EC sources and processes',[82] the long record of EU rejections, vetoes and
delays suggests the need for an alternative interpretation. At least in the
Turkish case, the quest for EU membership arose and developed independently from and mostly in opposition to the Union's 'sources and
processes' which, throughout the late 1980s and 1990s, were repeatedly
denied to this country. Turkey's unyielding endeavour to become an EU
member emanates primarily from a domestic set of socio-economic, ideological and political developments relating to the national process of
constructing a new, post-Kemalist identity. The origins of this process lie
in a phenomenon which both predates and supersedes the boundaries

of the European Communities, and has its own history in the late Ottoman Empire and the modern Turkish Republic:[83] this is the practice of adopting West European forms and types of behaviour as a means of faster modernization, a current known better among modern historians by the names of 'Europeanism' or 'Westernization'.[84] Consequently, the second core function of the Greek myth of a 'European Turkey' is to dislocate *Turkish Europeanism*[85] from its real national context in order to claim it as its own. This is, for example, how Simitis put it:

> In 1994 ... Turkey did not have its European orientation among its priorities. ... Today ... Turkey has elevated its entry in the Union to a top priority of its policy. This is the new framework ... we created.[86]

The appropriation of Turkish Europeanism by the Greek elites has been, of course, a vital precondition for their continuing support for Turkey's candidacy before a highly sceptical domestic audience. Ironically, however, it is the Turkish drive to become an EU member which simultaneously provides them with the historical reality they need for building and sustaining their national Greek myth.

Finally, the myth of a 'European Turkey' is also motivated by the deeply rooted ambivalence of Greek dualism. The elevation of Turkey's candidacy to a mythic status provides this contradictory diplomatic doctrine with an artificial form of stability and unity which it would not otherwise have. It enables it to appear coherent in maintaining a full commitment both to Greece's maximalist claims in Cyprus and the Aegean and to the Atlanticist policy of supporting Turkey's entry to the EU, when the attainment of all these objectives combined is improbable. The function of the myth in this regard is to provide a mechanism for constantly shifting forward the moment of the final decisions on Cyprus, the Aegean and Turkey's EU membership, in order to create an imagined sense of movement around a reality which remains unchanged. An example of how this mechanism operates is the statement made by the Greek foreign minister, Petros Molyviatis, at the launch of Turkey's accession talks in Luxembourg on 3 October 2005 under the previously agreed Framework of Negotiations:

> This is an historic agreement ... which, not immediately, but in due course, will change and replace the evil past and infamy of our region. It is the beginning of a new era. We are laying the foundations ... on which our relationship with Turkey will proceed, as well as the relationship between Turkey and the entire region. Greece and Cyprus

have succeeded in safeguarding all their positions and aims, on the basis of legally binding texts.[87]

The fact that six years after Helsinki, Greek policy is still announcing the 'beginning of a new era' and claims success in rescuing the terms agreed back then, suggests that in the meantime the elevation of Turkey's candidacy to a mythic status has brought about a gradual confusion of ends and means. In other words, from a means of solving the bilateral disputes in Cyprus and the Aegean, Turkey's candidacy became increasingly treated as an end in itself because it is regarded as the only policy capable of resolving the bilateral disputes. Furthermore, under Karamanlis this confusion appears to have grown increasingly into a full substitution, whereby the freezing of the Cyprus and Aegean disputes themselves has now been turned into a means of facilitating Turkey's candidacy.

Conclusion

The exposition of the mythic elements in Greek policy towards EU–Turkish relations was not intended here as a criticism of its basic conception. On the contrary, the prospect of Turkey's accession to the EU has been and remains the best option available to Greece for reaching a comprehensive settlement in Cyprus and the Aegean in the interests both of its own security and of a lasting regional peace. In revealing the different historical realities underlying the official and semi-official representations of this policy, the object was to warn against the deepening conflict between its stated aims on the one hand and the practices used to serve them on the other. The bifurcation of Greek policy into a mythic level which claims to be 'Europeanizing' and a real level which is continually reliant on Washington's triangular diplomacy with Ankara and Athens is the primary threat to its success and the chief cause of its hitherto limited achievements.

While an immediate end to this schizoid approach must not be expected as long as Turkey's accession talks are still subject to the EU's Kafkesque time-scales, progress in these talks will gradually force Greece to start closing the gap between the mythic and real dimensions of its policy. Historical precedent suggests that, when faced with such a pressure, Greek elites will once again resort to the extra-European solution of Washington's triangular diplomacy at the risk of further undermining the 'Europeanizing' mythic image of their policy. At the same time, however, Greek public opinion is highly unlikely to accept such a solution if it extends beyond the scope of Turkey's candidacy to include the core issues of Cyprus, the Aegean and Turkey's EU membership. The force of this opposition was made apparent during the Greek Cypriot referendum on the Annan Plan and has shown a worrying endurance in *Eurobarometer*'s surveys on Turkey's EU membership. Consequently, the only feasible option available to Greek elites would be to radically revise the present policy in such as a way as to make it truer to its mythic form, that is authentically to 'Europeanize' it.

Notes

1. 'The rule of law forms an essential element of all modern European national formations. In Turkey, by contrast, the concept of the rule of law is non-existent'; see Theodoros Pangalos, 'Elliniki Exoteriki Politiki ke Tourkia' (Greek Foreign Policy and Turkey), *Epetirida 1996* (Athens: Institute of International Relations – Sideris, 1996), p. 121.
2. Münevver Cebeci, 'CESDP: A Turkish Perspective', in Peter Xuereb, *Euro-Mediterranean Integration* (Msida: University of Malta, 2002), pp. 173–4; Semin Suvarierol, 'The Cyprus Obstacle on Turkey's Road to Membership in the European Union', in Ali Çarkoğlu and Barry Rubin, eds, *Turkey and the European Union* (London: Frank Cass, 2005), pp. 62–3.
3. Mehmet Uğur, 'Europeanisation and Convergence via Incomplete Contracts? The Case of Turkey', in Kevin Featherstone and George Kazamias, eds, *Europeanisation and the Southern Periphery* (London: Frank Cass, 2001), p. 235.
4. Ziya Öniş, 'Domestic Politics, International Norms and Challenges to the State: Turkey–EU Relations in the post-Helsinki Era', in Çarkoğlu and Rubin, eds, *Turkey and the European Union*, p. 23.
5. Pauline Green with Ray Collins, *Embracing Cyprus: The Path to Unity in the New Europe* (London: I.B. Tauris, 2003), pp. 82–4.
6. Ayten Gundogdu, 'Identities in Question: Greek–Turkish Relations in a Period of Transformation?', in *Middle East Review of International Affairs* 5 (2001), 1:6.
7. George Papandreou, 'Revision in Greek Foreign Policy', Western Policy Centre, Regional Report, January 2000, http://www.westernpolicy.org/publications/reports/2000/a/standpoint.asp
8. Zalmay Khalilzad, Ian Lesser and F. Stephen Larrabee, *The Future of Turkish–Western Relations* (Santa Monica, CA: RAND, 2000), p. 40; 'In a Shift, Greece Backs Turkey as EU Member', *International Herald Tribune*, 6 September 1999.
9. Robert Cox, *Approaches to World Order* (Cambridge University Press, 1996), p. 97.
10. Heinz Kramer, 'Turkey and the European Union: A Multi-dimensional Relationship with Hazy Perspectives', in Vojtech Mastny and R. Craig Nation, *Turkey Between East and West* (Boulder, CO: Westview Press, 1996), p. 216.
11. Uğur, 'Europeanisation and Convergence via Incomplete Contracts? The Case of Turkey', p. 234.
12. Suvarierol, 'The Cyprus Obstacle on Turkey's Road to Membership in the European Union', p. 64.

13. European Commission, *1998 Regular Report on Turkey's Progress Towards Accession*, p. 5.
14. This view is expressed by Mustafa Aydin, 'Contemporary Turkish–Greek Relations: Constraints and Opportunities'; Tozun Bahcheli, 'Turning a New Page in Turkey's Relations with Greece? The Challenge of Reconciling Vital Interests', in Mustafa Aydin and Kostas Ifantis, eds, *Turkish-Greek Relations: The Security Dilemma in the Aegean* (London: Routledge, 2004), pp. 32 and 97.
15. Thanos Veremis and Theodore Couloumbis, *Elliniki Exoteriki Politiki: Prooptikes kai Problimatismoi* (Greek Foreign Policy: Prospects and Reflections) (Athens: Sideris, 1994), p. 43. This was confirmed later by Papandreou himself: 'Turkey ... has also been upgraded in the EC. I remind you that Davos had no connection with the crucial confrontation of March. Davos came later'; in Andreas Papandreou, *I Ellada stis nees exelixeis* (Greece in the New Developments) (Athens: Echmi, 1992), p. 120.
16. *The Brussels Communiqué*, 3–4 March 1988, para. 7.
17. Institute of Political Studies and Education, *Themata Exoterikis kai Amyntikis Politikis* (Athens: Sideris, 1989), anonymous analysis, 25 May 1987, pp. 14–15.
18. Uğur, 'Europeanisation and Convergence via Incomplete Contracts?', pp. 234–5.
19. Mehmet Ogutcu, *Turkey's Place in the New Architecture of Europe: An Updated Assessment* (Bruges: Chatham House, 1992), p. 39.
20. Lisbon European Council, *Presidency Conclusions*, 26–27 June 1992, para. 2.C.
21. Theodoros Pangalos, 'I Elliniki Exoteriki Politiki mesa apo tis sxeseis Kuprou-Evropaikis Enosis' (Greek Foreign Policy Through Cyprus–EC Relations), in Sotiris Dalis, ed., *Evropaiki Enopoiisi ke Valkaniki Polydiaspasi* (European Integration and Balkan Fragmentation) (Athens: Sideris, 1994), p. 29.
22. George Bush Library, *Remarks at the Departure Ceremony for Prime Minister Suleyman Demirel of Turkey*, 11 February 1992.
23. Spiros Kaminaris, 'Greece and Middle Eastern Terrorism', *MERIA* 3 (1999), 2, www.ciaonet.org/olj/meria/meria_jun99.html
24. Alkis Kourkoulas, *Athens News Agency*, 16 September 1995. At that point the customs union agreement was still subject to ratification by the European Parliament.
25. *Anadolu News Agency*, 'Clinton Prods EU', quoted from 'Millet' and 'Hurriet', 28 February 1996.
26. Luxembourg European Council, *Presidency Conclusions*, 19–20 July 1993. The Commission, however, first presented its *Opinion* to the Council of Ministers on 10 April 1993.
27. Suvarierol, 'The Cyprus Obstacle on Turkey's Road to Membership in the European Union', p. 57.
28. Gundogdu, 'Identities in Question: Greek–Turkish Relations in a Period of Transformation?', pp. 1–2; Alexis Heraclides, 'The Greek–Turkish Conflict: Towards Resolution and Reconciliation', in Aydin and as Ifantis, *Turkish–Greek Relations*, p. 76.
29. Statement by Secretary of Defence, William Kohen, *US Department of Defence Brief*, 14 July 1999.
30. George Papandreou, interview in *Newsweek*, 21 February 2000.
31. Bill Clinton, interview in *To Vima*, 25 June 2000.
32. *Eleftherotypia*, 30 September 1999.

33. William H. Park, 'The Security Dimensions of Turkey–EU Relations', in Michael Lake, ed., *The EU & Turkey: A Glittering Prize or a Millstone?* (London: Federal Trust, 2005), p. 134.
34. *Cambridge Advanced Learner's Dictionary* (Cambridge University Press, 2004); *The Penguin English Dictionary* (Harmandsworth Penguin, 1985), p. 293.
35. *Brewer's Dictionary of Phrase and Fable,* (Leicester: Blitz, 1990), p. 439.
36. Uğur, 'Europeanisation and Convergence via Incomplete Contracts?', p. 235.
37. Papandreou, *I Ellada stis nees exelixeis* (Greece in the New Developments), p. 84.
38. Ogutcu, *Turkey's Place in the New Architecture of Europe: An Updated Assessment,* pp. 6, 14.
39. Kramer, 'Turkey and the European Union', pp. 215–16.
40. Bahcheli, 'Turning a New Page in Turkey's Relations with Greece?', p. 112.
41. Mine Eder, 'Populism as a Barrier to Integration with the EU', in Mehmet Ugur and Nergis Canefe, eds, *Turkey and European Integration: Accession Prospects and Issues* (London: Routledge, 2004), p. 57.
42. Yannis Papanicolaou, 'Realities and Perspectives: A Greek View on Turkey's European Ambitions', in Lake, *The EU & Turkey: A Glittering Prize or a Millstone?,* pp. 158, 160.
43. Heraclides, 'The Greek–Turkish Conflict: Towards Resolution and Reconciliation', p. 77.
44. Stelios Stavridis, '*Assessing the Views of Academics in Greece on the Europeanisation of Greek Foreign Policy: a Critical Appraisal and a Research Agenda Proposal*', Discussion Paper No.11, Hellenic Observatory, LSE, September 2003, p. 10.
45. Papanicolaou, 'Realities and Perspectives: A Greek View on Turkey's European Ambitions', p. 158.
46. Ogutcu, *Turkey's Place in the New Architecture of Europe: An Updated Assessment,* p. 84, footnote 198.
47. Heraclides, 'The Greek–Turkish Conflict', p. 76.
48. Helsinki European Council, *Presidency Conclusions,* 10–11 December 1999, para. 12, 9(b), 4.
49. George Papandreou, *Official Minutes of the Greek Parliament,* 17 December 2002.
50. Helsinki European Council, *Presidency Conclusions,* para. 4.
51. BBC, 11 December 1999, http://news.bbc.co.uk/1/hi/world/europe/ 558124.stm
52. George Papandreou and Ismail Çem, Joint Press Conference, 8 November 2001; Bahcheli, 'Turning a New Page in Turkey's Relations with Greece?', p. 96.
53. Brussels European Council, *Presidency Conclusions,* 16–17 December 2004, para. 23, bullet point 3.
54. *Kathimerini,* 22 November 2002.
55. Esra Çayhan, 'Towards a European Security and Defence Policy: With or Without Turkey?', in Çarkoğlu and Rubin, *Turkey and the European Union,* p. 52; Park, 'The Security Dimensions of Turkey–EU Relations', p. 134.
56. David Hannay, *Cyprus: The Search for a Solution* (London: Tauris, 2005), pp. 243–4.
57. European Council, *Presidency Conclusions,* 16–17 December 2004, para. 23, bullet point 1.
58. Hannay, *Cyprus: The Search for a Solution,* p. 237.

59. Aydin, 'Contemporary Turkish–Greek Relations: Constraints and Opportunities', p. 40.
60. *Hurriet*, 16 May 2003.
61. Costas Simitis, 'Press Conference at the Laaken European Council', 14 December 2001, *Official Greek Government Website*, http://www. government.gr/news/2001/december 17c 2001.html
62. On the popularity of this thesis among Greek academics, see Stavridis, *'Assessing the Views of Academics in Greece on the Europeanisation of Greek Foreign Policy'*, p. 7.
63. European Commission, *Standard Eurobarometer 63: Executive Summary*, July 2005, p. 31.
64. European Commission, *Eurobarometer 58: Executive Summaries – National Standard Reports for the member states*, Autumn 2002. p. 44; *Eurobarometer 63*, July 2005, p. 99.
65. Panayiotis C. Ioakimidis, 'The Europeanisation of Greece: An Overall Assessment', in Featherstone and Kazamias, p. 75.
66. Simitis, 'Press Conference at the Laaken European Council', 14 December 2001.
67. Costas Simitis, *Official Minutes of the Greek Parliament*, 17 December 2002.
68. Term used by the Council's President, Paavo Lipponen, in his controversial letter to Prime Minister Ecevit, 10 December 1999; full text cited in Hannay, *Cyprus: The Search for a Solution*, p. 115.
69. Georges Sorel, *Reflections on Violence* (New York: Collier, 1961) pp. 124–5 (first published in Paris: Rivière, 1908).
70. Christos Rokofyllos, quoted in *Greek–Canadian Vima*, 21 January 2000.
71. Costas Karamanlis, *Official Minutes of the Greek Parliament*, 15 December 1999.
72. Henry Tudor, *Political Myth* (London: Pall Mall Press, 1972), p. 15.
73. Roland Barthes, *Mythologies* (London: Vintage, 2000), pp. 142, 118 (first published in Paris: Seuil, 1957).
74. Ibid., pp. 128, 118.
75. BBC, *Text of Stability Pact Declaration*, 30 July 1999, http://news.bbc.co.uk/ 1/hi/world/monitoring/408363.stm
76. George Papandreou, *Time Europe*, 7 February 2000.
77. George Papandreou, 'A Total Balkan Approach', *Seton Hall Journal of Diplomacy and International Relations* (Summer/Fall 2000), p. 76.
78. Costas Simitis, *Address to the Southeast European Cooperation Process Summit of the Heads of State and Government*, Belgrade, 9 April 2003.
79. Hannay, *Cyprus: The Search for a Solution*, pp. 148–9.
80. *Phileleftheros*, 21 November 2002.
81. *Anadolu News Agency*, 21 November 2002.
82. Robert Ladrech, 'Europeanisation of Domestic Politics and Institutions: The Case of France', *Journal of Common Market Studies* 32 (1994), 1:70–1.
83. Albert Hourani, *Minorities in the Arab World*, (London: Oxford University Press, 1947), pp. 24–7; Lord Kinross, *Atatürk – The Rebirth of a Nation* (London: Weidenfeld & Nicolson, 1964), p. 473; Hakan Yilmaz, *Turkey: Within or Outside Europe? An Historical Perspective*, Seminar Paper, (IMEIS and Collingwood College, University of Durham: 2004), p. 7.
84. Gerard Delanty, *Inventing Europe* (London: Macmillan, 1995), pp. 97–8; Eric Hobsbawm, *The Age of Empire, 1875–1914* (London: Weidenfeld & Nicolson, 1987), p. 77; Hourani, *Minorities in the Arab World*, pp. 26–7.

85. When Turkish 'Europeanism' found more positive echoes in the EU, a parallel process of 'Europeanization' also began to occur; but this remains an auxiliary force, as the EU's long timescales for Turkey's pre-accession adjustment clearly indicate.
86. Simitis, *Official Minutes of the Greek Parliament*, 17 December 2002.
87. *Kathimerini*, 5 October 2005.

9
Turkey's Quest for EU Membership and the Cyprus Problem

Tozun Bahcheli

Introduction

Ever since the Turgut Ozal government first submitted Turkey's application for membership of the European Union (EU) in 1987, it has been widely assumed in many policy circles that Ankara would be required to actively promote a settlement on Cyprus in order to overcome the prospect of a Greek veto on its membership. While Ankara insisted that there ought to be no linkage between its EU membership and a political settlement on the island, Greek governments regularly reminded Ankara that the road to Brussels passed through Cyprus. However, as long as the prospects of Turkish accession were unpromising, Ankara saw no great incentive to revise its policy on Cyprus.

Pressure on Turkey regarding its stance in Cyprus mounted during the second half of the 1990s as EU members, prodded by Greece, appeared increasingly receptive to Cyprus's membership even at the risk of admitting the island before its communities reached a political settlement. The EU justified its receptivity regarding Cypriot membership by arguing that the prospect of admission would act as a catalyst to settle the Cyprus issue. For Ankara, however, the prospect of the EU admission of Cyprus without a settlement was unpalatable, as this would give the Greek Cypriot government a veto over EU policy toward Turkey.

While confronting it with the stick of Cyprus's impending accession, Brussels offered Ankara the carrot of improved chances for Turkish membership. At the Helsinki meeting of the European Council in December 1999, Turkey was officially declared a candidate to become an EU member. Although the EU's summit in Copenhagen in 2002 disappointed Ankara by refusing to grant an early date for the start of Turkey–EU accession talks, the government remained steadfast in pursuing

161

its European course. As the Turkish government proceeded in earnest to improve Turkey's human rights record to meet the requirements of the EU's 'Copenhagen criteria', it unsuccessfully tried to persuade European governments to defer Cypriot accession. Ankara also tried in vain to gain EU states' acceptance of its position that there be no linkage between Turkey's accession course and the settlement of the Cyprus issue.

Against the background of these failures, the determination of the newly elected Justice and Development Party (AKP) to advance Turkey's EU membership prospects set the stage for a new Turkish approach on the Cyprus issue. Over the objections of the Turkish Cypriot leader Rauf Denktash, the AKP government led by Recep Tayyip Erdogan supported negotiations based on the UN plan (known as the Annan Plan) that was first introduced on 11 November 2002 to settle the Cyprus issue. However, much to its later regret, the AKP government proved unsuccessful in applying adequate pressure on Denktash to support the Annan Plan at crucial stages during the UN-led negotiations in 2003. Having secured Cyprus's accession represented by the Republic of Cyprus, the Greek Cypriot leadership felt confident in rejecting the Annan Plan in the referendum of 24 April 2004. With the Greek Cypriot government bent on using the benefits of Union membership to extract concessions from the Turkish government, Ankara continues to be encumbered by the Cyprus issue as it seeks to advance Turkish prospects for EU accession.

Cyprus's EU membership course and Ankara's setbacks, 1990–2002

Since the island's partition in 1974, Turkey has supported the Turkish Cypriot position that a future settlement on the island should be negotiated by the island's communities on the basis of creating a bi-zonal, bi-communal federation. The forced movement of people in the course of the war in 1974 resulted in the creation of an ethnically homogeneous Turkish Cypriot entity in the north for the first time. This, and the presence of thousands of Turkish troops on the island, ensured that Ankara and the Turkish Cypriots would have a strong hand in negotiating a new settlement that would safeguard both Turkey's strategic interests and Turkish Cypriot security. In a bid to ostensibly strengthen its bargaining power, the Turkish Cypriot administration established the Turkish Republic of Northern Cyprus (TRNC) in 1983.

Against a strengthened Turkish and Turkish Cypriot bargaining power since 1974, Greek Cypriots benefited from the considerable advantage of representing the government of the Republic of Cyprus. As the only internationally recognized government on the island, the Republic of Cyprus used the trump card of international legitimacy in its successful endeavour to internationalize the Cyprus dispute and thereby pressure Turkey to withdraw its troops from the island. Many of the resolutions at the United Nations and other international forums broadly supported the Greek Cypriot position by calling for the reunification of the island and the withdrawal of foreign (read Turkish) troops. Moreover, in a bid to pressure Turkish Cypriots, the Greek Cypriot government imposed an economic embargo on the Turkish-Cypriot-administered north Cyprus. Turkey responded to the draconian embargo by providing generous financial aid to sustain the Turkish Cypriot state.

Although they have been unenthusiastic about any third-party intervention in Cyprus, Ankara and the Turkish Cypriot government reluctantly accepted the continued involvement of the United Nations in the island in both a peacekeeping and a mediating capacity since 1964. On the other hand, Turks objected to any EU involvement in Cyprus on the grounds that Greece's membership in the Union prevented Brussels from being an objective party in dealing with the Cypriot communities and with Turkey.

Turkish Cypriots objected when the Greek Cypriot government, acting as the Republic of Cyprus, applied for EU membership in 1990. At the time and subsequently, both Turkish Cypriots and Ankara warned Brussels against proceeding with the Greek Cypriot government's submission, made on behalf of all Cyprus, without a prior political settlement. Turkish Cypriots and Ankara raised legal objections as well. Thus, they cited the opinions of M.H. Mendelson who argued in reference to the 1960 constitution that 'art. 170 guaranteed most-favoured treatment to each of the Guarantors whereas, manifestly, if Cyprus became a member of the EU, Greece and the UK would have necessarily to receive more favoured treatment than Turkey'.[1] Brussels, however, disagreed with the legal objections. On the other hand, many European states were understandably reluctant to import into the Union an unresolved problem of this magnitude. Ankara and the Turkish Cypriots took comfort from indications of European reluctance to admit a divided Cyprus even as vigorous Greek promotion of the Cypriot membership cause softened European resistance by the mid 1990s.

Although Greece's EU partners were unhappy about the prospect of Cyprus's contested accession and Greek obstructionism on developing EU–Turkey relations, they found it difficult to adopt policies on Turkey and Cyprus to which Athens objected. Ultimately, the EU decision to move forward on Cypriot accession had less to do with the merit of the island's membership than with Greece's ability to sway its EU partners. In spite of the potential headaches Brussels would face by admitting a divided island, Greece extracted concessions to advance Cypriot accession each time its EU partners wished to promote Turkey's membership prospects.

Thus, when Greece lifted its veto to enable Brussels to offer a customs union to Turkey in 1995, it extracted a commitment from its EU partners to move forward with Cypriot accession. Subsequently, Greek pressures contributed to the EU Council's humiliating snub to Ankara in 1997: Turkey's bid to be designated a candidate was rejected while Cyprus was put on a fast track to join the EU. With Greek prodding, Brussels delivered another blow to Turkey when it agreed to begin accession talks with the Republic of Cyprus the following year, creating consternation in Ankara and among Turkish Cypriots.

Even after accession negotiations had begun, Turkish Cypriots and Ankara continued to hope that the reservations of some member states would dissuade Brussels from admitting a divided island and effectively importing the Cyprus conflict into the EU. In a significant indication of European reticence, the German, Dutch and Italian governments supported a French-sponsored declaration in November 1998 which stated that 'a political solution to the division and partial occupation of the island must be found as a matter of urgency as the only way to resolve problems that would arise in the accession process'.[2]

Ankara and the TRNC also hoped that, if the EU nevertheless moved in favour of accession, it would pressure Greek Cypriots to recognize Turkish Cypriot sovereignty as a price for admission. That would have been an ideal outcome for many Turkish Cypriots, who would have perceived it as paving the way for the simultaneous EU accession of the sovereign TRNC and the Republic of Cyprus (and, ideally, Turkey as well). All these hopes, however, appeared to be dashed by the EU's Helsinki Summit communiqué of 1999, which declared that the European Council

> underlines that a political settlement will facilitate the accession of Cyprus to the European Union. If no settlement has been reached by the completion of the accession negotiations, the Council's decision on accession will be made without the above being a precondition.[3]

While it protested the declaration on Cyprus, Ankara welcomed the affirmation by the EU presidency of Turkey's eligibility to become an EU member. However, despite the fact that the EU–Cyprus accession talks steadily progressed after the Helsinki declaration of 1999, Ankara doubted the warnings by Brussels regarding the latter's willingness to admit divided Cyprus. Turkish officials were reluctant to accept that Brussels would admit Cyprus and risk seriously damaging Europe's relations with Turkey. As Nathalie Tocci explained:

> [U]ntil late 2001, most Turkish policy-makers did not believe that the Union would proceed to integrate Cyprus as a divided island as stipulated in the Helsinki conclusions ... Many in Ankara failed to appreciate that by 1999, the European choice was not between Turkey and Cyprus, but rather between Turkey and the fifth enlargement, whose importance went beyond Cyprus and Turkey combined.[4]

While keen to advance Turkey's path to EU membership, Ankara and the Turkish Cypriot leadership took a hard line in response to indications from Brussels that Cypriot accession was virtually assured. Ankara tried to raise the stakes for the EU by repeating earlier warnings that the admission of Greek Cyprus would cement the division of the island, and damage Turkish–EU relations. Ismail Cem, Turkey's foreign minister, declared darkly that Turkey was prepared to take 'costly decisions' regarding Cyprus, suggesting that Ankara would be prepared to risk its EU membership for the sake of its Cyprus policy. Prime Minister Bulent Ecevit went a step further by warning that Turkey might annex the TRNC in the event of Cypriot accession.[5] Moreover, as the intermittent UN-sponsored proximity talks launched after Helsinki carried on with no progress, Ankara and the Turkish Cypriot leadership proceeded to take further steps to advance Turkey–TRNC integration.

These warnings might have made some EU governments uncomfortable regarding the admission of divided Cyprus, but none were prepared to provoke a Greek veto and risk the EU's enlargement. The EU's Copenhagen Summit on 12–13 December 2002 affirmed Cyprus's accession. Thereafter, it became obvious to Turkish policy-makers that Ankara could not dissuade EU states from admitting Cyprus. Whatever reservations regarding Cypriot accession some European governments had, Turkey's efforts to prevent or defer Cypriot accession had failed. Furthermore, while acknowledging that there was no formal link between the settlement of the Cyprus issue and Turkish accession, EU officials frequently reminded Ankara that an unresolved Cyprus issue would hamper Turkey's prospects. As the reality of impending Cypriot accession sank in, the EU and other third parties striving to secure a Cyprus settlement reminded Ankara that Turkey's and Turkish Cypriot interests could be safeguarded by ensuring that the Turkish community participated in the UN-led negotiations to secure the accession of Cyprus as a reunited federation. In the meantime, the EU's apparent resolve regarding Cypriot accession helped launch intense debates in Turkey concerning the merits of Ankara's Cyprus policy.[6]

The AKP and Turkey's new policy on Cyprus

When the AKP came to power in Turkey on 3 November 2002 with a comfortable parliamentary majority, domestic debates regarding the merits of Turkey's policy with regard to the Cyprus issue and the problem posed by Cypriot accession had been raging for some time. Upon assuming office, the new government wasted no time in signalling a serious intention to achieve Turkey's EU membership and that it would pursue a Cyprus policy different from that of its predecessors. The AKP government was in office for only eight days when UN Secretary-General Kofi Annan submitted his plan for a Cyprus settlement on 11 November 2002. At the same time as having urgently to attend such a vital and sensitive issue, the AKP government was burdened by the unfolding Iraq crisis as the Bush administration sought the Turkish government's help for its impending invasion.

The new government's declaration on the Cyprus issue was welcomed in numerous circles, particularly by international mediators. On the other hand, the Iraq War and the problems it created for Turkey's relations with the United States created a major distraction for Ankara during a period of intense international diplomacy and domestic debate on Cyprus. Having to confront two major urgent issues at once tested Erdogan's inexperienced government. Of the three senior members of the AKP, namely party leader Recep Tayyip Erdogan, Abdullah Gul and Bulent Arinc, only Gul had some experience in foreign affairs. Erdogan, a businessman who had served as mayor of Istanbul, had no prior background in international politics and scant exposure to national politics. In addition, the AKP leader had to overcome a court ban on holding political office due to a conviction for inciting religious hatred in 1988, before winning a seat in parliament and assuming the prime ministership on 14 March 2003.

In declaring that it would pursue Turkey's EU membership as a national imperative the AKP could count on the support of virtually all segments of Turkish society. In the same year that the AKP assumed the government, smarting from the effects of the severe economic crisis of 2000–1 and hoping for better economic times in Turkey, three-quarters of the Turkish public expressed support for EU membership.[7] The influential business community supported EU membership in the expectation that this would modernize the Turkish economy and boost prosperity. For minorities, including most Turkish Kurds, EU membership has represented hopes for better human rights. EU-driven reforms addressed Kurdish grievances: limited broadcasts in Kurdish have been allowed, opportunities for Kurdish education expanded, and conditions for Kurdish groups to engage in political activities have eased.

That the AKP, with its Islamist roots, has ardently championed EU membership is remarkably ironic. The leading members of the party who held senior positions in the previous (subsequently banned) Islamist parties, Refah (RP) and Virtue, consistently opposed Turkey's membership of the EU. Under the leadership of their veteran leader, Necmettin Erbakan, Turkey's Islamists viewed the EU as a Christian club and complained that Brussels discriminated against Turkey. Just a few years before his party took office, Turkey's foreign minister Abdullah Gul had declared that, 'a key aim of the RP was to protect Turkey's values against the EU'.[8]

In a departure from the stance of previous Islamist parties, the AKP astutely embraced EU accession as protection against the secularist establishment and a possible military takeover in defence of secularism in the future. In response to a principal EU demand to reduce the power of the military in Turkey, Erdogan deftly pushed through changes that have diminished the authority of the military over the civilian branch of government.

Although irritated by the Islamism of the party and suspicious of the motives of the AKP leadership, the powerful military has also endorsed EU membership in the belief that accession would safeguard Turkey's secular order and help preserve Turkey's territorial integrity. The Turkish military's support for EU membership has certainly made it easier for the AKP to pursue its reformist agenda.[9] The AKP government has also been fortunate that General Hilmi Ozkok, Turkey's chief of staff, threw his weight behind the government's reforms. Ozkok has supported other reformers in the military and sidelined those who opposed the government's liberalizing reforms.[10]

The popularity of EU membership in Turkish society helped the AKP in forging a strong consensus on pursuing EU accession. This contrasted with the inability of previous coalition governments that struggled to forge such a consensus on the issue. Erdogan's party enjoyed the considerable advantage of forming the first majority government in more than a decade. The elections had thoroughly discredited the three coalition parties that formed the previous government: none was able to win a parliamentary seat in the elections in 2002. The centre-left Republican People's Party (CHP) was the only other party that elected members and formed the opposition in parliament. Given its parliamentary strength, Erdogan's party was thus better equipped to take bold policy steps than former coalition governments that shuffled in and out of office at the average rate of one every year during the previous decade. The coalition led by Bulent Ecevit during 1999–2002 resisted a Cyprus settlement based on the reunification of the island and instead backed Denktash's call for a solution based on two sovereign states. By contrast, Erdogan accepted the reality that Turkey could not achieve its aspirations without supporting the UN efforts to achieve a settlement. He boldly declared on 2 January 2003: 'I am not in favour of the continuation of the policy that has been maintained in Cyprus over the past 30–40 years – We will do whatever falls on us. This is not Denktash's private matter.'[11]

However strong its mandate and its apparent resolve to settle the Cyprus issue, the AKP government ran into predictable opposition from Denktash and from various quarters at home soon after Erdogan declared the Annan Plan acceptable as a basis for negotiation in November 2002. In addition to CHP's opposition in parliament, the resistance to the Annan Plan came primarily from three quarters: the senior ranks of the Foreign Ministry, the Turkish military and president Ahmet Necdet Sezer.

In making its case, the AKP government emphasized the positives in the Annan Plan, namely the wide measure of autonomy Turkish Cypriots would exercise in the proposed federation, and the retention of Turkey's rights as a guarantor power over the objection of Greek Cypriots. The opposition to the Annan Plan, on the other hand, focused on what it considered to be its serious shortcomings: the dissolution of the TRNC and the abandonment of separate statehood for the Turkish community, the resettlement of large numbers of Turkish Cypriots, and Turkish Cypriot/Turkish security concerns arising from the withdrawal of the bulk of Turkish troops from the island. Opponents of a policy change also invoked the perennial complaint that Turkey was being pressured by European governments to make major concessions in Cyprus for the uncertain prospects of EU membership. Not surprisingly, the Turkish opponents of the Annan Plan rallied to support Denktash in his opposition to it.

Faced with the opposition from key sections of the Turkish political and military establishment, the AKP government's immediate reaction was one of vacillation. As veteran Turkish journalist Cengiz Candar put it, 'through inexperience' the government 'wavered and left a room for manoeuvre to Denktash and die-hards in Ankara who do not want a settlement.'[12]

That a settlement requiring major concessions and falling short of declared Turkish goals in Cyprus would provoke wrenching debates in Turkey was not surprising. Previous Turkish governments had supported the Turkish Cypriot leadership's goal of consolidating the TRNC. Ankara had backed Denktash as the latter moved away from a federal solution: hence its support of the Turkish Cypriot leader's call for a two-state confederation in 1998, and of plans for greater TRNC–Turkey integration to match that envisaged by (Greek) Cyprus and the EU. However, whereas the veteran Turkish leader Ecevit and Devlet Bahceli's nationalist MHP were steadfast supporters of Denktash's two-state policy in Cyprus, the same could not be assumed of other political leaders. Keen to advance Turkey's EU prospects, such former Turkish leaders as Turgut Ozal, Tansu Ciller and Mesut Yilmaz were willing to apply pressure on the Turkish Cypriot leader to show greater flexibility in intercommunal negotiations lest he jeopardize Turkey's EU prospects. Spurred with a more credible EU incentive, however, the AKP wasted no time in announcing a challenge to Denktash's policy.

While issues related to policy in Cyprus were widely if intermittently debated by policy-makers and the public in Turkey before 2002, the high stakes for Turkey in the imminent Cypriot accession to the EU meant that, unlike its previous counterparts, the AKP government did not have the luxury of postponing tough decisions on Cyprus. At the same time as it was criticized by opponents at home for being prepared to 'sacrifice' Cyprus and sell down Turkish Cypriots, the Erdogan government came under strong pressure by all the actors involved in the mediation process, namely the UN intermediaries, the United States, the United Kingdom and the EU, to apply sufficient pressure on Denktash to negotiate the terms of the UN plan in good faith.

Luckily for the AKP leadership, accusations by the opposition CHP and other nationalist groups that the government was preparing to sacrifice vital Turkish and Turkish Cypriot rights failed to shake the government's standing among the Turkish public. As vulnerable as it was in endorsing major concessions in Cyprus, numerous factors helped mitigate the capacity of the opposition to shake the resolve of the AKP leadership. During the course of the prolonged debates on the various revised versions of the Annan Plan, such influential groups as the Turkish Industrialists' and Businessmen's Association (TUSIAD) as well as many academics and newspaper columnists actively supported the government's stance on the Cyprus issue. Some columnists even declared the Annan Plan a victory for Turkey.[13]

Some Turks had long felt that the Cyprus issue had become an albatross around Turkey's neck and periodically bemoaned the high cost borne by Turkey for its commitment to the TRNC and Denktash's policies. It was no surprise, therefore, that some Turkish commentators complained that the future of 69 million Turks was jeopardized because of a policy geared for the benefit of 200,000 Turkish Cypriots.[14] Accordingly, many Turks became receptive to the government's argument that it was possible to secure a fair settlement in Cyprus in order to achieve progress toward EU membership.

The domestic support the AKP garnered for its Cyprus policy is additionally explainable by the diminution of Denktash's standing in Turkey as well as the TRNC. Although the Turkish Cypriot leader enjoyed the status of a national hero for many years in Turkey, particularly in nationalist circles, he has not been uniformly popular among all sections of Turkish society. In some circles he was viewed as being unduly obdurate in the never-ending negotiations to settle the Cyprus issue. The Turkish Cypriot leader's rejection of the Annan Plan was seen by some Turks as the most recent example of his inflexibility that threatened Turkey's larger interest in EU membership. Moreover, the unprecedented Turkish Cypriot challenge to Denktash over the settlement proposed by the UN hurt his standing in Turkey, as he was seen as having lost the support of his people.

Even with his reduced stature in Turkey, however, Denktash continued to receive critical support from the military–bureaucratic establishment in Turkey and restrain the AKP government as the latter tried to ensure that the Turkish Cypriot leader would remain engaged in the ongoing negotiations over the UN plan. Intense diplomatic efforts, including a series of summit meetings headed by the UN Secretary-General Kofi Annan himself, during February and March 2003, failed to secure an agreement between Greek and Turkish Cypriot leaders. Annan's main gambit was to pressure the Cypriot leaders to conduct separate referenda on the UN plan in their respective communities – in the hope that Greek Cypriots would not risk their EU membership by rejecting the plan, and that, if a majority of Turkish Cypriots supported the plan, it would force Denktash to acquiesce. But Denktash countered with a gambit of his own: after first securing the support of the Turkish military and senior ranks of the bureaucracy in Ankara, and defying the wishes of the AKP government he rejected holding a referendum in the TRNC.

Denktash's rejection of the revised version of the Annan Plan at the UN Secretary-General's summit meeting at The Hague during 11–12 March 2003 meant that the Greek Cypriot government was able to sign the EU Accession Treaty on 17 April 2003, and thereby secure membership of Cyprus without the Turkish-Cypriot-administered part of the island. The outcome was welcomed by Greek Cypriot nationalists and the recently elected president Tassos Papadopoulos, whose objections to the Annan Plan – though on entirely different grounds – were no less intense than those of the Turkish Cypriot leader.

The significance of missing the deadline at The Hague, and of the inexperience of the AKP government, has been subsequently acknowledged by Foreign Minister Abdullah Gul. In a candid interview with Fikret Bila of *Milliyet*, he declared: 'If I had two more months' experience, I would have concluded this matter [Cyprus] at The Hague in 2003.'[15] It was not until several months after the failed summit at The Hague that Erdogan managed to overcome the domestic opposition and obliged Denktash to return to the negotiating table. In February 2004, he compelled Denktash to resume negotiations with his Greek Cypriot counterpart based on the Annan Plan, and to accept the binding arbitration of the UN Secretary-General if no agreement could be reached.

Following the failure of the final bid to achieve a settlement that Greek and Turkish Cypriots would accept at the summit during 24–31 March 2004 in Bürgenstock, Switzerland, the UN Secretary-General then imposed a final draft settlement, representing the fifth revision of the original plan. This was put to simultaneous referenda in both parts of the island on 24 April 2004. Greek Cypriots were guaranteed EU membership regardless of how they voted. Thus, feeling they had nothing to lose, and encouraged by the opposition of President Papadopoulos, an overwhelming 75 per cent voted *no* to the Annan Plan. By contrast, 76 per cent of Turkish Cypriot voters defied the call of President Denktash to reject the plan and voted *yes*. As Greek Cypriots had anticipated, the Republic of Cyprus proceeded unhindered to full membership in the European Union on 1 May 2004. And the Turkish Cypriots, despite voting *yes*, were left out.

The AKP and Turkish Cypriots: ascendancy of pro-EU group in the TRNC

An immediate consequence of the submission of the Annan Plan was to bring into sharp relief the cleavages that existed in the TRNC concerning a future settlement of the Cyprus issue. Not all Turkish Cypriots thought that Denktash's two-state policy was viable and were apparently prepared to consider federal options. Denktash had declared his position unambiguously by rejecting the Annan Plan. Most Turkish Cypriots, however, were ambivalent. On the one hand, they singled out three provisions as being particularly problematic: the settlement of tens of thousands of Greek Cypriots in their constituent state, the recognition of Greek Cypriot title deeds in north Cyprus and the resettlement of tens of thousands of Turkish Cypriots. On the other hand, being tired of the adversities of years of isolation and faced with poor prospects, they were attracted by several other provisions of the plan, including the constitu-tionally equal status of the two communities, the wide measure of autonomy envisaged for the constituent states, Turkey's continuing role as a guarantor of their security and, not the least, the expected benefits of EU citizenship. The economic depression that has gripped north Cyprus since late 1999 naturally enhanced the economic appeal of the latter. Moreover, many Turkish Cypriots had concluded the Annan Plan repre-sented the best terms that they were ever likely to get and, if it failed, the Greek Cypriots would likely insist on even tougher terms in any future negotiations over reunification and EU accession.

This is why Denktash's resistance to the plan provoked unprecedented demonstrations among Turkish Cypriots in favour of EU membership, and calls for his resignation as the community's negotiator. In one of the largest demonstrations ever held by Turkish Cypriots, an estimated 50,000 to 60,000 (about a quarter of the entire community) marched on 14 January 2003 calling for negotiations based on the UN plan and Turkish Cypriot accession to the EU.[16]

Denktash has led the Turkish community for nearly forty years. He served as the Turkish Cypriot interlocutor in the UN-led intercommunal negotiations since 1968 until his retirement from the presidency in 2005. He won six consecutive presidential elections (as president of the Turkish Federated State of Cyprus in 1976 and 1981, and as president of the TRNC in 1985, 1990, 1995 and 2000). His charisma, strong national-ist credentials and political skills helped him forge a strong consensus in the Turkish community over many years, and retain Turkey's support for his policies. It was upon his initiative that the TRNC was founded in 1983, and he ardently sought to achieve its recognition.

However, Denktash's political support declined even before his last election as president in 2000. Growing opposition to his policies became especially pronounced once the UN Secretary-General submitted his settle-ment plan for Cyprus in November 2002. Although he declared himself to be above party politics, most Turkish Cypriots associated Denktash with the centre-right parties that led the government in the TRNC. The centre-left parties, the Republican Turkish Party (CTP) and the Communal Liberation Party (TKP), argued repeatedly that Denktash was not interested in achieving a federal solution and that he was bent on integrating the TRNC with Turkey.

Before the AKP assumed power, Denktash had been adept at securing the support of Turkish governments. He was particularly successful in forging a close working relationship with such Turkish leaders as Suleyman Demirel and Bulent Ecevit who led several governments in Ankara. Ecevit had ordered the Turkish army to the island in response to the Greek coup in 1974: he took a hard line on the Cyprus issue, arguing that the issue had been settled in 1974. The AKP government, on the other hand, emboldened the pro-settlement groups to mobilize the Turkish community in favour of the acceptance of the Annan Plan in order to achieve EU membership. The centre-left parties were joined by numerous non-governmental groups and organizations, including some former supporters of Denktash, to lead a successful campaign in favour of the Annan Plan.

With his standing greatly reduced in the TRNC, Denktash's critics could plausibly argue that he was unable to sustain the support of his people. This was not unwelcome to the AKP leadership and others who viewed him as obstructing Turkey's course to EU membership. Thus, the shared goal of pursuing EU membership and settling the Cyprus issue created an implicit alliance between the pro-settlement groups who campaigned against Denktash in the TRNC and the AKP government. During past Turkish Cypriot elections previous governments in Ankara did not hesitate to indicate their support for Denktash and the parties that supported his policies. By contrast, even though it assumed a seemingly neutral posture during the parliamentary elections in December 2003 and the referendum of 2004, there was no doubt that the AKP government preferred the anti-Denktash opposition to prevail.

The Cyprus issue and Turkey's EU prospects since the referenda

By charting a different course on the Cyprus issue, and ultimately prevailing over Denktash and opponents of the Annan Plan in Turkey, Erdogan won considerable acclaim internationally and helped secure the Turkish Cypriot *yes* in the referendum of 24 April 2004. However, the Greek Cypriot rejection of the Annan Plan in the referendum of April 2004 has denied the AKP government's goal of achieving a Cyprus settlement and removing the Cyprus issue as an obstacle in its pursuit of EU membership. Since entering the EU, the Republic of Cyprus has used the perennial legal card and its new leverage as a member to constrain the EU's efforts to end Turkish Cypriot isolation. The Papadopoulos government has obstructed the European plan to facilitate direct trade with northern Cyprus and provide economic assistance to the Turkish Cypriots promised by the EU Commission immediately after the referenda of April 2004. It has also threatened to use Cyprus's veto power during EU deliberations concerning Turkey's accession in a bid to wrest concessions from Turkey for a future settlement of the Cyprus issue. In this connection, it demanded that Turkey recognize the Republic of Cyprus as the legitimate government of the island.

Turkey has adamantly refused such recognition, which would seriously undermine the Turkish Cypriot administration's legal and political position. Moreover, as Quentin Peel has argued, Turkey's recognition of the Republic of Cyprus 'would amount to an admission that the Cyprus conflict is an internal matter and therefore nothing to do with the United Nations, which has spent years trying to mediate a peaceful resolution.'[17] In any case, the recognition of the Republic of Cyprus by the AKP government would inevitably provoke fierce opposition within Turkey. The sensitivity of this issue helps explain why Ankara pointedly issued a separate declaration that signing of the protocol to extend the customs union to ten new EU members, including Cyprus, in December 2005, should not be interpreted as recognition of the Republic of Cyprus.

The AKP government is keen to put the Cyprus issue behind it but is greatly frustrated that in the post-Annan environment the Greek Cypriot leadership has shown scant interest in a new UN initiative. The Papadopoulos government has calculated that Cyprus's EU membership has conferred an effective leverage to Greek Cypriots against Turkey and the TRNC, and that the tide is running in its favour. Accordingly, it has felt no urgency to revisit the Annan Plan, and instead has declared its preference to a 'European solution' in contrast to the Turkish/Turkish Cypriot commitment to a UN solution. Papadopoulos's only response, when pushed, has been to suggest changes which he knows would not be accepted by Turkish Cypriots and Ankara as a basis for new negotiations, such as removing Turkish Cypriot veto rights and strengthening the powers of the central government.[18] In his analysis of the nature of the demands for changes to the Annan Plan made by Papadopoulos, and their chances of acceptance, Tim Potier wrote:

> [T]hese demands are so far removed from the current text that it is impossible to regard them as merely a maximal opening rejoinder

before compromises can be reached in any later negotiations. Ankara would never accept them and it is extremely doubtful whether Washington or London would seek to place any kind of pressure to agree to most of them.[19]

The Greek Cypriot government could potentially derail Ankara's accession course[20] with the support from other EU members who may wish to block Turkey's path for reasons entirely unrelated to Cyprus.[21] Quite apart from the obstruction posed by the Greek Cypriot government, Ankara has had to contend with increasing resistance to Turkey's EU membership both among the European public and by some EU governments. According to a survey conducted by the European Commission in 2005, 52 per cent of EU citizens oppose Turkish membership whereas only 35 per cent support it. The survey reported 80 per cent of Austrians oppose membership as do 74 per cent of Germans.[22] Three of Europe's leading politicians, namely Nicholas Sarkozy, leader of the governing Union for a Popular Movement (UMP) in France, German Chancellor Angela Merkel and Austrian Chancellor Wolfgang Schussel, have declared their opposition to Turkey's membership. They have instead promoted the idea of a special partnership between Turkey and the EU, an option which Ankara has flatly rejected.

The AKP government has insisted that it remains steadfast in pursuing Turkey's EU course in spite of discouraging signs and opposition to Turkish membership from several EU members. However, Ankara's future commitment to pursuing membership cannot be taken for granted. Many Turks believe that the EU is asking Turkey to satisfy conditions that it has not asked of other membership candidates. Thus, they have been angered by the European Parliament's demand that Turkey admit it committed genocide against Ottoman Armenians in 1915, and by Austria's demand – even before accession talks have begun – that Ankara accept a 'privileged partnership' if the accession talks fail. When interviewed about the conditions Brussels has put forth for Turkish accession, a Turkish public relations manager voiced the frustration of many Turks when she stated: 'We have done everything they ask, we keep making sacrifices, and they keep adding more and more conditions – I am beginning to get fed up.'[23] It is not surprising, therefore, that support for EU membership, once as high as 75 per cent, dropped to 60 per cent by late 2005.[24]

More than fifty years after it first emerged, the Cyprus question remains high on the agenda of the Turkish government. Ankara is greatly frustrated that the Cyprus issue continues to complicate its accession course toward EU membership after it delivered its side of the bargain to the EU and helped deliver a *yes* vote in the Turkish Cypriot referendum of 2004. The AKP government's commitment to the EU accession course will ensure Ankara's continued interest in future initiatives to resolve the Cyprus issue. On the other hand, in future negotiations over Cyprus, the AKP government will be constrained by the diminished enthusiasm among Turks for EU membership, the apparent rise in nationalist sentiment in Turkish society and the risk of losing ground to the opposition which remains ready to exploit the Cyprus issue.

Notes

1. 'Summary of the Opinion of Professor M. H. Mendelson, QC, on the Application of the "Republic of Cyprus" to Join the European Union', *Perceptions* (September/ November 1999), p. 141.
2. Cited in Neill Nugent, 'EU Enlargement and the "Cyprus Problem" ', *Journal of Common Market Studies* 38 (2000), 1: 131–50, p. 134.
3. Helsinki European Council, 10–11 December 1999, *Presidency Conclusions*, para. 9 (b).
4. Nathalie Tocci, *EU Accession Dynamics and Conflict Resolution: Catalysing Peace or Consolidating Partition in Cyprus?* (Aldershot: Ashgate, 2004), p. 110.
5. 'Ecevit challenged the EU that if Greek Cypriots were admitted into the European club of democracies Ankara would either annex the Turkish Republic of Northern Cyprus or establish with the Turkish Cypriot state a "special relationship" that would make northern Cyprus its "autonomous part" '; *Turkish Daily News*, 5 November 2001.
6. As Lale Sariibrahimoglu put it: 'An implicit fight between Turkey's hawks and doves has reemerged in the face of increased pressure exerted upon Turkey by the EU over rapid action for a solution to the island. While doves argue that Turkey should make moves for a solution to the island, hawks insist that no concessions could be made over equal sovereignty of the Turkish Cypriots at any negotiating table': *Turkish Daily News*, 28 May 2001.
7. This is based on a survey conducted by two researchers at Bogazici University in Istanbul in 2002 which indicated that 74 per cent of the respondents would vote in favour of Turkey's membership should a vote be conducted on the issue. See Ali Carkoglu and Kemal Kirisci, '*Turkiye Dis Politikasi Arastirmasi*' (Survey of Turkish Foreign Policy), Department of Political Science and International Relations, Bogazici University, March 2002.
8. Abdullah Gul, interview given 23 December 1994 (Ankara), quoted in Philip Robins, 'Confusion at Home, Confusion Abroad: Turkey between Copenhagen and Iraq', *International Affairs* 79 (2003), 3: 547–66, p. 553.
9. For the Turkish military's approach to EU membership, see David L. Phillips 'Turkey's Dream of Accession', *Foreign Affairs* 83 (2004), 5: 86–97; and Ersel Aydinli, Nihat Ali Özcan and Dogan Akyaz, 'The Turkish Military's March Toward Europe,' *Foreign Affairs* 85 (2006), 1: 77–90.
10. See Phillips, 'Turkey's Dream of Accession.'
11. *New York Times*, 2 January 2003.
12. *Financial Times*, 15 December 2002.

13. Foremost among the pro-Annan columnists was veteran journalist Mehmet Ali Birand; see his 'Turks have won in Cyprus', *Milliyet* (Istanbul), 16 November 2002.
14. 'Why, mutter some Turkish diplomats, should 200,000 or so people in northern Cyprus scupper the European ambitions of 69 million plus Turks?'; *Economist*, 16 January 2003.
15. Interview with Fikret Bila, *Milliyet* (Istanbul), 20 December 2004.
16. Economist Intelligence Unit, Country Monitor, *Cyprus* (London: 20 January 2003).
17. *Financial Times*, 23 December 2004.
18. For a list of changes to the Annan Plan demanded by the Greek Cypriot government, see The Economist Intelligence Unit, Country Report, *Cyprus*, June 2005.
19. Tim Potier, 'Cyprus: Entering Another Stalemate?', Briefing Paper, Chatham House (November 2005), p. 4.
20. 'Tassos Papadopoulos, the president of Cyprus, has boasted that he has no fewer than 64 opportunities to veto and block the process: one at the beginning and one at the end, and two for each of the 31 technical chapters', *Financial Times*, 23 December 2004.
21. In reference to Greek Cypriot moves in the EU, *The Economist* wrote on 12 May 2005: 'Such gamesmanship is already receiving discreet encouragement in parts of Europe (for example, France and Austria) where a dust-up between Turkey and the EU would be welcome.'
22. *The Times*, 19 July 2005.
23. Reported in the *International Herald Tribune*, 30 September 2005.
24. 'Turkey and the EU: Will They Split Before They Marry?', *Spiegel online*, 3 October 2005.

10
Security Implications of Turkey's March Towards EU Membership

Mustafa Kibaroglu

Introduction

Contrary to what many believe, both inside and outside the country, Turkey's march towards membership in the European Union (EU) may cause serious deficiencies in its security. As a country which has traditionally taken a hard-line stance on security and defence matters, Turkey now seems to be adopting the 'soft-security' approach of the EU.[1] Turkey's dramatic shift in its stance, however, occurs at a time when membership in the EU cannot be seen on the horizon. Even the most optimistic analysts suggest a minimum of 15 years for full membership after the start of accession negotiations; these could well turn out to be a never-ending process. During the long time before attaining full membership, most of Turkey's security concerns will persist, if not worsen. This is particularly true of the issues with its Middle Eastern neighbours such as Iran and Syria. But in its dealings with these countries, Turkey cannot rely on the 'yet to be decided' security and defence policies of the EU as the Europeans themselves have not been able to put together a comprehensive document outlining their long-term policy objectives or the mainstays of a security and defence strategy for the Union.[2] Moreover, the attitude of most EU member states towards Turkey's southeastern neighbours has always been diametrically different from that of Turkey and there is no sign of change today.

Unless the 'EU-3' – namely the United Kingdom, France and Germany – are successful in finding a diplomatic solution regarding Iran's nuclear programme, their soft-security approach may well have allowed the latter enough time to develop nuclear weapons.[3] In that case, the regional balance of power would be dramatically tipped in favour of this potential rival of Turkey.[4] And the EU might do nothing substantial about it.

With heightened tension between Iran and the US following a possible failure of negotiations between Iran and the EU-3, Turkey might have to assume the pacifist European approach. A similar situation could apply to Turkey's relations with Syria. The aggressive intentions and the increasing military capabilities of these two countries may constitute a bigger threat to Turkey than is the case today. It may then be to Turkey's detriment to have taken the soft-security approach of the EU rather than the more confrontational US approach that might have thwarted the nuclear ambitions of the Iranian clergy.

While it is difficult to foresee what may take place in the future in the political and military arenas of the Middle East, there is room for optimism about a resolution of the conflict between Iran and the United States over the nuclear aspirations of the former. Iran is putting forward proposals for expanding the scope of the International Atomic Energy Agency (IAEA) inspections in the country to include measures that are more intrusive than the ones in force today. The 'objective guarantees' put forth by Iranian officials, which include 'permanent placement of IAEA inspectors as well as tamper-proof surveillance mechanisms in the nuclear facilities of Iran' are surely worth considering, at least for the sake of giving a chance to non-confrontational solutions.[5]

However, there is always the risk that Iran is buying time: that its diplomats are debating such ostensibly reasonable proposals while the radical clerical leaders are intensifying their clandestine efforts to surprise the world by suddenly walking out of the Non-Proliferation Treaty (NPT) with a couple of bombs in the basement. Given the depth and extent in the nuclear programme of Iran, such an eventuality can by no means be discounted as being mere speculation or an intellectual exercise. An Iranian diplomat has said that with its 'capability to detonate a nuclear device' Iran 'wants to join the Nuclear Club'.[6] Whether this is going to be as a *de facto* nuclear-weapons state or as a major supplier of civilian nuclear fuel cycles will depend on the decision which is 'yet to be taken by the Iranian leadership'. This decision 'will greatly depend on the outcome of the negotiations between the European Union (that is, EU-3) and Iran, and more importantly, on how the US will deal with Iran'.[7] The countries concerned, such as Turkey, should have contingency plans against this possibility.

A similar worst case scenario may apply to the future of Turkey's relations with Syria. The relationship apparently reached its zenith with President Ahmet Necdet Sezer's official visit to Damascus in April 2005 at a time when both countries had troubled relations with the United States, albeit for different reasons and to different degrees. The death of

Syrian President Hafez Al Assad and his son Bashar's ascent to power paved the way for historic developments in Turkish–Syrian relations. The attendance of Turkish President Sezer at Assad's funeral created some controversy in Turkey, but this courtesy was soon reciprocated by Bashar Assad's official visit to Turkey in 2004. The favourable climate continues. Perhaps Turkish authorities are trying to apply Turkey's fundamental foreign policy principle once laid out by Mustafa Kemal Ataturk, the founder and first president of the modern Turkish Republic: 'Peace at home, Peace in the world.'

Taking into consideration the fundamental changes in the regional and global security environments over the last decade, Turkish authorities may simply be looking forward to improving relations with their immediate neighbour, who, however, had long waged a war by proxy against Turkey by providing support to the separatist Kurdish terrorist organization, namely the PKK. This may be quite understandable from the political, economic and security standpoints. However, just as with the Iranian situation, a 'soft-security' attitude may well be giving time to the Syrian leadership, which is still fragile at home and wounded abroad. As this government consolidates and strengthens, it may come up with a more demanding attitude towards Turkey on traditionally controversial issues like the waters of the Euphrates and Tigris rivers, as well as Turkey's annexation of the Hatay district in 1939.

Against this background, this chapter aims at discussing the risk to Turkey of incautiously adopting the European approach. There are two main reasons for this risk. First, Turkey may not ever join the EU; if it does happen, this event is at least 10 years in the future. Second, were Turkey to join, the EU has no common foreign and security policy, or a European security and defence identity (ESDI), currently or on the horizon.[8] This chapter will adopt a cautious stance *vis-à-vis* the pace of possible developments in relations between Turkey and its principal Middle Eastern neighbours; it will criticize the foreign policy decisions of the political party in power in Turkey, the Justice and Development Party (AKP).

The long road ahead towards EU membership

Membership of the EU has long been official policy in Turkey, though not much had been specifically accomplished to that end. Successive governments have undertaken cosmetic initiatives, particularly at election time. More than four decades after the signing of the 1963 Ankara Agreement with the then European Economic Community (EEC),

Turkey was finally deemed eligible to begin accession negotiations in October 2005. Over the last couple of years Turkey has striven to comply with the Copenhagen political criteria that were designed to guide the former Eastern bloc countries towards full membership. Most of them have already become full members of the EU.

The usual process for full membership requires the national legislative bodies of each member state to approve admission after the completion of negotiations. But, in the case of Turkey, unlike that of any other candidate, referendums may be called, particularly in countries like Greece, Cyprus and France, where opposition to Turkey's membership is strongest.[9] This kind of challenge will make Turkey's membership all the more difficult, if not impossible.[10] There are several issues that make Europeans feel uneasy about Turkey's membership. These may be categorized under four broad headings: political, economic, cultural and military. With regard to political issues, Europeans are primarily concerned with the decision-making process in the EU that will certainly become further complicated with the inclusion of Turkey. Because of its population of 70 million and high birth-rate, the number of seats that Turkey will occupy in the European Parliament will equal those of each of the leading members of the Union such as Germany, France, Britain and Italy. Most Europeans see such an eventuality as a nightmare, particularly in view of their concerns about the level of democratic culture in Turkey, which they see as inadequate to meet European standards.[11]

Economic issues are no less frightening for the Europeans, again primarily due to Turkey's population, which is larger than the total of the ten new member states which joined the EU in 2004. Even the biggest, Poland, has only half of Turkey's population. While the EU is undergoing economic and financial difficulties in digesting the ten new members, it has serious concerns about Turkey's economic infrastructure, which is underdeveloped by European standards and less competitive in world markets. Furthermore, upgrading the industrial and service sectors in Turkey may require a lot of investment. However, the greatest difficulty may be the Turkish agricultural sector, which will certainly need huge subsidies that the EU cannot afford. Added to these is a worry that the Euro will be negatively affected by Turkey's persisting fragile financial system.

However, most analysts argue that neither the political nor economic problems constitute the major stumbling blocks for Turkey's eventual membership in the EU. To them, cultural issues are more sensitive problems, as they pertain to religious and traditional differences between Turkey and the rest of Europe and may not be resolved in the foreseeable future. In the post-9/11 world, differences over cultural issues have sharpened and moved to the point of confrontation. Europeans are getting more and more religious and more fearful and intolerant of Muslims as a reaction to some of the crimes committed by Islamic figures in the Middle East, such as the beheading of European aid workers or businessmen in Iraq, or the murder of Theo van Gogh, the Dutch film-maker, in the street in Amsterdam. Such events will most certainly add further to anti-Islamic sentiments in Europe and may also have a direct bearing on Turkey, whose population is predominantly Muslim.[12] In addition, bad memories of the past, in particular since the Ottoman times, still resonate within European society and contribute to the negative image of Turks and Turkey.

As for the security and defence issues, there are already problems between Turkey and some of the EU members such as Greece and Cyprus. Neither the Aegean problem with Greece nor the Cyprus issue has been resolved, even after the powerful intervention of UN Secretary-General Kofi Annan with a plan for the creation of a federal state on the island. Turkey's recognition of the whole island of Cyprus remains a problem; this would entail abandoning the self-proclaimed Turkish Republic of Northern Cyprus, which is recognized only by Turkey. Likewise, there is strong reaction within the Turkish society to the normalization of relations with Armenia. Even though Turkey formally recognized Armenia after the breakup of the Soviet Union, diplomatic relations have yet to be established. In other arenas, the Europeans are critical of Turkey's relations with the US and Israel. There is fear that Turkey will be the Trojan horse of the US, while its relations with Israel are seriously criticized especially since the military cooperation agreement of 1996.[13] In addition to all these problems, Turkey's relations with its Middle Eastern neighbours like Syria, Iraq and Iran are seen as problematic as the Europeans worry about upsetting whatever level of harmony they have achieved with these countries.

Taking all the above into account, it could be argued that, in the words of Zbigniew Brzezinski: '[T]he European Union will delay for as long as it can a clear-cut commitment to open its doors to Turkey.'[14] Even if a certain degree of loose commitment can be achieved on some of Turkey's security concerns, it is unlikely that Turkey and the EU will see eye-to-eye when it comes to dealing with the problems emanating from Turkey's Middle Eastern neighbours.

Different threat perceptions in Turkey and the EU

For a considerable time, Turkey has differed from Europe regarding the threat posed by the Middle East. During the cold war years the Middle

East was considered to be 'out of area' by Turkey's Western European allies within NATO for several reasons. First, Syria, Iraq and Iran (after the Islamic revolution in 1979) were not seen as posing a noteworthy threat to the Western European members of NATO, even though they developed strong relations with the Soviet Union. Second, these countries were current or potential trading partners of the Western European nations. And third, there were special historical relations between the key European allies and Middle Eastern countries in general, and Syria and Iraq in particular.

The European members of NATO had no desire to be placed in a quandary because their ally Turkey was involved in a conflict with its southern neighbours: a conflict which could eventually escalate into a superpower rivalry and nuclear exchange that would devastate all Europe. Therefore, in informal discussions, leading European members of NATO repeatedly made it clear to their Turkish counterparts that their loyalty to art. 5 (that is, alliance solidarity) of the 1949 Washington Treaty would only cover situations where Turkey had to be defended against its northeastern neighbour, the Soviet Union.[15] In that case, defending Turkey would be vitally important for the Europeans as Turkey's capability to resist would retard or even prevent a powerful Soviet assault on Western Europe.[16]

Dramatic changes have occurred since the end of East–West tension. After the collapse of the Soviet Union, concerns increased with the proliferation of weapons of mass destruction; large quantities of nuclear weapons and their component materials are stored in the former Soviet Union, often under conditions of inadequate safety and security. Europeans still do not think that Syria and Iran pose a threat even though these countries have tried to gain access to the arsenal of the former Soviet military. Since 'threat' is a combination of the capabilities and intentions of other states, Europeans consider that they are far beyond the military range of Iran and Syria, nor do they think that either of them would strike any European nation in the foreseeable future.

Clearly for Turkey and the EU to agree on this issue, one of them had to change their stance. It was essentially impossible for the EU to adjust its threat perceptions and security policies to match those of Turkey. Thus, the other option became imperative for the current government in Turkey if it wanted to begin accession negotiations with the Union. Therefore, the Turkish government apparently decided to adjust its foreign and security policies to those of the EU; these policies are, however, still in the making and are far from meeting Turkey's needs.

The threat posed to Turkey by Iran and Syria

Notwithstanding Turkey's attempt to adjust its stance to that of the EU, the threat posed to Turkey by Iran and Syria is real; their military capabilities include missiles that can hit strategic targets within Turkish territory. Also, these states have problems with Turkey. Syria, for instance, has long-standing claims on the waters of the Euphrates and Tigris rivers that originate mostly in Turkey and flow down to Syria and Iraq. Whereas Turkey suggests the allocation of the waters of this river basin according to the calculated needs of each riparian, Syria demands an arithmetic share of the waters, disregarding the many factors that may further worsen the water shortage in the region.[17]

Another potentially volatile and serious issue is Syria's persistent denunciation of the joining of Hatay province to Turkey in 1939 as the result of a referendum following the termination of the French mandate in Syria. Official Syrian maps persist in showing Hatay province within the boundaries of that country. There has been no change in the position or the rhetoric of the Syrian leadership even after the signing of the 1998 Adana Protocol between the two countries following a short-lived crisis over the accommodation of the leader of the Kurdish separatist organization (PKK) Ocalan in Damascus. Neither did the official visit of the Syrian President Bashar Assad to Turkey in early 2004 have any positive impact on the position of Syria. When asked to comment on the water issue as well as the Hatay issue, Assad made oblique statements suggesting the resolution of these problems be left to the future.

On the other hand, post-revolution Iran has serious concerns with the democratic principles and Western-style reforms in Turkey, which is a secular state by its constitution. The Iranian media incessantly curses Ataturk for having abolished the caliphate as well as the Sharia rule that was in force during the Ottoman Empire. In its stance towards Turkey, Iran has seemingly adopted an 'offence is the best defence' principle, especially in the 1980s and early 1990s. In order to prevent the potential penetration of Turkey's secular principles into Iran, clandestine Islamic fundamentalist propaganda directed at Turkish youth has become a major policy tool. Moreover, a series of assassinations of prominent secular Turkish intellectuals in the first half of the 1990s caused much deterioration of relations and showed how quickly the two countries could approach the brink of a hot confrontation had there been no parity in their military capabilities to force them to exercise restraint.[18]

These brief examples indicate that both Iran and Syria are fertile ground for increasingly hostile attitudes to Turkey. Were this hostility to be paired with superior military capability, the threat would be much greater. For the time being, Turkey can deal with these threats, one at a time, and with the help of NATO (probably without the European allies being on board). However, dealing with a combined threat from Iran and Syria may go beyond Turkey's capabilities. Furthermore, a nuclear-weapons-capable Iran would constitute a much bigger threat to Turkey and could have repercussions for its relations with Syria, who may want to use its strategic relationship with Iran as leverage against Turkey.

Relations with the United States and Israel

The pace of recent developments suggests that Iran is determined to acquire nuclear weapons manufacturing capability. Some Iranian hard-liners propose that even in the face of UN sanctions they should continue the nuclear programme.[19] Many scholars and official figures from the Non-Aligned Movement (NAM) countries as well as Islamic and Arab states are encouraging Iran to go ahead with developing nuclear weapons and to resist the pressures of the US and Europeans.[20] While they seem to consider that Iran's defiance of the US balances the hegemonic behaviour of the American administration, they also do not wish Iran to set a bad example by giving up under pressure.

With so much encouragement from many parts of the world, and with the example of North Korea, which has evaded all sanctions and international inspections, Iran may also follow the same path.[21] The Iranian leadership may imitate the North Korean nuclear weapons programme as they did with their ballistic missile programme. European countries would probably be unable to find a way to ensure that Iran's nuclear capability remains peaceful. At that point, the only countries both willing and able to deal with Iran's nuclear weapons ambitions would be the United States and Israel. Turkey should then carefully consider collaborating with the US in its policies aimed at increasing pressure on Iran. This would be separate from the diplomatic initiatives of the EU that are unlikely to yield a trustable modus operandi with that country.

Iran's gains in the nuclear field will be Turkey's net loss in the strategic balance that has existed between the two countries for centuries. Therefore, Turkey must do its utmost to stop Iran from weaponizing its nuclear programme. However, it cannot act alone. Nor can it act with the Europeans, who are not only reluctant to deal seriously with Iran's nuclear ambitions, but also incapable of doing anything concrete, such as persuading Iran to ratify the Additional Protocol of the International Atomic Energy Agency (IAEA) that it signed in November 2003 only after the long deliberations and the threat of use of force by the US. The Protocol, if ratified, would authorize the Agency to inspect 'any location' within the territory of Iran without exception.

Another 'no' crisis with the US is on the horizon

However, the possibility of collaboration between Turkey and the US seems remote due to a number of reasons. First, the current Turkish government is trying to adjust itself to EU standards in all areas including foreign and security policy; this requires adopting the soft-security approach of the Europeans, such as the exhaustion of diplomatic processes again and again. Second, prominent figures from the ruling Justice and Development Party (AKP) have repeatedly used religious overtones in their rhetoric with respect to the Palestine issue, the US Iraqi offensive and Iran's nuclear programme.[22] Third, those Turks who could be most critical of the AKP's foreign policy approach, the so-called *'ulusalci'* (secular nationalists) have become extremely wary of the intentions of the US and Israel *vis-à-vis* Iraq, particularly regarding the Kurds in northern Iraq.[23] This group of people believe that the US and Israel have secret plans to create an independent Kurdish state in Iraq that would lead to the disintegration of Turkey.[24] For this reason, anti-American and anti-Israeli feelings are gaining more and more ground in this group. While the *ulusalci* seem to be totally opposed to what they call the 'Islamists' in the government of Turkey, they in fact hold similar views to the Islamists in opposing the foreign policies of the US and Israel.

Against this background, Turkey's potential contribution to a hardline US policy towards Iran will be very limited, if not nil; this was also the case during the Iraq war in March 2003.[25] Because of their anti-American attitude, those secular nationalists in Turkey who would have otherwise been at the forefront of helping out the US in its dealings with Iran's nuclear weapons programme will most likely oppose collaboration between Turkey and the US. Yet this same group holds Iran responsible for the serial assassinations of Turkish secular nationalist intellectuals, as part of the Mullahs' desire to destabilize the regime in Turkey.

Critical decisions ahead

It seems that Iran has two windows of opportunity in the next couple of years, in exactly opposite directions. First, to quit nuclear ambitions and normalize relations with the US. And second, to accelerate and pass the crucial threshold enabling them to assemble a nuclear warhead. As for the first option, Iran knows that even if it abandons its nuclear ambitions, its relations with the US will not be significantly improved because of Israel's influence on US foreign policy. As long as Iran remains an Islamic fundamentalist state, its hostility towards the Jewish state of Israel will probably continue.[26] Some Iranian officials also believe that the US would still threaten them with regime change even if they quit their nuclear aspirations; after all, the American government acted the same way in Iraq. Added to these, are issues of national pride and prestige.[27] Because the Iranian leadership has difficulties arising from the public desire for more freedom, the government wants a strong issue for satisfying the demands to mobilize popular support. The nuclear row with the US has served two purposes: it has consolidated public support, and it has given Iran time to prepare.

For all these reasons, Iranian analysts believe that giving up the nuclear programme is not a good idea. As happened with North Korea, Iran may also benefit from developments that keep the US busy: the Iraq issue; polarization of domestic politics in the US; or new, shocking attacks by Al Qaeda, perhaps on prominent individuals. Should Iran as expected choose this path, it will use European diplomacy as armour and Turkey as a shield to protect it from a possible US military operation. As elaborated above, the current government in Turkey may serve Iran's purposes for two reasons: first, the reinforcement of anti-American and anti-Israeli feelings in the Turkish public domain both propagated and exploited by the politicians; and second, the adoption of the European soft-security approach in defence matters at a premature stage.

Conclusion

If Iran cannot be bound by stringent measures that would assure the international community that it is not developing nuclear weapons, Turkey's interest would then lie in helping the US to deal with the clerical regime. If Iran developed nuclear weapons, Turkey might be second on the hit-list, after Israel. Therefore, policy-makers and security analysts in Turkey should not be confused with the ongoing Europeanization debate or the role of Islam in foreign policy matters, neither of which will solve Turkey's ongoing security problems. Politicians should take a longer, broader perspective in security and defence and give serious thoughts to where Turkey's national interests lie. Mistakes committed at this stage in halting Iran's nuclear weapons ambitions may have negative repercussions for the security of Turkey in the longer term.

Notes

1. For an elaborate discussion on how the Turkish military approaches security issues, see Ali L. Karaosmanoglu, 'The Evolution of the National Security Culture and the Military in Turkey', *Journal of International Affairs* 54 (2000), 1: 199–216.
2. For a comprehensive discussion on this matter, see, for instance, Julian Lindley-French, 'The Revolution in Security Affairs: Hard and Soft Security Dynamics in the 21st Century', *European Security* 13 (2004), 1/2: 1–15.
3. The author is convinced that the efforts of the EU-3 that are directed at indefinitely halting Iran's uranium enrichment activities will not prove successful. This conviction is strengthened following a series of conversations with European as well as Iranian officials and scholars in conferences in Berlin, entitled 'Germany and Nuclear Nonproliferation', organized by the Aspen Institute and the Nonproliferation Education Center, 25–27 February 2005, and in Tehran, entitled 'Nuclear Technologies and Sustainable Development', organized by the Iranian Centre for Strategic Research, 5–7 March 2005.
4. See Mustafa Kibaroglu, 'Iran's Nuclear Ambitions May Trigger the Young Turks to Think Nuclear', *Carnegie Analysis*, 20 December 2004, http://www.ceip.org
5. See Kaveh L. Afrasiabi, 'The Peace Pipe's on the Table', *Asia Times*, 1 March 2005, http://www.atimes.com
6. Interview with Saeed Khatipzadeh, a career diplomat from the Iranian Ministry of Foreign Affairs, Tehran, Iran, 27 December 2004.
7. Ibid.
8. For a detailed discussion on how to strengthen the ESDI, see Adrian Hyde-Price, 'European Security, Strategic Culture, and the Use of Force', *European Security* 13 (2004), 4: 323–44.
9. Alain Juppé, former Prime Minister of France, expressed his concerns about Turkey's eventual membership and argued that 'the EU then will not be the EU of [their] dreams'. He went on to say that 'if and when Turkey becomes a member of the EU, [they] should rethink about the future of Europe and a new architecture with the EU will emerge'. Juppé made these remarks during an international conference on 'The US and Europe: Partnership or Competition', Boston University, Boston, MA, 16 November 2004.
10. For an account on the difficulties that Turkey faces in its relations with the EU, see Mohammed Ayoob, 'Turkey's Multiple Paradoxes', *Orbis* 48 (2004), 3: 451–63.
11. This view, which is also common to most European elite, was reiterated by Giorgios Dimitrakopoulos, a Greek member of the European Parliament, during a private conversation at Harvard University, 22 March 2005. Dimitrakopoulos also added that, based on his personal observations, the Europeans most fear migration of Turks in large numbers.
12. For a comprehensive coverage of a wide range of issues pertaining to Turkey's relations with the European Union, see Michael Bonner, 'Turkey, The European Union and Paradigm Shifts', *Middle East Policy* 12 (2005), 1: 44–71.

13. See Mustafa Kibaroglu, 'Turkey and Israel Strategize', *Middle East Quarterly* 9 (2002), 1: 6–65.
14. See Zbigniew Brzezinski, 'Hegemonic Quicksand', *National Interest* 74 (2003/04), p. 7.
15. Gen. Cevik Bir (Ret.), Second Chief of Turkish General Staff, 19 January 2005, Istanbul, Turkey.
16. See Mustafa Kibaroglu, 'La Turquie, les États-Unis et l'OTAN: une alliance dans l'Alliance' (Turkey, US, and NATO: an Alliance within the Alliance), *Questions Internationales* 12 (Mars–Avril 2005), pp. 30–2.
17. See Aysegul Kibaroglu, *Building a Regime for the Waters of the Euphrates–Tigris River Basin* (The Hague: Kluwer Law International, 2002).
18. The political climate between the two countries improved towards the end of the 1990s and in the early 2000s. However, it is too early to predict whether the current mood will survive, especially if the clerics manage to build nuclear weapons.
19. Conversations with Iranian scholars and officials during two consecutive conferences in Tehran in March 2005. The first of these conferences was on 'Persian Gulf Security', was organized by the Iranian Institute of Political and International Studies (IPIS), 1–3 March 2005. The second conference on 'Nuclear Technologies and Sustainable Development' was organized by the Iranian Centre for Strategic Research, 5–7 March 2005.
20. There were some 90 non-Iranian participants from 32 countries all over the world at the 'Persian Gulf Security' conference in Tehran, 1–3 March 2005, where the above-cited views were openly and forcefully declared repeatedly.
21. Ayatollah Hassan Rohani, Secretary of the Iranian Supreme National Security Council, clearly stated in his opening remarks at the conference on 'Nuclear Technologies and Sustainable Development', 5 March 2005, that should the Iran dossier be passed on to the United Nations Security Council by the Board of the IAEA, Iran would immediately withdraw from negotiations with the Europeans and would also reconsider its membership status in the Non-proliferation Treaty, hinting at the possibility of withdrawal.
22. One Deputy from the AKP, namely Mehmet Elkatmis, asserted that the American troops used atomic bomb against the Iraqi insurgents and committed genocide during the Fallujah offensive in November 2004. See Turkish media, 27 November 2004.
23. For a detailed account on the impact of the US and Israeli policies towards the Kurds of Iraq on Turkish–Israeli relations, see Mustafa Kibaroglu, 'Clash of Interest Over Northern Iraq Drives Turkish–Israeli Alliance to a Crossroads', *Middle East Journal* 59 (2005), 2: 246–64.
24. A quick look at the Turkish press in 2004 and early 2005 may demonstrate the sentiment of the Turks towards the US and Israel. See, for example, 'Israil devlet teroru yapiyor' (Israel commits state terrorism), *Hurriyet*, 5 June 2004, hhtp://www.hurriyetim.com.tr For a similar account, see Abdullah Karakus, 'Israil'in yaptigi teror' (Israel is terrorizing), 14 April 2004, *Milliyet*, http://www.milliyet.com.tr
25. See Mustafa Kibaroglu, 'Turkey Says No', *The Bulletin of the Atomic Scientists* 59 (2003), 4: 22–5.
26. An Iranian scholar, who wished not to be cited, said during a private conversation at the 'Nuclear Technologies and Sustainable Development' conference

in Tehran, 6 March 2005, that the impossibility of destroying Israel is now being acknowledged by many more Iranians. But it would be premature to conclude that the Iranian leadership might consider recognizing Israel even if such a development would considerably improve its relations with the US. One has to bear in mind that during the cold war period when Iran was one of the 'three pillars' (together with Israel and Egypt) of the United States in the Middle East, the Iranian Shah Reza Pahlavi did not dare to recognize the State of Israel.

27. Conversations with Iranian scholars and officials during the 'Persian Gulf Security' and the 'Nuclear Technologies' conferences, March 2005.

11
The US and Turkey's Quest for EU Membership

Omer Taspinar

Introduction

Relations between Turkey and the EU are taking place in a rapidly changing global context. An outlook that goes beyond political dynamics in Ankara and Brussels is therefore absolutely necessary. A broader analysis of Turkey–EU relations needs to take into consideration not only the transatlantic context but also tensions between the Islamic world and the West. This larger framework is particularly important for the United States, a main actor in both realms. Washington has been a staunch supporter of Turkey's European aspiration from very early on. Yet, in the wake of the 11 September 2001 attacks, the US stake in Turkey's EU membership has become even higher for three main reasons.

The first is related to the growing role of religion in mobilizing global conflicts. The shocking acts of Jihadist terrorism in America and Western Europe over the last few years have turned an otherwise unlikely scenario of 'the clash of civilizations' into global reality. Today, significant numbers of Muslims see the US-led global war against terrorism as a 'crusade' against Islam. Similarly, European and American attitudes towards Islam and Muslims are increasingly characterized by security concerns and the fear of terrorism. Such polarization along religious and cultural lines does not bode well for peace and security in Europe, the Middle East and the United States.

In such a polarized global context, the symbolism of a Muslim country seeking membership in an exclusive Western organization with a predominantly Christian population acquired tremendous importance. In other words, Turkey's EU membership has gained an unprecedented 'civilizational' dimension since 11 September 2001. This particular aspect of Turkey's EU quest matters greatly for the United States and all countries interested in proving the fallacy of an inherent clash between Islam and the West.

The second reason for analyzing Turkey–EU relations in a broader context is related to the implications of political dynamics within Turkey itself. Since 2002, Turkey has been pursuing its pro–EU reform agenda with much greater determination and energy under the leadership of a moderately Islamic government. This development is highly appreciated in Washington not only because it gives much needed intellectual ammunition to the argument that democracy, secularism and a pro-Western foreign policy are compatible with Islam, but also because democratization now tops the US foreign policy agenda in the broader Middle East.

Finally, it is important to note that Turkey–EU–US relations are part of a transatlantic context in flux. The lead-up to war in Iraq has created the worst transatlantic crisis ever. It also deeply strained internal dynamics within the EU. The second term of the Bush administration has been progressing more smoothly on the transatlantic front. Yet, Iran, Syria and the Israeli-Palestinian conflict still have the potential to polarize relations between America and Europe.[1] Turkey is greatly relevant in this transatlantic context, not only because it is a NATO member that recently started accession talks with the EU, but also because it shares borders with Iran, Syria and Iraq while enjoying good relations with both the Israeli and the Palestinian governments.

For all these reasons Washington's already firm support for Turkey's EU membership has become even stronger in the wake of the 11 September 2001 attacks. In other words, America's geostrategic rationale for Turkey's EU quest now acquired a potentially even more important civilizational dimension. Understandably, this American tendency to focus solely on the large picture contrasts sharply with the EU's more technical and scrutinizing approach to Turkey. For the EU, Turkey presents a foreign policy challenge more than a strategic opportunity. Turkey's size, uneven level of economic development, democratic standards, borders with dangerous regions and different religion are often perceived as liabilities, not as assets.

There is, moreover, an 'enlargement fatigue' within the EU that significantly complicates the current outlook towards Turkey. The EU, it is often argued, needs time to absorb its 2004 enlargement by ten new countries in Central and Eastern Europe. The fact that Turkey's population is almost as large as those of all the newcomers put together strengthens such a viewpoint. In addition, the EU is also in the midst of a profound political crisis, after French and Dutch voters unexpectedly rejected the

European Constitution in 2005. The two countries arguably did so because of serious concerns about high levels of unemployment and immigration. In both France and Holland, the *no* appeared to be bolstered by the subject of Turkey, which was seen as a country whose accession would lead to more immigration and unemployment in the EU.

Under such circumstances, US lobbying on Turkey's behalf – with an exclusive focus on the larger strategic picture – has the potential to backfire. In fact, Western Europeans often complain that Washington's vigorous support for Turkey lacks a detailed understanding of the inner machinations of the EU and the delicate financial and political balances between member countries. On the other hand, sweeping generalizations about European receptiveness (or lack thereof) to American support for Turkey can be misleading for a number of reasons. First of all, the EU is not a monolith. This is increasingly the case now that the EU has twenty-five members and no real common foreign and security policy. Second, much depends on the overall state of transatlantic relations. If relations are strained, as was the case during the lead-up to war in Iraq, American support for Turkey is likely to backfire or create the impression that Ankara may serve as Washington's Trojan horse within the EU. Yet, since the EU is often divided, certain member countries will always be more open to American positions than others.

In sum, the transatlantic dimension of Turkey–EU relations presents complex dynamics and challenges. Moreover, this complicated picture is further compounded by dynamics within Turkey. Rising anti-Americanism in Turkey and diminishing enthusiasm for the EU may become important determinants of Turkey's relations with the West. Turkey's frustration with the EU is a particularly worrisome development, which in certain ways overlaps with the factors leading to anti-Americanism. This chapter will therefore address Turkish–American–European relations without losing sight of Turkey's own changing views of the US and EU.

Turkish–American relations: from strategic ally to democratic model

As mentioned already, Washington has always valued Turkey's geostrategic importance. There is considerable continuity in this approach, which prioritizes American interests in regions surrounding Turkey. During the cold war, Turkey was the only NATO country sharing borders with the Soviet Union. As such, it served as a bulwark against Soviet expansion into the Middle East and the Eastern Mediterranean. Turkey's large army tied down some twenty-four Soviet divisions. Turkish–American relations still witnessed some ups and downs – the downs being mostly related to Cyprus. But the cold war paradigm defined the broader positive tone in relations.

The end of the cold war did not reduce Turkey's strategic importance, as many Turks feared would happen. During the 1990s Turkey remained a crucial strategic ally because of worsening regional instabilities in the Balkans, the Caucasus and the Middle East. The need to contain Iraq and Iran in the Gulf made Turkey and its NATO facilities all the more important. The United States flew thousands of sorties from the Incirlik base during the first Gulf War in 1991, and the US Air Force efficiently monitored the no-fly zone over Northern Iraq between 1992 and 2003 from Turkey. During the 1990s close cooperation between Ankara and Washington continued on issues ranging from military partnership in Bosnia and Somalia, to Caspian energy development with the construction of the Baku–Tbilisi–Ceyhan petroleum pipeline. In short, Turkey's geo-strategic importance and ability to share military burdens remained crucial for Washington.

In the aftermath of 9–11, Turkey's importance was no longer confined to geo-strategic location. What Turkey represented, as a unique democratic, secular and pro-Western country in the Islamic world became even more important than where Turkey was on the map. In many ways, Turkey came to be seen as a 'model' Muslim country worthy of emulation. In order better to appreciate this new take on Turkey, one needs to understand the crucial change in America's analysis of the Middle East after 9–11 attacks. The message brought to New York and Washington on that tragic day ended an erroneous premise about the state of affairs in the Middle East. Soon after the attacks, it became painfully clear that autocratic stability in the Middle East no longer provided security. To the contrary, the *status quo* had created the worst outcome for the United States by fuelling radical Islam and a proclivity for terrorism. The dysfunctional *status quo* had to be challenged.

This newfound willingness for change and democratization in the Middle East had realist and idealist undertones, often expressed simultaneously in the American debate leading to the invasion of Iraq. The realist voice prioritized security threats: weapons of mass destruction, terrorism, and the looming threat of potentially nuclear 9–11s. The idealist voice, on the other hand, attached equal importance to unleashing a democratic tsunami that would transform the region. Overall, the perception that underneath stable autocracies lay the most serious threats to US national security created a major sense of urgency for an activist agenda.

On the other hand, the idea of promoting democracy in the Arab world had to come to terms with a major US concern: the fear of the Islamist alternative. The likelihood of an Islamist electoral victory, under a 'one man, one vote, one time' scenario had always curbed America's enthusiasm for democratization in the Arab world. Yet, the attacks on US soil put such fears in perspective. An initial stage of Islamic proclivity in democratizing Arab countries increasingly appeared as a risk worth taking. This was particularly the case since the authoritarian *status quo* fuelled mass discontent and radical Islam, which in turn led to anti-Americanism and terrorism in the region. The logic behind such analysis was sound: the mosque is often the only social institution not totally suppressed by autocracies. All sorts of opposition to the regime therefore gathers in the mosque. These dynamics fuel the Islamization of dissent in the absence of alternative outlets to voice opposition.

Anti-Americanism is often the product of similar dynamics of repression. In most Arab autocracies, there is official tolerance only for anti-Israel demonstrations. Repressive regimes have, therefore, a vested interest in deflecting all sorts of dissent towards the legitimate plight of Palestinians. Domestic discontent is seldom allowed to address domestic political problems. As masses voice their frustration with Israel, they also turn increasingly anti-American, due to the special relationship between Israel and the United States. The resulting climate of frustration and humiliation in the Arab world provides an ideal breeding and recruitment ground for anti-American radicalism. The 9–11 attacks transformed this Arab predicament into a national security priority for the United States. The need for democratization, in turn, led to the search for democratic models that could be emulated in the Islamic world.

Within this new context, Turkey emerged as a natural choice. Turkey was not only the most democratic country in the Islamic world but it also shared borders with Syria, Iraq and Iran. Indeed, President George W. Bush and many prominent members of the US administration repeatedly praised Muslim Turkey as a model that merits emulation in the wider Islamic world. The strongest and most persistent pro-Turkish voice in the administration has been that of former Deputy Defense Secretary Paul Wolfowitz who offered a compelling case for the Turkish model in 2002:

> To win the war against terrorism we have to reach out to the hundred of millions of moderate and tolerant people in the Muslim world, regardless of where they live ... Turkey is crucial in bridging the dangerous gap between the West and the Muslim world. In the

United States we understand that Turkey is a model for those in the Muslim world who have aspirations for democratic progress and prosperity. Turkey gives us an example of the reconciliation of religious belief with modern secular democratic institutions.[2]

Similar beliefs have been voiced across the administration. For example, Condoleezza Rice called Turkey 'an excellent model, a 99 per cent Muslim country that has great importance as an alternative to radical Islam'. President Bush stated that Turkey 'provided Muslims around the world with a hopeful model of a modern and secular democracy'.[3]

Equally important became Turkey's role in discrediting those with a tendency to equate Islam with political violence and radicalism. Indeed, by illustrating that Islam could be perfectly compatible with democracy and secularism, Turkey and especially the moderately Islamic Justice and Development Party (AKP) government countered such extreme, yet occasionally vocal, viewpoints. As a result, Turkey's Muslim character gained unprecedented relevance in addition to its strategic importance. For instance, Turkey's active presence in the anti-terror alliance strengthened the claim that the American-led 'war on terrorism' is not a crusade against Islam. This is also why the leadership Turkey provided in the ISAF (International Security Assistance Force) in Afghanistan was very meaningful.

Ironically, America's admiration of Turkey as a model failed to take into consideration the scepticism about Turkey in the Arab world. Where Washington saw the only Muslim, democratic, secular and pro-Western country in the Middle East, most Arab countries saw a former colonial master that turned its back on Islam. Although the Arab world started paying more attention to Turkey after the arrival of the moderately Islamic AKP to power, the overall tendency remains to look at Turkey as a peculiar country with secularist proclivities and serious identity problems.[4] Yet one has to admit that the image of a democratizing and more Islamic Turkey that is relentlessly pushing for EU membership is intriguing – and potentially instructive – for Muslims all over the world.

Interestingly, perhaps more unexpected about America's promotion of the Turkish model has been the negative reaction within Turkey itself. The secular establishment of Turkey, as will be addressed later, did not appreciate the superpower's tendency to portray the country as 'moderately Islamic'. An important part of the problem is related to timing. Turkey's Kemalist sensitivities were already alarmed because of the arrival of AKP in power in 2002. As American officials began praising Turkey as a model in the Islamic world, the secular intelligentsia became increasingly distressed about global and domestic dynamics pushing Turkey towards the Middle East and the Islamic world rather than Europe. All these developments appeared to be coming at the expense of Turkey's Kemalist legacy and European self-perception. Yet it was not these looming concerns but a much more urgent problem that was to strain relations between Ankara and Washington.

The 2003 Iraq debacle

The rosy glow around Turkey in Washington faded somewhat in the lead-up to the US invasion of Iraq. On 1 March 2003, after six months of contentious military, political and financial negotiations between Ankara and Washington, the Turkish parliament denied US troops access to Iraq through southeast Turkey. After a heated debate in the Turkish Grand National Assembly, the resolution that was to grant transit rights to more than 60,000 US troops failed by the narrow margin of three votes.

This decision came as a shock to Washington and effectively curtailed America's ability to open a northern front against Baghdad during the invasion. Turkey's decision not only forced the Pentagon to change its original war plans, but also complicated the postwar situation. In fact, Secretary of Defense Donald Rumsfeld recently argued that the insurrection in Iraq is in large part the result of the absence of a northern front.[5] Without a northern front, Rumsfeld argued, Saddam's Republican Guards were able to retreat north and blend in with the civilian population. Turkey had obviously gained a place of its own in Secretary Rumsfeld's construct of 'Old' versus 'New' Europe thanks to the heartburn it gave Washington.

Turkey's minimal support for the United States was certainly an unexpected disappointment for American policy-makers. However, perhaps more importantly, frustration with Turkey provided a crucial litmus test for Washington's own commitment to democratization in the Middle East. The reason is simple. The regional picture that emerged prior to the war in Iraq was rather disturbing. Most authoritarian Arab governments, whose populations were overwhelmingly opposed to war in Iraq, decided to cooperate silently with the American effort anyway. In contrast, Turkey – the only Muslim democracy in the Middle East – refused to open its territories to the United States despite being offered billions of dollars in foreign and military aid. The irony was not lost on the superpower.

The easy trap would have been to react negatively against Turkey and display a tendency to punish. Such an outcome would have certainly

confirmed the sceptics' viewpoint that Washington's support for democratization is always contingent upon pro-American outcomes. Such a
serious blow to US sincerity about promoting democratization in the
Middle East was however avoided. Although disappointed, Washington
reacted with maturity: Turkey was a democracy and its parliamentary
process had to be respected. Not doing so would indeed have been self-
defeating for the grand project the United States was about to embark on
in Iraq and the broader Middle East.

It would still be naïve, however, to think that Turkish–American relations did not suffer a heavy blow because of Iraq. Turkey lost not only a
massive package of financial aid worth $6 billion but also any kind of
leverage it may have had over US policies in northern Iraq. The Iraq
episode strained Turkish–American relations particularly at the military
level. In fact, America's disappointment appeared to be more with the
Turkish military than with Turkish democracy. This point was clearly con-
veyed by former Deputy Defense Secretary Paul Wolfowitz in May 2003:

> Turkey, with a Muslim majority and a strong democratic tradition,
> remains an important model for a part of the world where the US is
> trying to move in a positive direction. However, for whatever reason,
> the Turkish military did not play the strong leadership role we would
> have expected.[6]

Despite America's irritation with the Turkish military, Turkey's importance as the most advanced democracy in the region remained crucial.
Despite its minimal cooperation in Iraq, Ankara still qualified for $1 billion
in economic aid in the president's supplementary war budget. US backing of IMF loans to Turkey also continued. Secretary of State Powell paid
a wartime visit to Ankara, where he once again described Turkey as a
model for a future Iraq. For its part Turkey, shortly after the war, offered
to send ten thousand Turkish peacekeepers to Iraq – a proposal that was
ultimately rejected by Baghdad.

The transatlantic context

Interestingly, some neoconservative American analysts have argued that
Turkey's Iraq policy was intended to score points with the EU, particularly
with France and Germany, who strongly opposed the invasion of Iraq.
Fouad Ajami, for instance, maintained that '[t]he Turks will soon realize
that no dosage of anti-Americanism will take Turkey past the gatekeepers
of Europe'.[7] It is certainly true that France and Germany were pleasantly

surprised by the Turkish parliament's refusal to cooperate with Washington. They even took it as a sign of democratic maturity. Yet it would be wrong to argue that Turkey's decision was motivated by factors other than its own domestic political and security concerns. Anxiety over the potential emergence of an independent Kurdistan in northern Iraq figured much more prominently in the Turkish domestic debate than the need to side with Europe in a transatlantic rift. Moreover, the fact that EU itself was clearly divided over Iraq would have diminished the impact of any Turkish intention to impress Europe with its resistance to Washington.

In any case, Turkey's decision did not lead the US to withdraw its support to Ankara *vis-à-vis* the EU. Washington continued strongly to back Turkey. Such support was already very robust, and arguably excessive, in December 2002 at the EU Copenhagen Summit, where Ankara hoped to get a firm date to begin accession negotiations. The EU, however, gave Turkey a 'conditional date'. Membership negotiations were to start soon after December 2004 – provided that Turkey continued to make democratic progress in the meantime. Some have argued that strong US lobbying on Turkey's behalf prior to the Copenhagen Summit was designed partly to secure Ankara's cooperation in Iraq.[8] This may indeed have been a policy consideration in Washington. Yet, it is important to note that Washington had always been very supportive of Turkey in the past, without expecting a particular quid-pro-quo.

For instance, in 1995 and 1999 – in two instances when the US support for Turkey proved more effective than in 2002 – there was no expectation that Turkey would return the favour with a specific policy. In 1995 the EU included Turkey in the customs union, an achievement that was optimistically interpreted by Ankara as a shortcut to full membership. Such high hopes were greatly disappointed in 1997, when the EU sidelined Ankara's candidacy for full membership at the Luxembourg Summit. In December1999, however, intensive US efforts prior to the Helsinki Summit played a positive role in putting Turkey's membership process back on track. Such US support was all the more valuable because Ankara had decided to cut all political relations with the EU in protest against the 1997 decision.

In that sense, the support Ankara received from Washington prior to the 2002 Copenhagen Summit was part of a well-established pattern in US policy toward Turkey–EU relations. In case there was an expectation of a quid-pro-quo, the fact that Turkey failed to cooperate with Washington did not lead to a change in US policy *vis-à-vis* Turkey's EU quest. This became abundantly clear at the NATO Istanbul Summit in

June 2004 where Washington continued its unwavering support for Ankara. During the summit President Bush strongly reiterated, at several occasions, that his administration remains a firm supporter of Ankara in the EU process. Such backing of Turkey, however, clearly irritated at least one important member of the EU. As a sign of ongoing transatlantic tensions, Jacques Chirac claimed that American meddling with Turkey–EU affairs was 'a bit like if France told the United States how they should manage their relations with Mexico'.[9]

These snapshots of Turkey–EU–US dynamics illustrate three main points. First, American support for Turkey's EU quest is strongly rooted in a strategic vision unlikely to be easily derailed. Drastic bilateral problems going beyond manageable policy disagreements could of course lead Washington to reconsider its relations with Turkey. Yet it is hard to imagine a situation where the United States would benefit from Turkey turning its back to Europe. Most Americans who follow Turkey are clearly aware of the role that the EU plays as a major catalyst for Turkish democratization. As Marc Grossman, a former under secretary of state who also served as US Ambassador to Turkey, argued:

> Americans are convinced that one of the European Union's most remarkable accomplishments has been its long-term strategy to spread democracy and prosperity to Europe's east and south through expansion. This is especially true of Turkey: its desire to join the Union has been a profound incentive for positive change.[10]

The second important point about Turkey–EU–US triangular dynamics is that the effectiveness of US support for Turkey's EU quest very much depends on the state of transatlantic relations. France and Germany will be less willing to take into consideration American talking points if EU–US relations are strained because of a crisis in the Middle East or elsewhere. It would, therefore, be unwise for Washington to incessantly lobby EU capitals when the mood in Europe is anti-American. A low-profile, behind-the-scenes American diplomatic support, without major public statements, would be much more effective. The opposite could do more harm than good, particularly in countries like France and Germany.

Finally, the role of the US should not be exaggerated as a primary determinant of Turkey–EU relations. Washington certainly plays an important and positive role by reminding its European partners of larger geo–strategic stakes involved in Turkey's European aspiration. The EU needs such reminding because it is often self-absorbed by internal problems or unwilling to assume global responsibilities commensurate with its economic power. Turkey, in such instances, is lucky to have the superpower on its side. Yet one should not forget that the most important factor that will determine the future of Turkey–EU relations is not Washington but the political dynamics within Turkey itself. Washington's influence with the EU can be helpful only if Turkey moves in the right direction with its political reforms.

Turkey's internal problems, and particularly the Kurdish question, may end up setting the tone in its relations with the United States as well as with the EU. For instance, Turkey's Kurdish policy could potentially alienate both the United States and the European Union. Especially if Iraq's potential disintegration exacerbates Turkey's Kurdish problem, growing anti-Americanism in Turkey, coupled with diminishing enthusiasm for the EU, may lead Ankara to reconsider its 'Western' orientation. The risk that Turkey could become more nationalistic and turn away from both the US and the EU should not be complacently downplayed on the grounds that Turkey has nowhere else to go. For instance, Ankara's frustration with the West may lead to a Eurasian strategy based on stronger relations with Russia and the Islamic world. In that sense, the factors leading to anti-Americanism and anti-EU feelings in Turkey have to be analysed carefully. The next section is an attempt to do so.

Anti-Americanism and Turkey's internal problems

In the last two years, the image of the United States in Turkey has become an unnoticed casualty of the war in Iraq. Poll after poll confirms that growing numbers of Turks perceive their NATO ally as a security problem, rather than a strategic partner. A 2005 BBC poll, for example, found that 82 per cent of Turks considered US policies in the Middle East a threat to peace and security.[11] In analysing Turkey's frustration with the United States, one needs to go beyond the Bush administration's negative global image. For instance, the German Marshall Fund's transatlantic survey of May 2005 showed that while anti-Americanism is in relative decline in Europe, the trend in Turkey is in the opposite direction.[12] Turkey seems to present a *sui-generis* case where anti-Americanism needs to be analysed in light of the country's own domestic dynamics and identity problems.

Before doing so, however, it is important to clarify a couple of points. First, let us define what we mean by anti-Americanism. In the Arab world, and increasingly in Turkey, anti-Americanism is fuelled primarily by disagreements with US foreign policy and not an intrinsic resentment against American culture, values or democracy. Quite the opposite: a majority of citizens in the Muslim world and in Turkey watch American movies, enjoy American food and want their children to study in the United States. Long lines in front of American Embassies for visa and green card applications often tell the same story: 'We love your country, but we hate your policies.'

In Turkey, disagreement with American policies is far from new. Turkish–American relations witnessed their fair share of ups and downs during the cold war, mostly in the form of Cyprus-centred episodes. These problems occasionally escalated to 'crisis' level, with abundant drama and posturing, as in the case of the 'Johnson Letter' in 1964 and the weapons embargo in 1974.[13] However, it is important to remember that such episodes took place in the context of a predictability provided by the cold war. These were, after all, times of global and domestic ideological polarization where anti-Americanism belonged to the realm of the left. Today, however, what often tends to be overlooked is the fact that Ankara and Washington no longer share a common enemy. For Turkey the 'Axis of Evil' is hardly a good substitute for the 'Evil Empire'. Iraq, Iran and, of course, North Korea never posed clear and present threats to Turkey. The Soviet menace, on the other hand, was all too clear. It brought predictability, as well as clear limits to Turkish–American differences.

Today, at the heart of Turkey's frustration with America lies the Kurdish issue. Iraq is particularly relevant here. The Kurdish agenda in post-Saddam northern Iraq has generated a deep distrust of the United States among the majority of Turks. This was already evident prior to the war. In fact, the Turkish military failed to support wholeheartedly the American invasion of Iraq because of concerns about the political and territorial integrity of Iraq.

Turkey's concerns were considerably aggravated during 2004 and 2005, as Iraqi Kurds appeared to pursue a maximalist political and territorial agenda, aimed at declaring the oil-rich province of Kirkuk as their regional capital. In the eyes of Ankara, the Kurds of Iraq were taking bold steps towards autonomy and independence under US watch. Making things worse was the fact that Turkey's own Kurdish nemesis – the PKK (Kurdish Workers Party) – also seemed to regain ground in both Turkey and Iraq. These developments put the United States in an extremely negative light in the eyes of Turkish public opinion. During 2005, a colourful example of Turkey's frustration with the United States was a best-selling novel depicting a Turkish–American war over Kirkuk in northern Iraq.[14] As conspiracy theories about Washington's willingness to create a Kurdish state became commonplace, few Turks seemed to remember that in 1999 the leader of the PKK was put behind bars in no small part thanks to the help of American intelligence – which located him in Nairobi, a few weeks after he was forced out of Damascus. Any attempt to understand the current wave of anti-Americanism in Turkey must acknowledge that the US is now on the wrong side of the Kemalist debate in Turkey by supporting the idea of Turkey serving as a 'model' for the Islamic world and by relying on the Kurds in Iraq. As previously mentioned, by promoting 'moderate Islam' the US alarms Turkish secularists. Although Washington has now erased 'model' from its Turkish political vocabulary – replacing it with creative formulas like 'source of inspiration' – the Kurdish problem is trickier to solve. America's strong partnership with the Kurds in Iraq, the new Iraqi constitution's loose federalism, the status of the oil-rich province of Kirkuk, and the Pentagon's reluctance to take action against PKK terrorists in northern Iraq all rattle the Kemalist guardians in the Turkish military.

What makes the Kurdish issue particularly relevant is that it strongly affects Turkey's perception of the European Union as well. After all, it is Brussels not Washington that demands that Ankara accept the Kurds as a national minority with distinct cultural and linguistic rights. In that sense, Turkey's anti-Americanism often overlaps with anti-EU feelings as well. In fact, anxiety about Kurdish nationalism is the common denominator of Turkey's anti-EU and anti-American feelings. For instance, a July 2005 opinion poll by a Turkish NGO found that 65.7 per cent of Turks believed that 'Western countries want to disintegrate Turkey like they disintegrated the Ottoman Empire in the past.' More interestingly, according to the same survey 51.4 per cent of Turks believed that 'the reforms required by the EU are similar to those required by the Treaty of Sèvres – which dismembered the Ottoman Empire in 1920'.[15]

The roots of Turkey's insecurity

Turkey's nervousness and insecurity about separatism and the Kurdish question has very deep roots. From the inception of the Turkish Republic in 1923, Kurdish dissent, coupled with political Islam as a second existential challenge, constituted in fact the 'twin threats' to Atatürk's project of creating a secular and homogeneous nation-state in Anatolia.[16] In that sense, Islamic and Kurdish dissent rejected Kemalist 'laicism' and 'Turkish nationalism'. Turkish secularism and nationalism were both deeply influenced by the French republican model. Turkey's secularism was modelled on French '*laïcité*' – based on the idea that religion should have no role in the public sphere.

As far as Turkish nationalism is concerned, the model was once again France. The Turkish Republic refused the concept of ethnic minorities and prioritized assimilation. All citizens were to become Turkish. In continuity with Ottoman traditions, the only officially recognized minorities were non-Muslims. Yet, Ottoman-style cosmopolitanism or multicultural tolerance was anathema in the new nation-state. All Muslims, including Kurds, were now considered Turks. Not surprisingly, these nationalist and secularist policies triggered a major Kurdish and Islamic backlash. From 1925 to 1938, a long series of Kurdish and Islamic uprisings had to be suppressed militarily. Inevitably, such powerful resistance to secularist nation-building traumatized the young Republic and led to an abiding suspicion of all things Kurdish and Islamic for years to come.

After the transition to multi-party democracy in the 1950s, neither Kurdish nationalism nor political Islam disappeared totally from Turkey's political agenda. Instead, for the next four decades, these identity problems were overshadowed by right-wing and left-wing ideological cleavages. During the cold war, Kurdish discontent was often expressed in terms of left-wing 'class struggle' while political Islam was part of the anti-communist struggle. By the 1990s however, these dynamics were no longer in place. After the cold war interlude, it became painfully clear that right-wing and left-wing ideological cleavages had indeed served to mask Turkey's underlying 'identity' problems.

By the mid-1980s, a major Kurdish insurrection was already under way. The separatist challenge posed by the PKK, a terrorist guerilla movement with considerable regional support, proved extremely costly. Between 1984 and 1999, in addition to a death-toll of 35,000 the conflict cost the Turkish economy an estimated $120 billion in military expenditures alone. As budget deficits soared, national inflation averaged 70 per cent during these years. The result was a lost decade of civil war, secular–Islamic polarization, authoritarian proclivities and economic crisis. Especially after the death of Turgut Ozal (prime minister 1983–91, president 1991–3) political instability became permanent. Nine different coalition governments ruled Turkey in the 1990s alone.

The Kurdish conflict and domestic instability clearly undermined Turkey's relations with the EU and prospects for democratization. To the dismay of Ankara, Europe saw in the Kurdish conflict the rebellion of an ethnic group whose cultural and political rights were denied by an authoritarian system dominated by the military. By the mid 1990s, things were going from bad to worse. As the war against the PKK continued to escalate, political Islam re-emerged as the second powerful domestic threat. The secular foundations of the Turkish Republic appeared to be rigorously challenged by the victories of the Islamic Welfare Party at local and national elections in 1995 and 1996. At the heart of the Turkish predicament was the failure to adapt Kemalism to the twenty-first-century 'liberal' democracy.

The Kemalist paradox

Defining Kemalism is a problematic issue. That Kemalism, in the context of the 1930s, represented a progressive political agenda based on establishing a secular Turkish nation-state is not contested. The modernization and Westernization dimension of the original project, put forward by Mustafa Kemal himself, is also widely accepted. What is more difficult, however, is to define what Kemalism represents in terms of Turkey's relations with the West in the context of the twenty-first century. There is, in fact, little agreement between Kemalists themselves about what Kemalism means exactly as a contemporary political project. This is understandable. Kemalism, after all, is already a success story. Modern Turkey is a secular nation-state and a democratic republic. There is certainly room for improvement in terms of establishing a truly 'liberal' democracy in Turkey. However, it would be unfair to blame Kemalism for such deficiencies. After all, liberalism was not on the global agenda of the 1930s. It is, therefore, possible to argue that the Kemalist project has successfully achieved its historic mission.

Today, in modern Turkey, it is this very success of Kemalism that transforms it into a conservative ideology. Having accomplished its goals, Kemalism today displays an understandable urge to preserve and protect what has already been achieved. This situation reduces Kemalism into a nationalist–secularist reflex against external and domestic threats rather than a coherent and progressive ideology. Especially for Turkey's politically powerful military that zealously safeguards Ataturk's legacy, Kemalism now amounts to 'protecting' the Republic from its perceived enemies: Kurdish nationalism and political Islam. Therefore, any deviation from the Turkish character of the nation-state or from the secular framework of the republic presents a challenge to Kemalist identity.

As far as the Kurdish question and political Islam are concerned, there is no room for ambiguity in the Kemalist position of the military. On the Kurdish front, the threat is conceptualized in the following manner. Any political assertion, no matter how minor, of Kurdish ethnic identity is perceived as a major security problem endangering Turkey's territorial and national integrity. A similarly alarmist attitude characterizes the military's approach to Islam. Islamic socio-political and cultural symbols in the public sphere – such as headscarves in public schools – are seen as harbingers of a fundamentalist revolution. Needless to say, such an alarmist approach to Kurdish and Islamic identity has been counter-productive for Turkish democracy.

This was particularly the case during the 1990s, when Turkey's Western credentials were no longer determined by cold war dynamics. After its application to the EU for full membership in 1987, Ankara needed to demonstrate its liberal and democratic credentials as a truly Western country. Such European scrutiny came at a time when Turkey was perceived as an illiberal country fighting for its own ethnic and religious identity. Despite such deeply rooted difficulties, it is all the more remarkable that Turkey managed to improve its badly tarnished relations with the EU – especially after the 1997 Luxembourg Summit – in the last few years. How did that happen? The answer requires a closer look at two seemingly contradictory factors: first, the Turkish state's success in defeating Kurdish separatism and taming political Islam, and second, the external dynamics that led the EU to reconsider it position at the 1999 Helsinki Summit.

On the domestic front the unwavering determination of the Turkish military to deal with the twin threats of political Islam and Kurdish nationalism produced unexpectedly satisfactory results by the late 1990s. The secular establishment first gained the upper hand against political Islam by forcing the Welfare Party out of power in 1997, in what came to be called a post-modern coup. The Kemalist backlash did not end there. By 1998 a major blow was inflicted against Kurdish terrorism. The apprehension and incarceration of PKK leader Abdullah Ocalan created a much-needed sense of victory against Kurdish terrorism. Soon after Ocalan's arrest, a militarily weakened and politically demoralized PKK declared a cease-fire. All these developments vindicated the logic of the Turkish military in rejecting political solutions to a conflict that lasted for fifteen years. With political Islam subdued and Kurdish nationalism defeated, the sense of siege that characterized the 1990s came to an end. The restoration of such domestic political confidence eased the transition to a more reformist mindset and facilitated the conceptualization of democratization as intentional rather than imposed.

The EU incentive

Despite such progress, it is far from certain that Turkey's internal dynamics would have been conducive to democratization on their own, without the help of external factors. In fact, the crucial catalyst for political liberalization came when the EU reversed course at the December 1999 Helsinki Summit and restored Turkey's candidacy for membership. Since Turkish democratic standards did not improve between 1997 and 1999, three major external factors played a positive role in the adjustment of the EU's position *vis-à-vis* Turkey.

The first and probably most important factor was the arrival of a government sympathetic to Turkish membership in Germany. Unlike the Christian Democrats who ruled Germany between 1982 and 1998, the SPD–Green coalition of Chancellor Schröder was not prejudiced against Ankara. Coming to power in 1998, the new government in Berlin not only changed Germany's antiquated citizenship laws – thus opening the possibility for German citizenship to 3 million Turks in Germany – but also followed a positive approach towards Turkey's eventual EU membership. Having the EU's largest country and budgetary contributor on its side significantly improved Turkey's European hopes.

To the surprise of many within the EU, Greece emerged as a second factor in support of Turkey. A breakthrough occurred in bilateral relations between Athens and Ankara in 1999 as the government of Greece decided that marginalizing Turkey outside Europe would create an unstable, impoverished and potentially more aggressive and nationalist neighbour. Consecutive earthquakes in Istanbul and Athens during the summer of 1999 also triggered a great deal of goodwill and sympathy between the two countries' populaces. As a result, Greece has turned from an ardent foe into a strong supporter of Turkey's European quest.

Finally, the third factor improving Turkey's chances in the 1999 Helsinki Summit was the United States. Throughout 1998 and 1999, the Clinton administration lobbied on behalf of Ankara in all EU capitals in an attempt to bring some strategic sense to European leaders' short-sighted approach to Turkey. These were crucial efforts since they came at a time when Turkey had decided to suspend its political relations with the EU in the aftermath of the 1997 Luxembourg Summit. The fact that transatlantic relations were much better under the Clinton administration greatly helped.

The 1999 Helsinki Summit was a crucial turning point in Turkey–EU relations in terms of putting Ankara on an equal footing with all other candidates. Thanks to this important step, EU membership became a major catalyst for Turkey in pressing for otherwise very difficult domestic reforms. It was therefore with such new hope that Turkey began the twenty-first century. Yet the country faced a severe financial crisis in 2001, which brought the end of an era for all political parties that governed during the lost decade of the 1990s.

Although Finance Minister Kemal Dervis, backed by the International Monetary Fund, restored a sense of economic stability in 2002, the political field was wide open in the general elections of November 2002. The impact of improved relations with the EU became all the more evident when the moderately Islamic AKP won in a landslide by campaigning on a pro-EU platform.

In doing so the newly established AKP managed to achieve two crucial objectives. First, the party gained a sense of legitimacy in the eyes of Turkey's Kemalist establishment. In other words, the military was much more willing to give the benefit of the doubt to a political party with a European vocation, rather than one with Islamist proclivities, as was the case with the Welfare Party. Second, thanks to its pro-EU stance, the AKP became more appealing for Turkey's business community, for the provincial middle classes and for liberal intellectuals. The AKP could not have achieved such widely based political legitimacy in the absence of the Helsinki Summit of 1999.

The AKP did not hesitate to embrace a pro-EU agenda because it pragmatically realized that Islamists desperately needed a liberal democracy for their own political survival. The new government attacked corruption, supported compromise on Cyprus and undertook further reforms of the Turkish judicial system, civil–military relations and human rights practices. By December 2004, the EU had concluded that Turkey fulfilled the criteria necessary to begin accession talks in October 2005. Ironically, the Turkish dream of joining the West seemed much closer thanks to a political party with Islamic roots. The symbolism of this achievement is a testament to the success of Turkish Westernization.

Challenges ahead

Yet, as previously mentioned, it is too early to celebrate. Europe suffers from an enlargement fatigue and the mood in Europe about Turkey is far from positive. Moreover, Ankara has embarked on a long and challenging process of membership negotiations that may very well last a decade or longer. Making things worse is the fact that Germany now has a Christian Democratic government willing to deal with Turkey in the framework of a 'privileged partnership'. Such views are enthusiastically shared by the French political elite, and especially Nicolas Sarkozy, a top candidate to become president in 2007. Under such circumstances Turkey will continue to need America's support. Since both Angela Merkel and Nicolas Sarkozy want to improve their countries' badly strained relations with the US, Washington may actually have some leverage. However, the US should pay perhaps more attention to Turkey's own political dynamics and find ways to address Turkey's concerns over Kurdish separatism in Iraq and southeastern Anatolia. The delicate balance of Turkey–EU–US dynamics will depend on the overall state of transatlantic relations and how Turkey's growing frustration with both the US and the EU evolves. It would certainly be a tragedy if the Kurdish question should lead to another lost decade in Turkey.

Notes

1. At the heart of the transatlantic rift, as Robert Kagan famously argued, may be the 'strategic culture' between Europe and United States. In that sense, the transatlantic rift can be seen as structural rather than contextual. Syria and Iran could potentially turn into new cases for testing this hypothesis, especially if Washington insists on keeping military options open while Europe exclusively focuses on diplomatic negotiations and economic sanctions. See Robert Kagan, *Of Paradise and Power: America and Europe in the New World Order* (New York: Random House, 2003).
2. Paul Wolfowitz, 'Turgut Ozal Memorial Lecture', delivered on 15 March 2002 at the Washington Institute for Near East Policy.
3. For the statements of Condoleeza Rice and President George W. Bush, see 'The Pentagon Talks Turkey', *American Prospect* 13 (2002), 16: 9–10.
4. Omer Taspinar, 'An Uneven Fit: The Turkish Model and the Arab World,' Analysis Paper No. 5 for the *Brookings Project on U.S. Policy Towards the Islamic World* (2003).
5. In March 2005, appearing on US television talk shows, Donald Rumsfeld stated that he wished US troops had not been 'blocked' from entering Iraq through Turkey, and asserted that this had enabled the postwar insurgency in Iraq to flourish. 'Given the level of the insurgency today, two years later, clearly if we had been able to get the 4th Infantry Division in from the north, in through Turkey, more of the Iraqi, Saddam Hussein, Baathist regime would have been captured or killed. The insurgency today would be less,' he said, adding that the resulting thrust of the US invasion through southern Iraq had enabled many insurgents to evade capture in the north. See *Agence France-Presse*, 21 March 2005, at http://www.turkishpress.com/news.asp?id=39081; see also CNN's coverage of Rumsfeld's statements at http://www.cnn.com/2005/WORLD/meast/03/20/iraq.anniversary, accessed 22 December 2005.
6. For a transcript of Paul Wolfowitz's interview with CNN Turk, see http://www.defenselink.mil/transcripts/2003/tr20030506-depsecdef0156.html
7. Fouad Ajami, 'The Falseness of Anti-Americanism', *Foreign Policy* 118 (September/ October 2003): 52–61.
8. See Ziya Onis and Suhnaz Yilmaz, 'The EU–U.S.–Turkey Triangle in Perspective: Transformation or Continuity?', *Middle East Journal* 59 (2005), 2: 265–84, p. 267.
9. 'EU Anger as Bush Calls for Turkish Membership', *Financial Times*, 30 June 2004.
10. Marc Grossman, 'America Should Be Ready to Fill the Void on Turkey', *Financial Times*, 16 September 2005.

11. The January 2005 BBC World Service Poll, which was conducted in 21 countries, indicated that a record 82 per cent of Turks perceived President Bush's policies as negative for global peace and regional security in the Middle East. See Karl Vick, 'In Many Turks' Eyes, U.S. Remains the Enemy', *Washington Post*, 10 April 2005, p. A21. According to the German Marshall Fund's 'Transatlantic Trends Survey' of September 2005, a slightly lower 77 per cent of Turks found the US administration's global leadership to be 'undesirable'; see the GMF report at: http://www.transatlantictrends.org/doc/TTKey Findings2005.pdf, accessed 22 December 2005.

12. See 'Overview of GMF Transatlantic Trends 2005', at http://www.transatlantictrends.org

13. One can hardly forget the words uttered by Prime Minister Ismet Inonu in 1964 (in reaction to President Johnson's letter warning that Turkey should not count on NATO support against the Soviet Union if it invaded Cyprus): 'If conditions change and events make a new order necessary, Turkey will certainly find its place in this new world order;' see Suha Bolukbasi, 'The Johnson Letter Revisited: Turkey's Policy toward Cyprus and Lyndon Johson's 1964 Letter to the Turkish Government', *Middle Eastern Studies* 29 (1993), 3: 505–25.

14. Orkun Uçar and Burak Turna, *Metal Firtina* (Metal Storm) (Istanbul: TimasYayınevi, 2004).

15. The Sèvres treaty of 1920 partitioned the defeated Ottoman Empire among victors of World War I and created an independent Kurdistan and Armenia in eastern Anatolia. For the poll numbers, see Ari Movement's 'Turkish Public Opinion about the USA and Americans', at :http://www.ari.org.tr/arastirma/ Turkish%20Public%20Opinion%20on%20the%20Americans%20&%20the %20United%20States.pdf

16. For a detailed study, see Omer Taspinar, *Kurdish Nationalism and Political Islam in Turkey: Kemalist Identity in Transition* (New York: Routledge, 2005).

12
The Iraq War and the Troubled US–Turkish Alliance: Some Conclusions for Europe

Ozlem Kayhan and Dan Lindley

Introduction

Since Turkey's foundation by Ataturk in 1923, the main goal of the country's leaders has been to bring the country into the ranks of the developed Western nations economically and politically. This Western orientation got firmly established after the country joined the North Atlantic Treaty Organization (NATO) in 1952 and signed an association agreement with the European Economic Community (EEC) in 1963. Although from time to time Turkey experienced problems in its relations with the United States (US) and the European countries, by the late 1990s it was recognized both as an important strategic ally by the US and as an official candidate member by the European Union (EU).

In fact, Turkey's ties with the EU and US have always been strongly connected to each other. Throughout the cold war years, Turkey developed close relations with both the US and Western European countries because Turkish foreign policy makers saw the country's association with these actors as an acknowledgement of Turkey's membership to the Western bloc as well as its Western identity. Moreover, in the post-cold-war period, the US advocated and lobbied for Turkey's participation in the EU because the presence of a pro-Western, stable and democratic Turkey substantially contributes to American interests in the Middle East, Caucasus and Central Asia. However, in the run-up to the Iraq War in 2003, Turkey's rejection of the US request to deploy American troops in Turkey to attack Iraq started a sequence of events which seriously damaged the relations between these two countries and which had important implications for Turkey's EU accession process.

This chapter discusses how the Iraq War and the weakened Turkish–American alliance have affected Turkey's EU project and explores the current trajectory of Turkey–US and Turkey–EU relations within the framework of the war in Iraq. First, we present a historical overview of the interaction between Turkey–EU and Turkey–US relations, specifically focusing on the continuous US efforts to make Turkey part of the EU. Then, we discuss the ways in which the Iraq War and the weakened Turkish–American alliance have affected Turkey's EU accession process. In this discussion, we first argue that Turkey's rejection of the US request to open a northern front to attack Iraq via Turkish territory helped Turkish political leaders to focus on fulfilling the membership criteria during this period and to start accession negotiations in October 2005. Second, we show that the US 'war on terror' helped bring Islamic issues to the fore throughout Europe and that this increased concerns in the EU about admitting Turkey, which has a predominantly Muslim population of 70 million. Third, we argue that the troubled Turkish–American alliance in the Iraq War, when coupled with Turkey's problems in its EU accession process, show that Turkey should not see its relations with the US and the EU as mutually exclusive, but instead as mutually reinforcing. Turkey is either going to move towards the West or it is not, and as it is devoted to doing so, it must develop a balanced foreign policy towards both the US and the EU. Finally, we briefly discuss the future of Turkey's foreign policy towards its two Western partners. We acknowledge that in light of the current state of affairs the future of Turkey's relations with the US and the EU still holds a substantial amount of uncertainty.

Turkey–US–EU relations: a historical overview

The efforts to make Turkey a modern Westernized state have their roots in the eighteenth-century Westernization process of the Ottoman Empire. The deterioration of Ottoman military superiority from the seventeenth century onwards and the continuous defeats of the empire mainly by the European countries led to several efforts by the political and military elites to restore the power of the Ottoman state internally and externally. These reform efforts mostly involved looking to Europe as a model and importing its military technology, lifestyle and way of thinking in order to reinstate the empire's status *vis-à-vis* the European countries.[1]

The establishment of the Republic of Turkey in 1923 was a new and ambitious step in this two-century-old modernization project. After Ataturk founded the republic, he and his colleagues made a substantial effort to create a Western secular state structure and established their main goal as bringing Turkey to the ranks of the contemporary civilization, that is, to the ranks of the developed European countries.

Turkey's Westernization project acquired new momentum after World War II.[2] In the postwar period, Turkey's political elites saw the future of their country's Westernization in the parallel processes of establishing close relations with both the US and Western European countries as well as acquiring membership in the institutions of the Western alliance such as the Council of Europe and NATO.

Turkey's interaction with the US in this period developed mostly as a result of these countries' security concerns. Although Turkey–US relations were based on trade during the late Ottoman and early republican times, the post-World-War-II developments placed Turkey in a central position in the efforts to contain the Soviet Union.[3] This new era for Turkish–American alliance started with the 1947 Truman Doctrine, which granted economic and military aid to Turkey and Greece with the aim of preventing these two countries from falling to communism. Turkey's participation in the Korean War in 1950 and its admission to NATO in 1952 strengthened the Turkish–American security partnership.

However, this alliance was never without problems during the cold war. Turkey–US relations suffered from several setbacks such as the increasing anti-American sentiments in Turkey in the 1960s; the 1964 Johnson Letter, which stated that if Turkey intervened in Cyprus, NATO might not defend Turkey in case of a Soviet attack during the intervention and that American military equipment could not be used by Turkish forces in Cyprus;[4] American insistence on stopping poppy cultivation in Turkey in 1972; and the imposition of an arms embargo on Turkey by the US Congress as a response to the 1974 Turkish intervention in Cyprus.[5] But despite the emergence of these problems, Turkey and the US built an overall successful strategic alliance during the cold war period.

Turkey's relations with Europe throughout the cold war cannot be understood in isolation from its ties with the US because during those years the Turkish political elite did not see the country's ties with Western Europe and the US as separate from each other. Turkey perceived Western European countries and the US as its two partners in a single 'Western Alliance'. Thus, Turkey's relations with Western Europe in general and its conclusion of an association agreement with the EEC in 1963 in particular was seen in Turkey mainly as a means to strengthen the country's security-related ties with the West.[6]

The nature of the Turkey–US–EU interaction began to change with détente from the 1970s onwards. As a result of the diminishing hostility between Western and Eastern bloc countries in this period and the subsequent reduction of the security concerns, the political and economic dimensions of the Turkey-EEC relationship began to attract increasing attention.[7] Consequently, in the 1970s and 1980s Turkey and the Western European countries confronted some difficult issues, including the creation of a customs union, Turkey's poor human rights record and the failure of its democratization efforts.[8] This emphasis on political and economic issues increased even more after the cold war and has substantially shaped Turkey–EU relations since then.

In spite of the change in the nature of Turkey's interaction with the European countries, Turkey–US relations continued to reflect a strong security dimension even with détente and the end of the cold war. While the Soviet threat waned after the collapse of the Soviet Union in 1991, the instability and the importance of the regions that surround Turkey ensured that the Turkish–American alliance would continue to revolve around the geopolitical interests and security considerations of these two countries.[9] Specific security-related issues included the 1991 Gulf War, ethnic violence in the Balkans in the 1990s, and Turkey's proximity to the Middle East and Caspian oil.

Although the relaxation of the East–West tension and the subsequent end of the cold war changed the nature of Turkey–US–EU interaction, these developments did not fully eliminate the fact that Turkey–US and Turkey–EU relations have been closely connected to each other. In the post-cold-war world, this interconnection showed itself mostly in the continuous American efforts to advocate and lobby for Turkey's full membership in the EU.

US Republican and Democrat administrations alike have encouraged the EU's enlargement efforts since the establishment of the EEC in 1957. For the US, each wave of enlargement signified a further extension of the European zone of economic and political stability.[10] However, Turkey's EU membership bid has a more distinctive meaning for American foreign policy than the accession of the rest of the candidate countries to the EU.

In an era in which American strategic interests have focused on dealing with the instability and chaos in the Balkans, Caucasus, Central Asia and the Middle East, it is crucial for the US that Turkey stays strongly anchored to the West as a stable, modern, secular and democratic ally. Needless to say, Turkey's accession into the EU is the best way to achieve this goal without imposing much burden on the US to keep Turkey as a stable country.[11] Moreover, Turkey's EU membership process acquired the utmost importance after the 9–11 attacks. As the US war on terror has created problems for America's relations with the Muslim world, it is important for the US that Turkey, which has a predominantly Muslim population, remains a close American ally and a model democracy for the Islamic world.[12]

The US has a number of other strategic interests in a strong and democratic Turkey. First, Turkey provides a buffer and a staging ground with airbases as the US looks towards the Middle East, all of which became even more important in the era of the US war on terror. Futhermore, Turkey is the most stable and politically preferable exit route for Caspian energy sources and is a bulwark and buffer against instability in the Caucasus region. During much of the 1990s, the US developed its strategy of gaining access to Caspian oil through the Baku–Tbilisi–Ceyhan pipeline, which, along with the associated gas line still under construction, terminated in Turkey. This route for the pipeline was strategically important for the US, which did not want to see the route go through Russia or Iran. Finally, Turkey is one of the most powerful members of NATO, and the US is on Turkey's side in the centuries old game of using Turkey to stem Russia's southward ambitions. An overview of the economic strength, population, military expenditures and military forces of some of the major players in the region (Table 12.1) shows that Turkey is a key ally for the US. Expenditure per active soldier is given to provide a rough indicator of the quality of forces.

Some suggest that the US wants Turkey in the EU to weaken, not strengthen the Union. These sceptics argue that once Turkey enters the

Table 12.1 Strategic overview of some major players in the Middle East

	Gross national product (GNP, billions of US dollars)	Population (millions)	Military expenditure (billions of US dollars)	Military forces, active plus reserve (in thousands)	Expenditure per active soldier (thousands of US dollars)
Turkey	297	70	10.1	515 + 379	19.6
Iraq	23	26	0	180	?
Iran	148	68	4.1	420 + 350	9.8
Syria	22	18	1.6	308 + 354	5.2
Russia	1,400	143	14.1	1,037 + 20,000	13.6
Greece	202	11	4.1	164 + 325	25.0

Notes: Figures are for latest year given. Russian dollar figures are purchasing power parity estimates. Iraq is in a state of flux.

Source: International Institute for Strategic Studies, *The Military Balance, 2005–2006*.[13]

EU, the US will use it as a Trojan horse to divide the EU and undermine its decision-making capacity.[14] However, this argument is false. At a time when the key events of geo-strategic interest are the rise of China and India, most in the US want to strengthen the West as a whole. Whether it wants to deal with terrorism, turmoil in the Middle East, ethnic conflict in Africa, or the rise of other great powers, the US is better off with a strong Europe. Despite its squabbles with Europe, and occasional signals from Europe that it is trying to balance against the US, Europe and the US both need each other to be strong. The former US President Bill Clinton's words from his speech in Istanbul in July 2002 clearly show this line of thinking:

> America cannot remain as the only superpower forever ... Therefore, we should develop ourselves to become part of the group that shares our own common values. This is the reason why I support the EU. Of course, one day the EU will surpass the United States economically. But if we belong to the same group with our common values, who cares![15]

American diplomatic efforts for Turkey's EU membership bid became most evident in the mid 1990s when Turkey and the EU were in the process of signing a customs union treaty. During the talks, the US pressured the EU and lobbied for this customs union agreement in order to help Turkey gain the European Parliament's consent.[16] Moreover, after the 1997 Luxembourg Summit, where Turkey was excluded from the EU's post-cold-war enlargement process, Turkish political elites turned to the US for help in convincing the EU member states to include Turkey as a candidate country in the enlargement process. Finally, when Turkey was officially declared a candidate country at the 1999 Helsinki Summit, it was argued that American lobbying by several important figures such as Nicholas Burns, Marc Grossman and Mark Parris substantially contributed to this positive outcome.[17] Thereafter, the US regularly involved itself in successive decisions of the EU regarding Turkey's membership process. For example, before the 2002 Copenhagen Summit, where Turkey received a tentative date for the initiation of membership negotiations, the Bush administration pushed the European member states to accelerate Turkey's accession. President George W. Bush even made telephone calls to the French president Jacques Chirac and to the Danish prime minister Anders Fogh Rasmussen – who held the EU presidency at the time – about Turkey's case.[18] Likewise in 2005 when the European leaders were discussing whether to let Turkey start accession negotiations on 3 October, the US secretary of state Condoleezza Rice made telephone calls to the European leaders to help solve the problem over the issue of Cyprus's possible admission in NATO and contributed to the ending of a deadlock over Turkey's accession. Also after the EU decision to start accession negotiations with Turkey was made, Rice organized a meeting with the ambassadors of the EU member states in Washington and discussed the advantages of making Turkey part of Europe.[19]

The above examples show clearly that the US – especially from the mid 1990s onwards – has been closely involved in Turkey's EU accession process and has lobbied firmly for Turkish membership. However, this should not give the impression that American backing has always been welcomed by the EU and has positively influenced every outcome. In fact, from time to time the US support for Turkey's membership has caused annoyance on the part of the European member states and has been seen as interference in their internal affairs.[20] The 2004 NATO Istanbul Summit provided a very noticeable example of the EU resentment against American lobbying for Turkey's EU membership. During that summit, President Bush talked about the importance of admitting Turkey to the EU as a full member. After this speech, President Chirac said that President Bush 'not only went too far, but he has gone into a domain that is not his own'.[21] Chirac also added that Bush's demand was 'a bit like if France told the United States how they should manage their relations with Mexico'.[22] But despite this European resentment of American lobbying for Turkey from time to time, the continuous US support has contributed positively to Turkey's progress towards EU accession in several occasions, including the 1995 customs union talks and the 1999 Helsinki Summit. In addition to the US lobbying for Turkey's EU project, the Turkish–American alliance has also provided psychological comfort for Turkey. Whenever Turkey's relations with the EU deteriorated, the Turkish governments have usually turned to their American partners for help. This has ensured that Turkey's Western orientation would continue despite the country's problems with its European partners.

The Iraq War and the Turkish–American alliance: implications for Turkey–EU relations

Although Turkish–American relations suffered from periodic setbacks from the 1960s onwards, relations were firmly positive at the time of the 9–11 attacks on the World Trade Center and the Pentagon. In 1999, the Turkish–American alliance was characterized by the then US President

Bill Clinton as a 'strategic partnership', which meant that 'the strategic cooperation is multi-dimensional and multi-faceted, involving a wide range of overlapping interests in Europe, the Caucasus, Central Asia and the Middle East'.[23]

When the Bush administration declared war on terrorism in the immediate aftermath of 9–11, Turkey acted as a partner in the war against the Taliban. Turkey granted the use of its airspace to the US during the Afghan War and then deployed Turkish special forces troops to Afghanistan. The Turkish government also provided logistical and intelligence support to the US war effort and participated in the International Security Assistance Force (ISAF) after the fall of the Taliban regime. Moreover, Turkey took over the command of ISAF from June 2002 to February 2003 and from February 2005 to August 2005.[24]

However, when the US decided to declare war on Iraq as the next stage of its war on terror, Turkey was unwilling to participate in this endeavour. Despite the Turkish–American negotiations in 2002–3 about the potential role of Turkey in a future Iraq War and despite the $24 billion American offer to Turkey in loans and credits, the Turkish Grand National Assembly (TGNA) could not muster enough votes to allow American troops to open a northern front to attack Iraq from Turkey on 1 March 2003.[25] Turkish–American relations deteriorated even further after this decision owing to a number of ensuing events such as the American troops' detention of eleven Turkish special forces soldiers in Sulaymaniya in the summer of 2003 – based on the claim that these forces were planning to assassinate the Kurdish governor of Kirkuk – Turkey's reference to the US military actions in Falluja as genocide, and Turkish uneasiness about the civilian deaths in during US military operations against the insurgents in Talafar.[26]

There were two major reasons why the Turkish parliament declined to open a second front in the Iraq War from Turkey. First, the US war effort was enormously unpopular in Turkey. According to the polls, more than 90 per cent of the Turkish people opposed the war in Iraq and it was not possible for the members of the governing Justice and Development Party, who constituted the majority in the Parliament, to ignore such a vast number. Therefore, the outcome of the voting in the Grand National Assembly represented the almost unanimous Turkish public opinion.[27] Second, the parliament's negative response to the deployment of American troops on Turkish soil reflected the reluctance of the major Turkish political and military actors to involve Turkey in a US war against Iraq. While on the one hand political leaders and military officers were concerned about the legitimacy of such a war, on the other hand they were uneasy about the possible postwar instability and chaos in Iraq. For example, although the Turkish armed forces did not explicitly state their apprehension about the Iraq War, they were concerned that if Iraq got out of control and/or an independent Kurdish state was established in northern Iraq, this could have significant consequences for Turkey's Kurdish population. These potential consequences included a rise in the separatist sentiments among Turkey's Kurdish minority and an increase in Kurdistan Workers Party (PKK) terrorism in the region.[28]

In the aftermath of the 1 March 2003 vote, a number of commentators suspected that Germany's and France's opposition to the war negatively influenced Turkey's stance and resulted in the parliament's rejection of the motion to open a northern front from Turkey. The theory was that, as an aspirational EU member, Turkey rejected the US request in order to align its foreign policy with France and Germany and to gain a favourable position in the eyes of these two major EU members.[29] However, given the high level of public disapproval of the Iraq War in Turkey and the political and military elites' concerns about the implications of this war for Turkey's Kurdish issue, it is difficult to agree with the argument that the Turkish parliament rejected the opening of a northern front in order to gain the favour of the major EU countries. Instead, it is more accurate to say that Turkey's concerns about the US war in Iraq moved Turkish foreign policy closer to the Franco-German position in this period.[30]

No matter what caused the Turkish parliament's to refuse to allow US troops in Turkey to attack Iraq, this decision triggered a sequence of events which seriously damaged relations between Turkey and the US and which had important implications for Turkey's EU accession process. It is worth noting, though, that Turkey still offered some passive but real assistance to the US during the Iraq campaign. Turkey granted the US permission to use its airspace to carry American troops to northern Iraq in March 2003, supported the rotation of the US troops via Incirlik airbase, and approved the use of Incirlik as a cargo hub for the US operations in Iraq and Afghanistan.[31]

The first important impact on Turkey's EU project by the Iraq War and the newly weakened Turkish–American alliance was that the country's relative disengagement from the war provided a favourable environment for the Turkish government to focus on its EU accession process. If Turkey had accepted to play a more active role in the Iraq War alongside the US, including playing host to thousands of ground troops, it would not have been easy for the government to spend considerable time and resources on meeting the EU accession criteria and starting negotiations in October 2005. Turkish political and military leaders would have concentrated most of their attention on the issues of national security and this would have no doubt hindered the major democratic openings in Turkey. Without democratic progress, Turkey would not have moved as far along its path towards full EU membership.

As a result of Turkey's increased focus on its EU project, significant democratization reforms were carried out in 2003 and 2004. In contrast to the reforms undertaken after the 1999 Helsinki Summit, where Turkey was officially declared a candidate country, the reforms of 2003 and 2004 addressed the most controversial elements of the Turkish political structure. This included the role of the military in Turkish politics, the anti-terror law, the Turkish criminal code and the issue of broadcasting in local languages. For example, the sixth harmonization package abolished art. 8 of the anti-terror law, which defines separatist propaganda as a crime, and allowed broadcasting in local languages and dialects. The seventh harmonization package curtailed the powers of the National Security Council (NSC) – which was seen as the main body through which the military exerted its influence on Turkish politics – and turned it into an advisory body, reduced the frequency of the NSC meetings from once a month to every other month and made the military budget subject to the Court of Accounts' review in August 2003.[32] Arguably, it would have been difficult to carry out these extensive reforms had Turkey been more enmeshed in the Iraq War.

The second outcome of the Iraq War for Turkey's EU membership process revolves around Turkey's identity as a predominantly Muslim country. The 9–11 attacks on the US by radical Muslims brought the problem of Islamic fundamentalism to the forefront. The increase in the number of terrorist incidents by radical Islamist groups, which followed the US declaration of the war on terror and particularly its military campaign in Iraq, intensified discussions about a clash of civilizations and the incompatibility of Islam with the West. These events and discussions led to an increase in anti-Muslim sentiments in Europe and negatively affected Turkey's EU accession process.

In fact though, the EU's worries about admitting a predominantly Muslim country as a full member are not new and they started long before the US war in Iraq. Several European politicians have openly expressed such concerns since the 1990s. For example, in 1997 the then German chancellor Helmut Kohl and the Dutch politician Wilfred Martens stated that '[t]he EU is a civilization project and within this civilization project Turkey has no place'.[33] As a result of such statements, Turkey accused the EU of being a 'Christian club' several times and of excluding Turkey from Europe for religious reasons.[34]

However, the events that took place after the US declaration of its war on terrorism gave a new dimension to the already existing uneasiness about admitting Turkey into the EU. In the wake of the 9–11 attacks, Turkey joined the US efforts to fight against terrorism and emphasized that there was no connection between terrorism and religion. Furthermore, Turkish political leaders continuously affirmed their country's Western, secular and democratic orientation in order to distance Turkey's image from the radical Islamist groups.[35] Also, a number of political leaders in the US and Europe frequently repeated that the US-led war on terrorism was not against Islam. But unfortunately these efforts were not enough to keep Turkey's EU membership process from being affected by the growth of anti-Muslim sentiment in Europe.

Terrorist attacks by radical Islamist organizations on Europe increased after 9–11 and gained new momentum after the US declared war against Iraq. Such terrorist incidents mostly targeted those European countries that participated in the Iraq War alongside the US. The Istanbul bombings, where British targets (as well as synagogues) were attacked in November 2003, the Madrid train bombings in March 2004, which were committed by Muslim immigrants of Moroccan descent, and the bombings in London's underground trains in July 2005, for which Al Qaeda claimed responsibility, are examples of this situation.[36]

The Islamic issues that came to the fore throughout Europe in the aftermath of 9–11 and especially with the US invasion of Iraq had two important consequences for Turkey's EU membership process. First, the terrorist acts of Islamic fundamentalists increased awareness about the EU governments' failure to integrate their approximately 15–18 million Muslim population into the European society.[37] This strengthened the feelings of 'us' versus 'the other', 'Islam versus the West' in these EU countries and confirmed 'the other's' hostility and willingness to use violence against their host societies.[38] As a result, discrimination against Muslims increased substantially in Europe. According to a survey on religious attitudes conducted on behalf of the *Wall Street Journal*, more than 50 per cent of the Western Europeans viewed Muslims living in Europe with suspicion in September–October 2004. The number reached over 70 per cent in certain countries such as Netherlands and Sweden.[39] Not surprisingly, this situation had a negative impact on Turkey's EU accession process because Turkey's full membership means the inclusion of 70 million more Muslims into European society. It is possible to observe this negative attitude towards Turkey's aspiration to full EU membership in the statements of several European politicians. For example, in 2002 the former French President Valéry Giscard d'Estaing declared that 'Turkey is not a European country' and that Turkey's membership in the EU would mean 'the end of Europe'.[40] Also, in 2004 German Chancellor Angela Merkel stated that 'Turkey does not fit into the EU because it is "culturally different" '.[41] Second, the successive terrorist acts by radical Muslim groups in Europe created a fear in the minds of European publics that Turkey's membership in the EU will 'make it easier for Islamist terrorists to attack from within'.[42] Such fears probably increased with the discovery of several Islamist terror cells in European countries.

In sum, the events that followed the 9–11 attacks and especially the US war in Iraq brought Islamic issues to the forefront and negatively affected Turkey's EU membership process. The Turkish government argued that their country's full membership could weaken arguments about a rising clash of civilizations and build a bridge between Europe and the Muslim world, but this did not protect Turkey's accession process from increasing anti-Muslim sentiment in Europe.

The third major influence of the US war in Iraq and the weakened Turkish–American alliance on Turkey's EU membership process is a rather circular one. We argued above that Turkey's refusal to play a more central role in the Iraq War helped the political elites to focus their full attention on fulfilling the Copenhagen criteria and to start accession negotiations in October 2005. However, despite this positive outcome, the events on the path to the October 2005 decision decreased the optimism for the EU project.

It was hard for Turkey to hear continuous intra-EU discussions about how Turkey's full membership with its poor economic conditions and predominantly Muslim population will impose a tremendous burden on the EU countries, to contemplate European arguments that Turkey has to recognize Cyprus in order to become a full member, to see the rejection of the EU Constitution by the referenda in France and Netherlands, and to witness the inability of the EU to agree over the organization's budget. All these difficulties with and within the EU clearly showed that Turkey cannot afford to consider its relations with the EU and the US as two mutually exclusive policy options in this era and that it should follow a more balanced policy towards its Western partners.[43]

Turkish political leaders once again had to acknowledge that Turkey's EU accession process would be a 'long and winding road',[44] as characterized by the late President Turgut Ozal. They realized that a weakened Turkish–American alliance was not the best foreign policy tool at hand when Turkey needs substantial support for its accession process. As a result, Turkey decided to formulate a more balanced foreign policy towards the EU and the US.

Since the initiation of its relations with the US and the EU, Turkey usually opted to turn to one of its Western allies when it felt disappointed and excluded by the other. For example, after the 1964 Johnson Letter, which stated that NATO might not defend Turkey if the Soviet Union attacked it during a possible Turkish intervention in Cyprus, and after the 1975 arms embargo, which was imposed on Turkey by the US Congress, Turkish political leaders turned to Europe and focused their attention on improving their relations with the Western European countries.[45] Likewise, in the post-cold-war period when Turkey–EU relations weakened owing to Turkey's shortcomings in its democratization and human rights records, Turkey turned to the US and built a strong strategic partnership with the latter.[46]

However, the recent developments with regard to Turkey's EU membership process changed the dynamics of this interaction. As an EU candidate, which started accession negotiations, Turkey no longer really has the luxury to suspend political dialogue and turn to the US whenever it gets frustrated by European attitudes, actions or decisions. On the other hand, Turkey cannot choose Europe over the US and disregard its relations with the US altogether because American backing and lobbying is a valuable asset for Turkey in its challenging EU accession process. This expectation is based on the positive US role in the conclusion of the 1995 customs union treaty and in the 1999 Helsinki decision to grant official candidate status to Turkey.[47] Further, the US has long had a better understanding than the European countries of Turkey's foreign policy priorities and security concerns. This was clearly seen in the Turkish–American cooperation regarding the construction of the Baku–Tbilisi–Ceyhan pipeline and the important role the US played in the capture of the PKK leader Abdullah Ocalan in 1999.[48] Therefore, Turkey will continue to need US help in its security and defence related considerations.

As a result of their need for a more balanced approach towards Turkey's relations with Europe and the US, Turkish political leaders made substantial efforts to mend the country's relations with the US in the aftermath of the 1 March 2003 decision. As mentioned above, Turkey opened its airspace to US aircraft going to Iraq, allowed transit passage of American troops via Turkey, and declared full support in the US's Greater Middle East democratization project. Turkey even agreed to send troops to Iraq to fight against the insurgency alongside the US, but this plan fell through as a result of Iraqi opposition to Turkish intervention.[49]

The fact that the US took some steps in alleviating the economic and political isolation of Turkish Cypriots such as sending a trade delegation to Turkish Cyprus in February 2005 and using Ercan Airport, which is on the Turkish side of the island, during this visit shows that there is progress in restoring the Turkish–American alliance.[50]

The future of Turkey–US–EU relations

When one looks at the current state of the Turkey–EU and Turkey–US partnerships, an obvious fact is that uncertainty surrounds Turkey's future relations with these two actors. On the one hand, Turkey made substantial progress in fulfilling the Copenhagen criteria and started accession negotiations with the EU in October 2005. On the other hand, uneasiness about the idea of Turkey's full membership still exists in the EU. First, several European leaders point out problems with Turkey's economy, democracy, human rights record and policies towards the Kurdish minority. Second, the ongoing Cyprus issue also creates obstacles in Turkey's accession process. The island of Cyprus has been divided between the Greek and Turkish sides since Turkey's military intervention in 1974.

In the latest attempt to resolve this issue, UN Secretary-General Kofi Annan proposed the Annan Plan to unify the island. This was put to referendum in April 2004; 65 per cent of the Turkish Cypriots voted in favour of it and 76 per cent of the Greek Cypriots voted *no*. In the aftermath of the referendum, European politicians were glad to see that Turkey made a substantial effort to resolve the Cyprus issue. A number of European leaders promised that they would take action to decrease the isolation of the Turkish Cypriots in the international arena. However, the Greek Cypriots entered the EU in May 2004, and the EU has failed to take serious action to alleviate the isolation of the Turkish side of the island. On the contrary, politicians such as French President Jacques Chirac and Prime Minister Dominique de Villepin stated that Turkey could not start accession negotiations and become a full EU member without resolving the issue of recognition of Cyprus. Finally, in major EU countries such as France and Germany, politicians question Turkey's Europeanness and raise doubts about the rationality of admitting a predominantly Muslim country. As an alternative to full membership, a number of European politicians such as former French President Valérie Giscard d'Estaing, German Chancellor Angela Merkel and French Interior Minister Nicolas Sarkozy suggest that Turkey should have a 'privileged partnership' with the EU.

Concerning the future of Turkey's alliance with the US, there has been considerable improvement in Turkish–American relations since Turkey's rejection of American troop deployments and disagreements over subsequent events in Iraq. Turkish Prime Minister Tayyip Erdogan's recent visits to the US and his support for the US's Greater Middle East democratization project were welcomed by the US. The American opening to the Turkish Cypriots in order to help ease their economic and political isolation strengthened this positive atmosphere as did Secretary of State Condoleezza Rice's telephone calls to the European leaders when they were discussing the initiation of accession negotiations with Turkey in October 2005.

However, this does not guarantee a problem-free Turkish–American alliance in the future. There are several areas of potential disagreement between Turkey and the US policy. First, any number of problems can be envisioned with the Kurdish population in Turkey and in Iraq. Indeed, Turkey is lukewarm about the role of the Kurds in the future of Iraq and its possible implications for Turkey's Kurdish minority. A number of Turkish politicians and military officers believe that an independent Kurdish state in the region will result in an increase in the Kurdish separatist sentiments in Turkey and a subsequent rise in PKK terrorism.[51]

These concerns reflect a long and bloody history. Turkey fought against the PKK from 1984 to 1999, until the organization's leader Abdullah Ocalan was captured in Kenya. The PKK, which caused more than 35,000 deaths in Turkey, declared a cease-fire after Ocalan's capture. However, this cease-fire was renounced in June 2004.[52] According to some estimates, around 1200–2000 PKK militants have entered Turkey from Iraq since the end of this cease-fire and they have carried out 109 attacks.[53] As a result, Turkey is concerned about the recurrence of PKK terrorism and has asked the US to take action against the PKK militants in northern Iraq, including arresting the organization's leadership cadres.

However, the US has different interests in Iraq and has not done much to help Turkey fight the PKK. In turn, Turkish political and military leaders are concerned about the lack of an effective US policy initiative against the PKK, and some have argued that Turkey has the right to carry out trans-border operations in order to combat the PKK.[54] Others are beginning to consider what additional steps can be taken to adjust to the new reality of a strong Kurdish political presence in northern Iraq. This situation has important implications for Turkish–American relations because Turkish public opinion is increasingly blaming the US for the recurring PKK violence since it is the US military, working with Kurdish militias and Kurds in Iraqi uniforms, that operate in and control northern Iraq now.[55] Moreover, if Turkey decides to conduct trans-border operations in northern Iraq, this could vastly complicate matters with both the US and the Iraqi government.

Second, Turkey and the US disagree on how to deal with Syria and Iran. Although both the US and Turkey are in favour of democratization in these countries, they promote different ways of achieving this objective. Turkey endorses a policy of engagement mainly because it is a neighbour of Iran and Syria and has trade relations with these countries. Moreover, Turkey knows that Syria and Iran's cooperation could be helpful in Turkey's fight against PKK terrorism since both Iran and Syria have Kurdish minority populations and they share Turkey's concerns about the possibility of an independent Kurdish state in the region.[56] In contrast to the Turkish position, the US pursues a policy of isolation and forceful action, if necessary, towards Syria and Iran and has been applying economic sanctions against these countries. Such divergence in the American and Turkish attitudes became evident when the US tried to prevent Turkish President Ahmet Necdet Sezer's visit to Syria in summer 2005.[57] These examples show that the Turkish–American alliance will in the future continue to experience obstacles that are due to differences in their foreign policy attitudes.

What kind of a policy should Turkey develop towards the EU and the US in the months and years to come? Without a doubt, Turkey should make a concurrent effort to improve its relations with both the EU and the US. Although Turkey is disappointed with the arguments of several European leaders against Turkey's membership, it is important to keep in mind that Turkey's EU project is a 'civilizing mission' for the country's leaders to bring Turkey into the ranks of the Western developed nations.[58] It is possible that Turkey's commitment to the West may backslide, either because Europe becomes more polarized and/or because Turkey itself becomes less committed to Western values. We do not believe this is in the best interests of anyone.

The most fitting way to respond to the challenges against Turkey's accession process is to develop Turkey economically and politically and to change the European image that Turkey's membership will bring more burden than benefit to the EU. In order to achieve this goal, the Turkish political elites should continue with the EU harmonization reforms, which played a very important role in the decision to open accession negotiations with Turkey in October 2005. On the other hand, during this process, Turkey should also try to improve its relations with the US. There is no doubt that a strong Turkish–American alliance is in the interests of both of these countries. Despite certain differences in policies,

Turkey and the US share similar interests in issues such as bringing stability and democracy to the Middle East, the Caucasus and Central Asia, taking advantage of the energy resources of the Caspian basin, and showing that Islam is compatible with democracy and modernity. Moreover, a close relationship with the US can be a strong bargaining tool for Turkey in its EU accession negotiations and in its attempts to solve the Cyprus issue. Although it is highly likely that Turkey's EU membership will move Turkish foreign policy away from the US and bring it closer to some European positions, a Turkey which is firmly anchored to the West is in the best interests of the US.[59] It is also true that the common interests between the US and EU far outweigh their differences, and that these common interests are only likely to grow. Thus, in the following months and years, Turkey should avoid seeing its relations with the US and the EU as mutually exclusive and should give its full attention to improving its relationship with both of these Western partners.

Notes

1. F. Stephen Larrabee and Ian O. Lesser, *Turkish Foreign Policy in an Age of Uncertainty* (Santa Monica, CA: Rand, 2003), p. 45.
2. Soli Ozel, 'It Truly Is a Long and Winding Road: The Saga of EU–Turkey Relations', in *AICGS/DAAD Working Paper Series: Turkey and the European Union* (2004), p. 3.
3. Larrabee and Lesser, *Turkish Foreign Policy in an Age of Uncertainty*, pp. 159–62. Also see Cagri Erhan, 'Main Trends in Ottoman–American Relations', in Mustafa Aydin and Cagri Erhan, eds, *Turkish–American Relations: Past, Present and Future* (New York: Routledge, 2004), pp. 3–25.
4. For the full text of the 1964 Johnson Letter, see 'Correspondence Between President Johnson and Prime Minister Inonu, June 1964, as Released by the White House, 15 January 1966', *Middle East Journal* 20 (1966), 3: 386–93.
5. Yalim Eralp, 'An Insider's View of Turkey's Foreign Policy and Its American Connection', in Morton Abramowitz, ed., *The United States and Turkey: Allies in Need* (New York: Century Foundation Press, 2003), pp. 110–11; George S. Harris, 'U.S.–Turkish Relations', in Alan Makovsky and Sabri Sayari, eds, *Turkey's New World: Changing Dynamics in Turkish Foreign Policy* (Washington, DC: Washington Institute for Near East Policy, 2000), pp. 192–6; Heinz Kramer, *A Changing Turkey: The Challenge to Europe and the United States* (Washington, DC: Brookings Institution Press, 2000), p. 224.
6. Atilla Eralp, 'Turkey and the European Union in the Post-Cold War Era', in Makovsky and Sayari, *Turkey's New World: Changing Dynamics in Turkish Foreign Policy* (Washington, DC: Washington Institute for Near East Policy, 2000), p. 173.
7. Ibid.
8. Ibid., see also Larrabee and Lesser, *Turkish Foreign Policy in an Age of Uncertainty*, p. 49.
9. Michael M. Gunter, 'The U.S.–Turkish Alliance in Disarray', *World Affairs* 167 (2005), 3: 113–23.

10. Kristin Archick, 'European Union Enlargement', *CRS Report for Congress* (7 March 2005), p. 6; Engin Soysal, 'US, EU and Turkey', Center for Strategic and International Studies, http://www.csis.org/media/csis/events/050404_summary.pdf, p. 1; Marc Grossman, 'Americans Should be Ready if the EU Misses its Chance with Turkey', *Financial Times* (16 September 2005).
11. Morton Abramowitz, 'The Complexities of American Policymaking on Turkey', in Morton Abramowitz, ed., *Turkey's Transformation and American Foreign Policy* (New York: Century Foundation Press, 2000), p. 159; Alan Makovsky, 'U.S. Policy Toward Turkey: Progress and Problems', in Abramowitz, *Turkey's Transformation and American Foreign Policy*, p. 245; Morton Abramowitz, 'Introduction: The United States and Turkey: New Opportunities, Old Problems', in Abramowitz, *The United States and Turkey*, p. 17; Cengiz Candar, 'The Post-September 11 United States Through Turkish Lenses', in Abramowitz, *The United States and Turkey*, pp. 169–70; Henry J. Barkey, 'The Endless Pursuit: Improving U.S.–Turkish Relations' in Abramowitz, *The United States and Turkey*, p. 216; Ozel, 'It Truly is a Long and Winding Road', p. 8; F. Stephen Larrabee, 'American Perspectives on Turkey and Turkish-EU Relations', in *AICGS/DAAD Working Paper Series: Turkey and the European Union* (2004), pp. 26–7; 'The Effects of the Iraq War on the U.S.–Turkish Relationship', Transcript, Council on Foreign Relations (6 May 2003), http://www.cfr.org/publication/6024/effects_of_the_iraq_war_on_the_us_turkish_relationship.html
12. David L. Phillips, 'Turkey's Dreams of Accession', *Foreign Affairs* 83 (2004), 5: 86–97; Ziya Onis and Suhnaz Yılmaz, 'The Turkey–EU–US Triangle in Perspective: Transformation or Continuity?', *Middle East Journal* 59 (2005), 2: 265–85; 'Cook: Despite Some European Qualms, Turkey Will Eventually Join the EU' (5 October 2004), Council on Foreign Relations, http://www.cfr.org/publication/7427/cook.html
13. All figures are from the International Institute for Strategic Studies, *The Military Balance, 2005–2006* (London, IISS 2005), pp. 98, 191, 188, 209, 158 and 71 in order of the countries given in table.
14. Kemal Kirisci, 'Between Europe and the Middle East: The Transformation of Turkish Policy', *Middle East Review of International Affairs* 8 (2004), 1: 39–51 pp. 42, 47.
15. Cited in Candar, 'The Post-September 11 United States Through Turkish Lenses', p. 170.
16. Abramowitz, 'The Complexities of American Policymaking on Turkey', p. 179; Eralp, 'An Insider's View of Turkey's Foreign Policy and Its American Connection', p. 117; Barkey, 'The Endless Pursuit: Improving U.S.–Turkish Relations', p. 215; Makovsky, 'U.S. Policy Toward Turkey: Progress and Problems', p. 245.
17. Murat Yetkin, 'Sizden Beklentimiz AB Yolunda Basarili Sonuc' (Our Expectation from You is Successful Outcome on the Path to the EU), *Radikal* (18 May 2005); Erdal Guven, 'Ya ABD Ya AB mi? Yok Oyle Bir Sey' (Either the USA or EU? There Is Nothing Like That), *Radikal* (15 March 2002); Omer Taspinar, 'AB'nin Esnek Geometrisi' (EU's Flexible Geometry), *Radikal* (3 May 2005); Kramer, *A Changing Turkey*, pp. 195, 198; Cengiz Candar, 'Some Turkish Perspectives on the United States and American Policy Toward Turkey', in Abramowitz, *Turkey's Transformation and American Foreign Policy*,

pp. 148–9; Onis and Yılmaz, 'The Turkey–EU–US Triangle in Perspective: Transformation or Continuity?'; Barkey, 'The Endless Pursuit: Improving U.S.–Turkish Relations', pp. 215–16.

18. Michael S. Teitelbaum and Philip L. Martin, 'Is Turkey Ready for Europe?', *Foreign Affairs* 82 (2003), 3: 97–111, http://www.foreignaffairs.org/20030501faessay11222/michael-s-teitelbaum-philip-l-martin/is-turkey-ready-for-europe.html; 'Turks Look West; Will It Look Away?', *New York Times* (13 December 2002); 'Bush: AB Icin Omuz Omuza' (Bush: Shoulder to Shoulder for the EU), *Radikal* (11 December 2002); 'Bush–Erdogan Gorusmesinde Ilginc Diyaloglar' (Interesting Diologues in Bush–Erdogan Meeting), *Radikal* (11 December 2002); 'Baskan Bush Verdigi Sozu Tuttu' (President Bush Kept the Promise He Made), *Radikal* (12 December 2002).

19. 'Rice'a Sukran Sunuldu' (Gratitude Was Presented to Rice), *Radikal* (6 October 2005).

20. Abramowitz, 'The Complexities of American Policymaking on Turkey', p. 180; Larrabee, 'American Perspectives on Turkey and Turkish–EU Relations', p. 27.

21. William Safire, 'Beware of Certitude', *New York Times* (30 June 2004). Also see Onis and Yilmaz, 'The Turkey–EU–US Triangle in Perspective: Transformation or Continuity?'; Mike Allen, 'Bush Chides U.S. Allies on Mideast; In Speech, He Exhorts Move to Democracy', *Washington Post* (30 June 2004).

22. Cited in Omer Taspinar, 'Changing Parameters in U.S.–German–Turkish Relations', *AICGS Policy Report*, 18 (16 February 2005), pp. 27–8, American Institute for Contemporary German Studies, http://www.brookings.edu/fp/cuse/analysis/taspinar20050216.htm

23. 'Turkish–U.S. Relations', http://www.turkishembassy.org/governmentpolitics/regionsnorthamerica.htm; see also Mark Parris, 'Starting Over: U.S.–Turkish Relations in the Post-Iraq War Era', *PolicyWatch* 732 (26 March 2003), Washington Institute for Near East Policy, www.washingtoninstitute.org/media/parris/parris0403.htm; 'The Effects of the Iraq War on the U.S.–Turkish Relationship'; Serkan Demirtas, 'Portre: Turk–Amerikan Iliskileri' (Portrait: Turkish–American Relations), *Radikal* (13 June 2005); Bulent Aliriza, 'Turkiye ve ABD Yeni Arayista' (Turkey and the USA Are in a New Search), *Radikal* (8 June 2003).

24. Gandar, 'The Post-September 11 United States through Turkish Lenses', p. 152; Helena Kane Finn, 'Turkey and the War on Iraq: It isn't Just About Money', Council on Foreign Relations Presentation (20 February 2003), http://www.cfr.org/publication.html?id=5540; featuring Lt Gen. Ethem Erdagi, 'The ISAF Mission and Turkey's Role in Rebuilding the Afghan State', *PolicyWatch* 1052 (18 November 2005), Washington Institute for Near East Policy, http://www.washingtoninstitute.org/templateC05.php?CID=2403

25. The Turkish Grand National Assembly voted 264–250 in favour of the motion. However, because of the 19 abstentions, the 'yes' votes could not form the absolute majority of the representatives who participated in the voting process.

26. Dexter Filkins, 'Turkey Says U.S. Has Detained Some of Its Soldiers in North Iraq', *New York Times* (6 July 2003); Max Boot, 'West Should Welcome Turkey', *Los Angeles Times* (16 December 2004), http://www1.cfr.org/pub7566/max_boot/west_should_welcome_turkey.php; Mark Parris, 'Allergic

Partners: Can U.S.–Turkish Relations Be Saved?', *Turkish Policy Quarterly* 4 (2005), 1: 49–58; Mark Parris, 'U.S.–Turkish Relations', *Testimony Before the House Committee on International Relations*, http://www.washingtoninstitute.org/templateC07.php?_CID=240; Murat Yetkin, 'Irak'ta Tehlikeli Gelismeler' (Dangerous Developments in Iraq), *Radikal* (11 September 2004).

27. Omer Taspinar, 'The Turkish Turnaround', *The Daily Times* (14 October 2003); 'The Effects of the Iraq War on the U.S.–Turkish Relationship', Transcript, Council on Foreign Relations (6 May 2003).

28. 'Cook: Despite Some European Qualms, Turkey Will Eventually Join the EU'; Bulent Aliriza, 'Seeking Redefinition: U.S.–Turkish Relations After Iraq', *CSIS Turkey Update* (5 June 2003); Gunter, 'The U.S.–Turkish Alliance in Disarray', p. 119; Onis and Yılmaz, 'The Turkey–EU–US Triangle in Perspective: Transformation or Continuity?'

29. Max Boot, 'West Should Welcome Turkey'; Gunter, 'The U.S.–Turkish Alliance in Disarray', 119.

30. Onis and Yılmaz, 'The Turkey–EU–US Triangle in Perspective: Transformation or Continuity?'; Mark Parris, 'Allergic Partners: Can U.S.–Turkish Relations be Saved?', *Turkish Policy Quarterly* 4 (2005), 1, http://turkishpolicy.com/default.asp?show=spr_2005_Parris

31. 'Turkey Lets US Use Its Airspace' (21 March 2003), http://news.bbc.co.uk/2/hi/europe/2871817.stm; 'Incirlik Permission Granted Days Ago', *Turkish Daily News* (26 April 2005); Murat Yetkin, 'Turkiye Uzerinden Gizli Operasyonlar' (Clandestine Operations Through Turkey), *Radikal* (15 May 2005).

32. Harmonization Package – 59th Government, http://www.byegm.gov.tr/on-sayfa/uyum/uyum-ingilizce-59hukumet.htm

33. Available at http://www.worldhistoryplus.com/e/europeanUnion.html; Bruce Kuniholm, 'Turkey's Accession to the European Union: Differences in European and US Attitudes, and Challenges for Turkey', *Turkish Studies* 2 (2001), 1: 30.

34. Eralp, 'An Insider's View of Turkey's Foreign Policy and Its American Connection', p. 134.

35. Ibid., p. 127; Candar, 'The Post-September 11 United States Through Turkish Lenses', p. 147.

36. Robert S. Leiken, 'Europe's Angry Muslims', *Foreign Affairs* 84 (2005), 4, http://www.foreignaffairs.org/20050701faessay84409/robert-s-leiken/europe-s-angry-muslims.html.

37. It is quite difficult to find the exact number of the Muslims living in Europe. First, several European countries do not have data on religious groups. Second, the size of the Muslim community is a sensitive issue in Europe. And third, the statistics change according to how Europe is defined. For example, including Turkey as part of Europe changes the number. Approximately 15–18 million is the number of Muslims in the 25 EU countries. See 'An Uncertain Road: Muslims and the Future of Europe', *The Pew Forum on Religion and Public Life* (October, 2005), The Pew Research Center, http:// pewforum.org/publications/reports/muslims-europe-2005.pdf, p. 3.

38. See Jeffrey Young, 'Madrid Bombing Anniversary: One Year Later', *Voice of America* (10 March 2005), http://www.globalpolicy.org/empire/terrorwar/analysis/2005/0310madridanniv.htm

39. 'Anti-Muslim Bias "Spreads" in EU', http://news.bbc.co.uk/2/hi/europe/4325225.stm; Marc Champion, 'Europe's Claim to Be a Land of Multicultural Tolerance is Being Sorely Tested', *Wall Street Journal* (15 December 2004). Also see 'Findings of the GfK Survey on Religious Attitudes in Europe', http://www.gfk.hr/press_en/religion.htm
40. 'Too Big for Europe?', *Economist* (14 November 2002); 'Turkey Entry "Would Destroy EU" ' (8 November 2002), http://news.bbc.co.uk/2/hi/europe/2420697.stm; Teintelbaum and Martin, 'Is Turkey Ready for Europe?'.
41. Soner Cagaptay, Duden Yegenoglu and Ekim Alptekin, 'Turkey and Europe's Problem with Radical Islam', *PolicyWatch* 1043 (2 November 2005), Washington Institute for Near East Policy, http://www.washingtoninstitute.org/templateC05.php?CID=2391
42. Young, 'Madrid Bombing Anniversary: One Year Later'.
43. Craig S. Smith, 'Turks, Nervous About European Prospects, Turn to U.S.', *New York Times* (11 June 2005).
44. Ozel, 'It Truly is a Long and Winding Road', p. 4.
45. Kramer, *A Changing Turkey*, p. 184.
46. Ian O. Lesser, 'Beyond "Bridge or Barrier": Turkey's Evolving Security Relations with the West' in Makovsky and Sayari, *Turkey's New World: Changing Dynamics in Turkish Foreign Policy*, p. 217; Candar, 'Some Turkish Perspectives on the United States and American Policy Toward Turkey', p. 148.
47. See Onis and Yılmaz, 'The Turkey–EU–US Triangle in Perspective: Transformation or Continuity?', and Morton Abramowitz, 'Turkey at a Crossroads', *Wall Street Journal* (29 June 2005).
48. Larrabee and Lesser, *Turkish Foreign Policy in an Age of Uncertainty*, p. 68.
49. Gunter, 'The U.S.–Turkish Alliance in Disarray', p. 121; Parris, 'Allergic Partners: Can U.S.–Turkish Relations Be Saved?'.
50. Soner Cagaptay, 'Changing Turkish Public Attitudes Toward the United States: Premises and Prospects', *PolicyWatch* 969 (7 March 2005), The Washington Institute for Near East Policy, http://www.washingtoninstitute.org/templateC05.php?CID=2272; Murat Yetkin, 'Buyuk Ortadogu'ya Evet' (Yes to the Greater Middle East), *Radikal* (9 June 2005).
51. Ozel, 'It Truly Is a Long and Winding Road', pp. 8–9.
52. Soner Cagaptay and Emrullah Uslu, 'Is the PKK a Threat to the United States and Turkey', *PolicyWatch* 940 (10 January 2005), The Washington Institute for Near East Policy, http://www.ciaonet.org/pbei/winep/policy_2005/2005_940/index.html
53. Ibid.; Murat Yetkin, 'Ankara'da PKK Asabiyeti Yukseliyor' (Anxiety over PKK is Rising in Ankara), *Radikal* (15 July 2005).
54. Yetkin, 'Ankara'da PKK Asabiyeti Yukseliyor' (Anxiety over PKK is Rising in Ankara); 'Zebari Uyardı: Irak'a Girmeyin' (Zebari Warned: Do Not Enter Iraq), *Radikal* (25 July 2005).
55. Soner Cagaptay, 'Turkey at a Crossroads: Preserving Ankara's Western Orientation', *Policy Focus* 48 (October 2005), p. 1, Washington Institute for Near East Policy, www.washingtoninstitute.org/html/pdf/CagaptayBook Web.pdf
56. See Kemal Kirisci, 'Turkey and the United States: Ambivalent Allies', *Middle East Review of International Affairs* 2 (1998), 4, http://meria.idc.ac.il/journal/1998/issue4/jv2n4a3.html; Soner Cagaptay, 'Can the U.S. Win Turkey Over in 2005? Understanding EU Dynamics and Confidence Building in Iraq',

PolicyWatch 939 (7 January 2005), Washington Institute for Near East Policy, http://www.washingtoninstitute.org/templateC05.php?CID=2216

57. 'ABD ile Yeni Kriz' (New Crisis with the USA), *Radikal* (14 March 2005).
58. Eralp, 'Turkey and the European Union in the Post-Cold War Era', p. 177.
59. For specific examples, see Morton I. Abramowitz, Richard R. Burt, Donald K. Bandler, Frances G. Burwell, William Drozdiak and Eric Melby, 'Turkey on the Threshold: Europe's Decision and U.S. Interests', *Policy Paper* (August 2004), Atlantic Council of the United States, http://www.ciaonet.org/pbei/acus/abm01/abm01.pdf, pp. 23–4.

Bibliography

Abramowitz, Morton, ed., *The United States and Turkey: Allies in Need* (New York: Century Foundation Press, 2003).

Abramowitz, Morton, ed., *Turkey's Transformation and American Foreign Policy* (New York: Century Foundation Press, 2000).

Adamson, Fiona B., 'Democratisation and the Domestic Sources of Foreign Policy: Turkey in the 1974 Cyprus Crisis', *Political Science Quarterly* 116 (2001), 2: 277–303.

Ahmad, Feroz, *Turkey: The Quest for Identity* (Oxford: Oneworld Publications, 2003).

Ahmed, Mohammed M. A. and Michael M. Gunter, eds, *Kurdish Exodus: From Internal Displacement to Diaspora* (Sharon, MA: Ahmed Foundation for Kurdish Studies, 2002).

Ahmed, Mohammed M.A. and Michael M. Gunter, eds, *The Kurdish Question and the 2003 Iraqi War* (Costa Mesa, CA: Mazda, 2005).

Arikan, Harun, *Turkey and the EU: an Awkward Candidate for EU Membership?* (Burlington: Ashgate, 2003).

Aydin, Mustafa and Cagri Erhan, eds, *Turkish–American Relations: Past, Present and Future* (New York: Routledge, 2004).

Aydin, Mustafa and Sinem Akgul Acimese, 'Waiting for December 2004: Turkish Blues for the EU', *International Spectator* 39 (2004), 3: 111–125.

Aydinli, Ersel, Nihat Ali Ozcan and Dogan Akyyaz, 'The Turkish Military's March Toward Europe', *Foreign Affairs* 85 (2006), 1: 77–90.

Bahcheli, Tozun, 'Searching for a Cyprus Settlement: Considering Options for Creating a Federation, a Confederation, or Two Independent States', *The Journal of Federalism* 30 (2000), 1–2: 203–16.

Bahcheli, Tozun, *Greek–Turkish Relations since 1955* (Boulder: Westview Press, 1995).

Balassa, Bela, ed., *European Economic Integration* (Amsterdam: North-Holland, 1975).

Baldwin, Richard E., 'Measurable Dynamic Gains from Trade', *Journal of Political Economy* 100 (1992), 1: 162–74.

Balkir, Canan and Allan M. Williams, eds, *Turkey and Europe* (London: Pinter, 1993).

Barkey, Henri J., ed., *Reluctant Neighbor: Turkey's Role in the Middle East* (Washington, DC: U.S. Institute of Peace, 1996).

Barkey, Henri J. and Graham E. Fuller, *Turkey's Kurdish Question* (New York: Rowman & Littlefield, 1998).

Borzel, Tanya, *Shaping States and Regions: The Domestic Impact of Europe* (Cambridge University Press, 2001).

Brauer, Jurgen, 'Survey and Review of the Defense Economics Literature on Greece and Turkey: What Have We Learned?', *Defence and Peace Economics* 13 (2002), 2: 85–107.

Bruinessen, Martin van, *Agha, Shaikh and State: The Social and Political Structures of Kurdistan* (London: Zed, 1992).

Çarkoğlu, Ali and Barry Rubin, eds, *Turkey and the European Union: Domestic Politics, Economic Integration and International Dynamics* (London: Frank Cass, 2003).

Chaliand, Gerard, ed., *A People without a Country: The Kurds and Kurdistan* (New York: Olive Branch, 1993).

Christou, George, *The European Union and Enlargement: The Case of Cyprus* (London: Palgrave Macmillan, 2005).

Clarke, George R.G., 'How the Quality of Institutions Affects Technological Deepening in Developing Countries', Policy Research Working Paper No. 2603, Washington, DC, World Bank (2001).

Constas, Dimitris, ed., *The Greek–Turkish Conflict in the 1990s: Domestic and External Influences* (New York: St Martin's Press, 1991).

Couloumbis, Theodore, *The United States, Greece and Turkey: The Troubled Triangle* (New York: Praeger, 1983).

Dervis, Kemal, Daniel Gros, Faik Oztrak and Yusuf Isik, 'Turkey and the EU Budget: Prospects and Issues', Centre for European Policy Studies, EU–Turkey Working Paper No. 6 (2004).

Diez, Tomas, ed., *The European Union and the Cyprus Conflict: Modern Conflict, Postmodern Union* (Manchester University Press, 2002).

Droutsas, Dimitris and Panayotis Tsakonas, 'Turkey's Road Map to the European Union: Implications for Greek–Turkish Relations and the Cyprus Issue', *Hellenic Studies* 9 (2001), 1: 77–100.

Eagleton, William, Jr, *The Kurdish Republic of 1946* (London: Oxford University Press, 1963).

Entessar, Nader, *Kurdish Ethnonationalism* (Boulder: Lynne Rienner, 1992).

Featherstone, Kevin and George Kazamias, eds, *Europeanization and the Southern Periphery* (Portland: Frank Cass, 2001).

Featherstone, Kevin and Claudio M. Radaelli, eds, *The Politics of Europeanization* (Oxford: Oxford University Press, 2003).

Fernandez, Raquel, 'Returns to Regionalism: an Evaluation of Non-Traditional Gains from Regional Trade Arrangements', Brussels, Centre for European Policy Studies, Working Paper No. 1634 (1997).

Fisher, Ronald, 'Cyprus: The failure of Mediation and the Escalation of an Identity-based Conflict to an Adversarial Impasse', *Journal of Peace Research* 38 (2001), 3: 307–26.

Frankel, Jeffrey and Andrew Rose, 'An Estimate of the Effect of Common Currencies on Trade and Income', *Quarterly Journal of Economics* 117 (2002), 2: 437–66.

Gellner, Ernest, *Nations and Nationalism* (Ithaca, NY: Cornell University Press, 1983).

Ghareeb, Edmund, *The Kurdish Question in Iraq* (Syracuse, NY: Syracuse University, 1981).

Gill, Stephen, 'European Governance and New Constitutionalism: Economic and Monetary Union and Alternatives to Disciplinary Neoliberalism in Europe', *New Political Economy* 3 (1998), 1: 5–26.

Green Cowles, Maria, James Caporaso and Thomas Risse, eds, *Transforming Europe: Europeanization and domestic change* (Ithaca, NY: Cornell University Press, 2001).

Griffiths, Richard T. and Durmus Ozdemir, *Turkey and the EU Enlargement: Processes of Incorporation* (Istanbul Bilgi University Press, 2004).

Gulnur, Aybet and Meltem Muftuler-BAC, 'Transformations in Security and Identity after the Cold War: Turkey's Problematic Relationship with Europe', *International Journal* 55 (2000), 4: 567–82.

Gunduz, Aslan, 'Human rights and Turkey's Future in Europe', *Orbis* 45 (2001), 1: 15–30.

Guney, Aylin, 'The USA's Role in Mediating the Cyprus Conflict: A Story of Success or Failure?', *Security Dialogue* 35 (2004), 1: 27–42.

Gunter, Michael M., 'The U.S.–Turkish Alliance in Disarray', *World Affairs* 167 (2005), 3: 113–23.

Gunter, Michael M., *The Kurdish Predicament in Iraq: A Political Analysis* (New York: St Martin's Press, 1999).

Gunter, Michael M., *The Kurds of Iraq: Tragedy and Hope* (New York: St Martin's Press, 1992).

Gunter, Michael M., *The Kurds and the Future of Turkey* (New York: St Martin's Press, 1997).

Haas, Peter M., 'Compliance with EU Directives: Insights from International Relations and Comparative Politics', *Journal of European Public Policy* 5 (1998), 1: 17–37.

Hall, Robert E. and Charles I. Jones, 'Why Do Some Countries Produce so Much More Output per Worker than Others?', *Quarterly Journal of Economics* 114 (1999), 1: 83–116.

Halliday, Fred, *The Middle East in International Relations: Power, Politics and Ideology* (Cambridge University Press, 2005).

Harrison, Glenn W., Thomas W. Rutherford and David G. Tarr, *Economic Implications for Turkey of a Customs Union with the European Union* (Washington, DC: World Bank, 1996).

Hassanpour, Amir, *Nationalism and Language in Kurdistan, 1918–1985* (San Francisco, CA: Mellen Research University Press, 1992).

Izady, Mehrdad, *The Kurds: A Concise Handbook* (Washington, DC: Crane Russak, 1992).

Jawad, Sa'ad, *Iraq and the Kurdish Question, 1958–1970* (London: Ithaca, 1981).

Joseph, Joseph S., 'The Cyprus Problem, the EU and the Annan Plan', in Thomas Giegerich, ed., *The EU Accession of Cyprus: Key to the Political and Legal Solution of an 'Insoluble Ethnic Conflict?'* (Baden-Baden: Nomos, 2006), pp. 189–97.

Joseph, Joseph S., *Cyprus: Ethnic Conflict and International Politics, from Independence to the Threshold of the European Union* (London: Macmillan, 1997).

Joseph, Joseph S., 'Leaving the EU Door Ajar for Turkey', *Hellenic Studies* 12 (2004), 2: 31–40.

Joseph, Joseph S., 'The Spill-Over Effect of Cross-Boundary Ethnic Bonds in a Conflict Situation: The Greek-Cypriot–Turkish Triangle', *Thetis* 3 (1996), pp. 311–24.

Jung, Dietrich (with Wolfango Piccoli), *Turkey at the Crossroads: Ottoman Legacies and a Greater Middle East* (London: Zed Books, 2001).

Kagan, Robert, *Of Paradise and Power: America and Europe in the New World Order* (New York: Random House, 2003).

Kaldor, Mary, *Global Civil Society: An Answer to War* (Cambridge: Polity Press, 2003).

Kalyvas, Stathis, *The Rise of Christian Democracy in Europe* (Ithaca, NY: Cornell University Press, 1996).

Kardam, N., *Turkey's Engagement with Global Women's Human Rights* (Burlington, VT: Ashgate, 2005).

Keohane, Robert O. and Helen V. Milner, eds, *Internationalization and Domestic Politics* (Cambridge University Press, 1996).

Ker-Lindsay, James, 'Remaining Engaged: Turkish–US Relations in the Post-Iraq Era', *Hellenic Studies*, 12 (2004), 1: 91–106.

Keridis, Dimitris and Dimitris Triantafillou, eds, *Greek–Turkish Relations in the Era of Globalization* (Washington, DC: Brassey's, 2001).

Kerim Yildiz, *The Kurds in Syria: The Forgotten People* (London: Pluto Press, 2005).

Kibaroglu, Mustafa, 'Clash of Interest over Northern Iraq Drives Turkish–Israeli Alliance to a Crossroads', *Middle East Journal* 59 (2005), 2: 246–64.

Kinzer, Stephen, *Crescent and Star: Turkey Between Two Worlds* (New York: Farrar, Strauss and Giroux, 2001).

Kirisci, Kemal, 'Between Europe and the Middle East: The Transformation of Turkish Policy', *Middle East Review of International Affairs* 8 (2004), 1: 39–51.

Kirisci, Kemal, 'The Enduring Rivalry between Greece and Turkey: Can *Democratic Peace* Break It?', *Alternatives* 1 (2002), 1: 38–50.

Kirisci, Kemal, 'The December 2004 European Council Decision on Turkey: Is It an Historical Turning Point?', *Middle East Review of International Affairs* 8 (2004), 4: 39–51.

Kirisci, Kemal and Gareth M. Winrow, *The Kurdish Question and Turkey: An Example of a Trans-State Ethnic Conflict* (London: Frank Cass, 1997).

Knill, Christoph, *The Europeanisation of National Administrations* (Cambridge University Press, 2001).

Kollias, Christos, 'The Greek–Turkish Conflict and Greek Military Expenditure, 1960–1992', *Journal of Peace Research* 33 (1996), 3: 217–28.

Koohi-Kamali, Farideh, *The Political Development of the Kurds in Iran: Pastoral Nationalism* (New York: Palgrave Macmillan, 2003).

Kramer, Heinz, *A Changing Turkey: The Challenge to Europe and the United States* (Washington, DC: Brookings Institution Press, 2000).

Krebs, Ronald R., 'Perverse Institutionalism: NATO and the Greco-Turkish Conflict', *International Organization* 53 (1999), 3: 343–77.

Kreyenbroek, Philip G. and Stefan Sperl, eds, *The Kurds: A Contemporary Overview* (London: Routledge, 1992).

Lake, Michael, ed., *The EU and Turkey: A Glittering Prize or a Millstone?* (London: Federal Trust for Education and Research, 2005).

Larrabee, F. Stephen and Ian O. Lesser, *Turkish Foreign Policy in an Age of Uncertainty* (Santa Monica, CA: Rand, 2003).

Larrabee, Stephen, 'The EU Needs to Rethink Its Cyprus Policy' *Survival* 40 (1998), 3: 25–29.

Lejour, Arjan M., Ruud A. de Mooij and Clem H. Capel, 'Assessing the Economic Implications of Turkish Accession to the EU', The Hague, CPB Netherlands Bureau for Economic Policy Analysis, Working Paper No. 56 (2004).

Lewis, Bernard, *The Emergence of Modern Turkey*, 2nd edn (London: Oxford University Press, 1968).

Lohrmann, Astrid-Marina, 'Development Effects of the Customs Union between Turkey and the European Union', *Russian and East European Finance and Trade* 36 (2000), 4: 26–44.

Loizides, Neophytos, 'Crisis Management in the Eastern Mediterranean', *Hellenic Studies* 12 (2004), 1: 39–56.

Loizides, Neophytos, 'Greek–Turkish Dilemmas and the Cyprus EU Accession Process', *Security Dialogue* 33 (2002), 4: 429–42.

Makovsky, Alan and Sabri Sayari, eds, *Turkey's New World: Changing Dynamics in Turkish Foreign Policy* (Washington DC: Washington Institute for Near East Policy, 2000).

Mango, Andrew, *The Turks Today* (London: John Murray, 2004).

McDowall, David, *A Modern History of the Kurds* (London: Tauris, 1996).

Mehmet, Ozay, *Islamic Identity and Development: Studies of the Islamic Periphery* (London: Routledge, 1990).

Meho, Lokman I., compiler, *The Kurds and Kurdistan: A Selective and Annotated Bibliography* (Westport, CT: Greenwood, 1997).

Meho, Lokman I. and Kelly L. Maglaughlin, compilers, *Kurdish Culture and Society: An Annotated Bibliography* (Westport, CT: Greenwood, 2001).

Morris, Chris, *The New Turkey: The Quiet Revolution on the Edge of Europe* (London: Granta Books, 2005).

Moustakis, Fotios, *Greek–Turkish Relationship and NATO* (New York: Frank Cass, 2003).

Moustakis, Fotios and Rudra Chudhuri, 'Turkish–Kurdish Relations and the European Union: An Unprecedented Shift in the Kemalist Paradigm?', *Mediterranean Quarterly* 16 (2005), 4: 77–89.

Moustakis, Fotios and Michael Sheehan, 'Democratic Peace and the European Security Community: The Paradox of Greece and Turkey', *Mediterranean Quarterly* 13 (2002), 1: 69–85.

Muftuler-BAC, Meltem, 'The Never-Ending Story: Turkey and the European Union', *Middle Eastern Studies* 34 (1998), 4: 240–58.

Mutlu, Servet, 'Ethnic Kurds in Turkey: A Demographic Study', *International Journal of Middle East Studies* 28 (1996), 4: 517–41.

Nachmani, Amikam, *Turkey: Facing a New Millennium: Coping with Intertwined Conflicts* (Manchester University Press, 2003).

Nugent, Neill, 'EU Enlargement and the Cyprus Problem', *Journal of Common Market Studies* 38 (2000), 1: 131–50.

O'Ballance, Edgar, *The Kurdish Revolt, 1961–1970* (Hamden, CT: Archon, 1973).

Oguzlu, Tarik, 'Is the Latest Turkish–Greek Détente Promising for the Future?', *European Security* 12 (2003), 2: 45–62.

O'Leary, Brendan, John McGarry and Khaled Salih, eds, *The Future of Kurdistan in Iraq* (Philadelphia: University of Pennsylvania Press, 2005).

Olson, Robert, ed., *The Kurdish Nationalist Movement in the 1990s: Its Impact on Turkey and the Middle East* (University Press of Kentucky, 1996).

Olson, Robert, *The Emergence of Kurdish Nationalism and the Sheikh Said Rebellion 1880–1925* (Austin: University of Texas Press, 1989).

Onis, Ziya, 'Turkey, Europe and Paradoxes of Identity: Perspectives on the International Context of Democratization', *Mediterranean Quarterly* 10 (1999), 3: 109–36.

Onis, Ziya and Suhnaz Yilmaz, 'The Turkey–EU–US Triangle in Perspective: Transformation or Continuity?', *Middle East Journal* 59 (2005), 2: 265–84.

Ozbudun, Ergun, *Contemporary Turkish Politics: Challenges to Democratic Consolidation* (Boulder: Lynne Rienner, 2000).

Ozdalga, Elisabeth, *The Veiling Issue: Official Secularism and Popular Islam in Modern Turkey* (Surrey, UK: Curzon Press, 1998).

Ozkececi-Taner, Binnur, 'The Impact of Institutionalized Ideas in Coalition Foreign Policy Making: Turkey as an Example, 1991–2002', *Foreign Policy Analysis* 1 (2005), 3: 249–78.

Pettifer, James, *The Turkish Labyrinth: Atatürk and the New Islam* (London: Penguin, 1998).

Phillips, David L., 'Turkey's Dreams of Accession', *Foreign Affairs* 83 (2004), 5: 86–97.

Pope, Nicole, and Hugh Pope, *Turkey Unveiled: A History of Modern Turkey*, 2nd edn (Woodstock, NY: Overlook Press, 2004).

Prodromou, Elizabeth, 'Reintegrating Cyprus: The Need for a New Approach', *Survival* 40 (1998), 3: 5–24.

Psomiades, Harry, *The Eastern Question: The Last Phase. A Study in Greek–Turkish Diplomacy* (New York: Pella, 2000).

Riemer, Andrea, 'The Long and Winding Road of EU–Turkish Relations after Copenhagen', *Hellenic Studies* 11 (2003), 1: 57–78.

Risse, Thomas, Stephen C. Ropp and Kathryn Sikkink, eds, *The Power of Human Rights: International Norms and Domestic Change* (Cambridge University Press, 1999).

Robins, Philip, 'Confusion at Home, Confusion Abroad: Turkey between Copenhagen and Iraq', *International Affairs* 79 (2003), 3: 547–66.

Rodrik, Dani, Arvind Subramanian and Francesco Trebbi, 'Institutions Rule: The Primacy of Institutions over Geography and Integration in Economic Development', *Journal of Economic Growth* 9 (2004), 2: 131–65.

Rumelili, Bahar, 'Liminality and Perpetuation of Conflicts: Turkish–Greek Relations in the Context of Community Building by the EU', *European Journal of International Relations* 9 (2003), 3: 213–48.

Sajoo, Amyn B. ed., *Civil Society in the Muslim World: Contemporary Perspectives* (London: Tauris, 2002).

Samatar, Ahmed I., *Hybrid Geographies in the Eastern Mediterranean: Views from Bosphorus* (St Paul, MN: Macalester College, 2005).

Schimmelfenning, Frank and Ulrich Sedelmeier, eds, *The Europeanization of Central and Eastern Europe* (Ithaca, NY: Cornell University Press, 2005).

Shankland, David, *Islam and Society in Turkey* (Huntingdon: Eothen Press, 1999).

Siegl, Erik, 'Greek–Turkish Relations: Continuity or Change?', *Perspectives: Central European Review of International Affairs* 18 (2002): 40–52.

Smith, Ron, Martin Sola and Fabio Spagnilo, 'The Prisoner's Dilemma and the Greek–Turkish Arms Race', *Journal of Peace Research* 37 (2000), 6: 737–50.

Smolny, Werner, 'Macroeconomic Consequences of International Labour Migration: Simulation Experience from an Econometric Disequilibrium Model', in Hans-Jurgen Vosgerau, ed., *European Integration in the World Economy* (Berlin: Springer, 1991), pp. 376–412.

Stansfield, Gareth, *Iraqi Kurdistan: Political Development and Emergent Democracy* (London: Routledge Curzon, 2003).

Storesletten, Kjetil, 'Fiscal Implications of Immigration: a Net Present Value Calculation', *Scandinavian Journal of Economics* 105 (2003), 3: 487–506.

Straubhaar, Thomas and Rene Webber, 'On the Economics of Immigration: Some Empirical Evidence from Switzerland', *International Review of Applied Economics* 8 (1994), 2: 107–29.

Talmon, Stefan, 'The Cyprus Question before the European Court of Justice', *European Journal of International Relations* 12 (2001), 4: 727–50.

Taspinar, Omer, *Kurdish Nationalism and Political Islam in Turkey: Kemalist Identity in Transition* (New York: Routledge, 2005).

Teintelbaum, Michael S. and Philip L. Martin, 'Is Turkey Ready for Europe?', *Foreign Affairs* 82 (2003) 3: 97–111.

Tocci, Nathalie, 'Europeanization in Turkey: Trigger or Anchor for Reform?', *South East European Politics and Society* 10 (2005), 1: 73–83.

Tocci, Nathalie, *EU Accession Dynamics and Conflict Resolution: Catalysing Peace or Consolidating Partition in Cyprus?* (Aldershot: Ashgate, 2004).

Tocci, Nathalie, 'Anchoring Turkey to the EU: Domestic and Foreign Policy Challenges', *Hellenic Studies* 12 (2004), 1: 107–22.

Togan, Subidey, 'Turkey: towards EU Accession', *World Economy* 27 (2004), 7: 1013–46.

Triantaphyllou, Dimitrios, 'Greek–Turkish Relations: Problems for Europe', *Hellenic Studies* 12 (2004), 1: 75–90.

Tsakonas, Panayotis, 'Turkey's Post-Helsinki Turbulence: Implications for Greece and the Cyprus Issue', *Turkish Studies* 2 (2001), 2: 1–40.

Ugur, Mehmet and Nergis Canefe, eds, *Turkey and European Integration: Accession Prospects and Issues* (London: Routledge, 2004).

Ugur, Mehmet, *The European Union and Turkey: An Anchor-Credibility Dilemma* (Aldershot: Ashgate, 1999).

Veremis, Thanos, 'The Transformation of Turkey's Security Considerations', *International Spectator* 40 (2005), 2: 75–84.

Viner, Jacob, *The Customs Union Issue* (New York: Carnegie Endowment for International Peace, 1950).

Vojtech, Mastny and R. Craig Nation, eds, *Turkey Between East and West: New Challenges for a Rising Regional Power* (Boulder, CO: Westview Press, 1996).

White, Paul, *Primitive Rebels or Revolutionary Modernizers? The Kurdish National Movement in Turkey* (London: Zed, 2001).

Yavuz, M. Hakan, '*Provincial* not *Ethnic* Federalism in Iraq', *Middle East Policy* 11 (Spring 2004), pp. 126–31.

Yildiz, Kerim, *The Kurds in Iraq: The Past, Present and Future* (London: Pluto Press, 2004).

Yildiz, Kerim, *The Kurds in Turkey: EU Accession and Human Rights* (London: Pluto Press, 2005).

Zahariadis, Nicholaos, 'A Framework for Improving Greek–Turkish Relations', *Mediterranean Quarterly* 11 (2000), 4: 98–116.

Zeff, Eleanor and Ellen Pirro, eds, *The European Union and the Member States: Cooperation, Coordination and Compromise* (Boulder, CO: Lynne Rienner, 2001).

Zurcher, Eric J., *Turkey: A Modern History*, 3rd edn (London: Tauris, 2004).

Index

Notes: n = note; t = table; **bold** = extended discussion or heading emphasized in main text.

Printed in the United States
89591LV00001B/73/A